The Political Economy of Science, Technology, and Innovation in China

There are a variety of reasons underlying the remarkable development of science and technology (S&T) and innovation in post-1978 China. This book seeks to achieve an understanding of such development from an institutional or a political economy perspective. Departing from the literature of S&T and innovation studies that treats innovation as a market or an enterprise's behavior in the Schumpeterian sense, Sun and Cao argue that it involves politics, institutions, and the role of the state. In particular, they examine how the Chinese state has played its visible role in making innovation policies, allocating funding for R&D activities, making efforts to attract talent, and organizing critical R&D programs. This book appeals to scholars in S&T and innovation studies, political economy, innovation governance, and China studies as well as policymakers and business executives.

YUTAO SUN is a professor at the School of Economics and Management, Dalian University of Technology, China, and a former Marie Curie Fellow at the University of Nottingham, UK. He has published in international journals including *Science* and *Research Policy*. He is the author of *China and Global Value Chains: Globalization and the Information and Communications Technology Sector* (co-authored, 2018).

CONG CAO is a professor at Nottingham University Business School China, University of Nottingham Ningbo China. His most recent books include *GMO China: How Global Debates Transformed China's Agricultural Biotechnology Policies* (2018) and *Innovation in China: Challenging the Global Science and Technology System* (co-authored, 2018).

The Political Economy of Science, Technology, and Innovation in China

Policymaking, Funding, Talent, and Organization

YUTAO SUN
Dalian University of Technology, China

CONG CAO
University of Nottingham Ningbo China

CAMBRIDGE
UNIVERSITY PRESS

CAMBRIDGE
UNIVERSITY PRESS

Shaftesbury Road, Cambridge CB2 8EA, United Kingdom

One Liberty Plaza, 20th Floor, New York, NY 10006, USA

477 Williamstown Road, Port Melbourne, VIC 3207, Australia

314–321, 3rd Floor, Plot 3, Splendor Forum, Jasola District Centre, New Delhi – 110025, India

103 Penang Road, #05–06/07, Visioncrest Commercial, Singapore 238467

Cambridge University Press is part of Cambridge University Press & Assessment, a department of the University of Cambridge.

We share the University's mission to contribute to society through the pursuit of education, learning and research at the highest international levels of excellence.

www.cambridge.org
Information on this title: www.cambridge.org/9781108490580

DOI: 10.1017/9781108854269

First published 2023

A catalogue record for this publication is available from the British Library.

Library of Congress Cataloging-in-Publication Data
Names: Sun, Yutao, author. | Cao, Cong, 1959– author.
Title: The political economy of science, technology, and innovation in China : policymaking, funding, talent, and organization / Professor Yutao Sun, Dalian University of Technology, China, Professor Cong Cao, University of Nottingham Ningbo China.
Description: New York : Cambridge University Press, 2023. | Includes bibliographical references and index.
Identifiers: LCCN 2022058471 | ISBN 9781108490580 (hardback) | ISBN 9781108854269 (ebook)
Subjects: LCSH: Information technology – Economic aspects – China. | Technological innovations – China. | Science – Economic aspects. | Technology and state – China.
Classification: LCC HC430.I55 S8656 2023 | DDC 338.4/70040951–dc23/eng/20230206
LC record available at https://lccn.loc.gov/2022058471

ISBN 978-1-108-49058-0 Hardback

*To Fengchao Liu, Denis Fred Simon, Jinqin Su, and Richard P. Suttmeier,
mentors, colleagues, collaborators, comrades, and friends*

Contents

Figures

Tables

Acknowledgments

We have accumulated enormous debts in the process of researching on, writing about, and publishing this book. To start, we would like to express our gratitude to Fengchao Liu, Denis Fred Simon, Jingqin Su, and Richard P. Suttmeier for their aspiration, encouragement, and support over the years. We are extremely fortunate to have them as mentors, colleagues, collaborators, comrades, and friends, to whom we dedicate the book to show our appreciation. Indeed, the book bears some of our joint efforts.

In 2008, with a scholarship from the China Scholarship Council, Yutao visited the Pennsylvania State University where Denis, a professor at the university, introduced Yutao to Cong, which started our more-than-a-decade and immensely productive collaboration. In 2012, a Marie Curie International Incoming Fellowship from the European Union's Seventh Framework Programme (302303/911303) enabled Yutao to spend two years at the University of Nottingham in the UK working with Cong. In fact, much of the foundation of the book was laid there and then. Subsequently, grants from the National Natural Science Foundation of China (71922005; 71774091) have made it possible for us to further our collaborative research.

Joe Ng, the commissioning editor of Cambridge University Press, not only invited us to write a book on science, technology, and innovation in China but also has steered us through the entire process of the publication. We received critical and constructive comments made by three anonymous reviewers on the proposal and first draft. Pete also provided an early feedback to our proposal. Christian Green led the production of the book, which also involved Balaji Devadoss and AG Rajan Shamili. We appreciate their efforts and especially their accommodation of the change at the stage of proofreading, prompted by a drastic reorganization of China's S&T system that was announced at the 14th National People's Congress of China. We feel obligated to update the book somewhat to reflect the change and its implications for China's science, technology, and innovation going forward.

We want to thank our co-authors – Lengchao Liu, Denis Fred Simon, Rongyu Guo, and Shuai Zhang. Their inputs into the research and writing were valuable. We also have benefited from our able research assistants, Ling Jiang, Rui Cao, and Xiaowen Yu, who helped with data collection and a variety of tedious but important tasks. Finally, we want to thank our families for their support, caring, and tolerance during our research and writing.

The permissions of the publishers allow us to use substantial materials in our previous publications, which also are appreciated:

Liu, F., Simon, D.F., Sun, Y. & Cao, C. (2011). China's innovation policies: Evolution, institutional structure, and trajectory. *Research Policy*, 40(7): 917–931. doi:10.1016/j.respol.2011.05.005

Sun, Y. & Cao, C. (2014). Demystifying central government R&D spending in China: Should funding focus on scientific research? *Science*, 345(6200), 1006–1008. doi:10.1126/science.125347

Sun, Y., Guo, R. & Zhang, S. (2017). China's brain gain at the high end: An assessment of Thousand Youth Talents Program. *Asian Journal of Innovation and Policy*, 6(3), 274–294. doi:10.7545/ajip .2017.6.3.274

Sun, Y. & Cao, C. (2018). The evolving relations between government agencies of innovation policymaking in emerging economies: A policy network approach and its application to the Chinese case. *Research Policy*, 47(3), 592–605. doi:10.1016/j.respol.2018.01.003

Sun, Y. & Cao, C. (2021). Planning for science: China's "grand experiment" and global implications. *Humanities and Social Sciences Communications*, 8, 215. doi:10.1057/s41599-021-00895-7

Sun, Y. & Cao, C. (2021). Mission-oriented mega-R&D programs: Governance and policy. *Innovation and Development Policy*, 3(2), 110–134. doi:10.3724/SP.J.2096-5141.2021.0007

Abbreviations

AAAS	American Association for the Advancement of Science
ABOC	Agricultural Bank of China
ACFIC	All-China Federation of Industry and Commerce
ACFTU	All-China Federation of Trade Unions
ACWF	All-China Women's Federation
BRICS	Brazil, Russia, India, China, and South Africa
CAC	Office of the Central Cyberspace Affairs Commission
CAE	Chinese Academy of Engineering
CAS	Chinese Academy of Sciences
CASS	Chinese Academy of Social Sciences
CAST	China Association for Science and Technology
CBIRC	China Banking and Insurance Regulatory Commission
CBRC	China Banking Regulatory Commission
CCCCYL	Central Committee of the Chinese Communist Youth League
CDB	China Development Bank
CIBC	Commerce and Industry Bank of China
CIRC	China Insurance Regulatory Commission
CMA	China Meteorological Administration
CMC STC	Science and Technology Committee of the Central Military Commission
COSTIND	Commission of Science, Technology, and Industry for National Defense
CPC	Communist Party of China
CPC CC	Communist Party of China's Central Committee
CPC CC CEW	CPC CC Commission on Enterprise Work
CPC CC DOO	CPC CC Department of Organization

CPC CC DOP	CPC CC Department of Propaganda
CPC CC FAO	CPC CC Foreign Affairs Office
CPPCC	National Committee of the Chinese People's Political Consultative Conference
CSRC	China Securities Regulatory Commission
CSTC	Central Science and Technology Commission
EIBOC	Export–Import Bank of China
GAC	General Administration of Customs
GAPP	General Administration of Press and Publication
GAQSIA	General Administration of Quality Supervision, Inspection, and Quarantine
GAS	General Administration of Sport
GDP	Gross domestic product
GERD	Gross expenditure on research and development
GFS	Government Finance Statistics
GII	Global Innovation Index
GVC	Global value chain
IP	Intellectual property
IPR	Intellectual property right
KIP	Knowledge Innovation Program
MCT	Ministry of Culture and Tourism
MEE	Ministry of Ecology and Environment
MEM	Ministry of Emergency Management
MEPS	Mega-Engineering Programs
MLP	Medium and Long-term Plan for the Development of Science and Technology (2006–2020)
MMRDs	Mission-oriented mega-R&D programs
MNR	Ministry of Natural Resources
MOA	Ministry of Agriculture
MOARA	Ministry of Agriculture and Rural Affairs
MOCA	Ministry of Civil Affairs
MOE	Ministry of Education
MOF	Ministry of Finance
MOFA	Ministry of Foreign Affairs
MOFCOM	Ministry of Commerce
MOHRSS	Ministry of Human Resources and Social Security
MOHURD	Ministry of Housing and Urban-Rural Development

MOIIT	Ministry of Industry and Information Technology
MOJ	Ministry of Justice
MOLR	Ministry of Land and Resources
MOMB	Ministry of Machine Building
MOMI	Ministry of Mechanical Industry
MOPS	Ministry of Public Security
MOST	Ministry of Science and Technology
MOT	Ministry of Transport
MOWR	Ministry of Water Resources
MSP	Mega-Science Programs
NAC	National Copyright Administration
NAO	National Audit Office
NASSP	National Administration of State Secrets Protection
NBS	National Bureau of Statistics
NCMCPDSRS	National Commission on the Management and Coordination of Post-Doctoral Scientific Research Stations
NDRC	National Development and Reform Commission
NEA	National Energy Administration
NFGA	National Forestry and Grassland Administration
NFSRA	National Food and Strategic Reserves Administration
NHC	National Health Commission
NIS	National Innovation System
NLGST	National Leading Group for Science and Technology
NPC	National People's Congress
NSFC	National Natural Science Foundation of China
NSTPs	National S&T Programs
OCMCCSC	Office of the Central Mental Civilization Construction Steering Committee
OECD	Organization for Economic Co-operation and Development
OSTP	Office of Science and Technology Policy of the USA
OMB	Office of Management and Budget of the USA
PBOC	People's Bank of China

PLA DGL	People's Liberation Army Department of General Logistics
PLA GAD	People's Liberation Army General Armament Department
R&D	Research and Development
SA	Standardization Administration
SAA	State Archives Administration
SAFE	State Administration of Foreign Exchange
SAFEA	State Administration of Foreign Experts Affairs
SAIC	State Administration of Industry and Commerce
SAMR	State Administration for Market Regulation
SASAC	State-owned Assets Supervision and Administration Commission
SASTIND	State Administration of Science, Technology and Industry for National Defense
SAT	State Administration of Taxation
SATCM	National Administration of Traditional Chinese Medicine
SC GO	State Council General Office
SC HMO	State Council Hong Kong and Macau Affairs Office
SC OCAO	State Council Overseas Chinese Affairs Office
SC PAD	State Council Leading Group Office of Poverty Alleviation and Development
SCOPSR	State Commission Office for Public Sector Reform
SDPC	State Development and Planning Commission
SEC	State Economic Commission
SEI	Strategic Emerging Industries
SETC	State Economic and Trading Commission
SIPO	State Intellectual Property Office
SMEs	Small and Medium-sized Enterprises
SNA	Social network analysis
SOA	State Oceanic Administration
SOEs	State-owned enterprises
SPC	State Planning Commission
SPCC	Supreme People's Court
SPP	Supreme People's Procuratorate
SSTC	State Science and Technology Commission

S&T	Science and Technology
TTP	Thousand Talents Program
WIPO	World Intellectual Property Organization
YTTP	Youth Thousand Talents Program

Introduction

In 1978, soon after China initiated the reform and opening-up policy, the American Association for the Advancement of Science (AAAS) Board of Directors organized a three-week visit to China aiming to arrange cooperation between AAAS and its counterpart, the China Association for Science and Technology (CAST). Afterward, in 1979, *Science*, the flagship journal of AAAS, published a special issue, "China in Transition." One of the papers (Abelson, 1979), "Education, Science, and Technology in China," for the first time raised a very critical and provocative question: "Why hasn't China developed faster and more extensively?"

Forty-five years later, China has become not only the second largest economy in the world but also a juggernaut in science, technology, and innovation. If visiting China today, the AAAS delegation might end up with a completely different but somehow hyped question: "When will China impose a serious overall threat to the competitiveness and scientific leadership of the USA?"

There is no doubt that the development of science, technology, and innovation in post-1978 China has been nothing short of remarkable. With increasing and sustained government and societal efforts, in 2021, China reported to spend RMB2.79 trillion ($439 billion, current US dollars) on research and development (R&D) (NBS, 2022). This was twice as much as that of six years ago and 56 times that of 1995 when the "rejuvenating the nation with science, technology, and education (*kejiao xingguo*)" strategy was proposed. In 2019, China's R&D expenditure reached $525.7 billion (PPP US dollars), accounting for about 22 percent of the global total and close to the level of the USA ($668.4 billion, or 28 percent of the global total) (NSB & NSF, 2022: 23). In 2021, China's R&D intensity, or gross expenditure of R&D (GERD) as a percentage of gross domestic product, reached 2.44 percent, more than tripled since 1996. China's R&D intensity reached 2 percent in 2013 for the first time and has maintained or surpassed this level thereafter. Although China did not fulfill the R&D intensity target set in the *Medium and Long-Term Plan for the Development of Science and Technology (2006–2020)* (MLP) for 2020, which is 2.5 percent, it has retained the momentum to help transform the nation's economic structure and stimulate the next stage of economic and social development by technology and innovation. The country is likely to set an even more ambitious target for its R&D intensity. Presumably, the level will be 3 percent for the next 15-year MLP (2021–2035), which the Chinese government has been formulating.[1]

China's talent pool is the largest in the world. In 2020, China's R&D personnel reached 5.24 million person-year in full-time equivalent terms, more than any other country in the world (NBS, 2021: Table 20–21). Its human resources pipeline is full as a result of the expansion of higher education that started in the late-1990s. In 2020, the number of undergraduate graduates in China reached 7.97 million and postgraduates 662,451 with 66,176 at the doctoral level (MOE, 2021).

China has become the world's most prolific country for knowledge production. Measured by the number of papers published in journals catalogued by *Science Citation Index (SCI)*, a bibliometric database compiled by Clarivate Analytics, China has ranked first in the world for quite a number of years. China's share of top 0.1 percent high-impact papers in Scopus, another bibliometric database, has grown from less than 1 percent in 1997 to about 20 percent in 2016 (Yang, 2016). China has witnessed continuous growth in patent applications and grants of domestic resident invention patents and patents with the Patent Cooperation Treaty (PCT), an international patent law treaty. In 2021, the number of PCT applications filed by Chinese inventors reached 69,540, putting China first in the world for the first time, ahead of the USA (59,570). Huawei Technologies, China's largest telecommunications equipment maker, ranked first with 6,952 PCT patent applications (WIPO, 2022). In addition, China's number of "triadic" patents – a set of patents filed with the European Patent Office, the

---

[1] In fact, the innovation-driven development strategy, released by the Communist Party of China's Central Committee and China's State Council in May 2016, stipulated to increase China's R&D intensity to 2.8 percent by 2030 (Communist Party of China's Central Committee and the State Council, 2016).

US Patent and Trademark Office, and the Japan Patent Office for the same invention, by the same applicant – has grown from less than 100 per year before 2000 to more than 5,000 in 2018 (OECD, 2022).

China also has become increasingly technologically sophisticated. Since the establishment of Zhongguancun in Beijing, the capital, as the first high-tech park, China has witnessed quite a number of its cities that rival Silicon Valley and the world's other high-tech zones. And three clusters of big-science research infrastructures in Beijing's Huairou, Shanghai's Zhangjiang, and Anhui's Hefei have turned these cities into the nation's comprehensive science centers. China is among the leaders in the number of leading high-tech companies, including those emerging "unicorns" valued at $1 billion and over, venture capital investment, high-tech trades, Internet and especially mobile Internet users, and volume of e-commerce. Overall, the Global Innovation Index, an index produced by Cornell SC Johnson College of Business, INSEAD, and the World Intellectual Property Organization to benchmark the innovation ecosystem performance of more than 130 economies, ranked China the 12th in 2021, a significant improvement over the 34th in 2012 (WIPO, 2021).

Indeed, various quantitative measures – from rapidly rising expenditure on R&D, a larger and high-quality talent pool, to impressive scientific publication and patenting statistics – indicate that China has been on its rapidly rising trajectory to becoming a formidable player, if not a superpower yet, in science, technology, and innovation. More importantly, China's catching up with and even leapfrogging Western countries in certain areas of science and technology (S&T) has to do with its possession of institutional capacity to mobilize human, financial, and material resources to achieve high-priority, national-development objectives (Suttmeier, 1981; Xue, 1997). Major accomplishments in national defense as well as in certain fields of basic research and technologies are just some of the examples. Meanwhile, the general inefficiency of transferring R&D achievements to production, even amid the reform of the S&T system that started in 1985, also makes it clear that overcoming structural uncertainty of China's science, technology, and innovation system is imperative if the system were to meet the demand for successful innovation in an increasingly market-oriented and knowledge-based economy (Breznitz & Muphree, 2011).

Why Another Book on Science, Technology, and Innovation in China?

In this book, we seek to achieve an understanding of China's development in science, technology, and innovation from an institutional or a political economy perspective. Over the years, scholars have tried to explain China's innovation from the enterprise's or economic perspective in the context of the enterprise-centered innovation system (Zhang *et al.*, 2009; Fuller, 2016; Yip & McKern, 2016; Lindtner, 2020). However, in examining the extent to which the Chinese state has led innovation (Appelbaum *et al.*, 2018), most of the studies are neither systematic nor comprehensive.

We were not that satisfied with the literature as science, technology, and innovation are more than a market or an enterprise's behavior in Joseph Schumpeter's sense but involve politics, institutions, and the role of the state. Indeed, behind China's innovation is the undeniable role of the Chinese state. Therefore, in around 2010, we started to work together. We have collected data from government and other credible sources, painstakingly demystifying and piecing together information on policy documents, R&D expenditure, and talents, among others. We have interviewed policymakers, policy analysts, academics, entrepreneurs, and other stakeholders involved in science, technology, and innovation activities and governance to achieve an appreciation of the evolving structure, process, operation, and characteristics of China's S&T system. We have actively participated in and contributed to the studies of China's science, technology, and innovation so as to accumulate first-hand knowledge and come up with new and insightful findings, some of which have been well received in the scholarly and policy communities.

In the ensuing years, we also have looked for a novel perspective and given serious thoughts to and tried to solve some of the burning questions pertaining to science, technology, and innovation in China. They include: What are the key government agencies handling S&T and innovation within the Chinese state and what are their respective roles? What are the structure and change of the relations between these government agencies? How do these government agencies and their relations play a role in making S&T and innovation policy, funding scientific research, attracting talents, and organizing R&D programs? Having accumulated enough material, we feel that it is the time to tackle the above-mentioned questions by writing this book. We hope that our efforts represent a right step toward achieving a more thorough and nuanced understanding of science, technology, and innovation in China.

Structure of the Book

We organize our discussions on the political economy of science, technology, and innovation in China in seven chapters. The first chapter reviews the political economy of science, technology, and innovation literature, including the evolution from the national innovation system to a political economic approach, and proposes a conceptual framework to open the "black box" of the state related to S&T and innovation activities.

The second chapter is about how China's innovation policies have evolved to reflect our changing and supposedly better understanding of innovation by China's policymakers. It carries out a quantitative analysis of 630 innovation policies issued by China's central government ministries from 1980 to 2019. In fact, China has shifted its S&T and industrial policy-centered innovation strategy to pursuing a more coordinated innovation-oriented economic development by giving increasing attention to a portfolio of policies that also include financial, tax, and fiscal measures. There has been a gradual departure from the pattern in which innovation policies were formulated by one single government agency, therefore steering China to a different and probably more promising innovation trajectory.

Taking the policy network approach, the third chapter investigates three mechanisms – policy agenda, power concentration, and heterogeneity dependence – underlying the evolution of inter-government agency relations in China. Operationally, the chapter adopts a social network analysis–based method to quantitatively study China's innovation policy network. The findings show that the formal policy network for innovation has not only sustained through the intervention of policy agenda but also become self-organized because of policy network's nature of power concentration and heterogeneity dependence. The presence of such mixed mechanisms in the evolution of China's innovation policy network differs from the findings from industrialized countries where self-organization plays a central role. The findings advance our theoretical understanding of the evolution of innovation policy network and have implications for policymaking in emerging economies.

China's rapid growth of R&D expenditure has attracted wide attention from the international scientific and policy communities. We try to open the "black box" of China's central R&D expenditure based on an analytical framework of "funding–performing" in the fourth chapter. Specifically, the chapter solves a major mystery regarding China's central government's R&D expenditure – who spends how much on what. By using data released by central government agencies with mission in S&T and innovation between 2011 and 2020, we find that the allocation of the central R&D expenditure has become decentralized and diversified, which has posed new challenges for China's R&D budget management. Much of the public money has financed scientific research, but the nation's overall R&D funding has been oriented toward development research, thus pointing to a possibility that China's efforts to build an enterprise-centered innovation system may lack a solid scientific foundation. The findings are helpful for understanding China's S&T budgeting process and spending patterns as well as funding structure.

In examining the effect of Chinese talent-attracting programs launched by the Chinese government, with few exceptions, studies have rarely assessed these programs empirically and pertinently. We intend to fill the gap by evaluating an important central government program – the Youth Thousand Talents Program – in the fifth chapter. We start with proposing a transnational migration matrix of the academics to clarify the dynamic mechanism of achieving an academic brain gain at the high end. The transnational migration matrix suggests that the academics with high ability have competitiveness in both overseas and domestic academic job markets and can especially enjoy a higher salary and academic reputation in the host (overseas) academic job market due to its more mature mechanism of academic evaluation relative to their home country. The results show that some scholars whose last employer's academic ranking is among the world's Top 100 have stronger willingness to return, and the negative effect of academic ranking decreases with time passing. Compared to scholars with an overseas tenure-track position, those with a tenure position or a permanent position tended to stay overseas, the rate of their staying

abroad increased with ages. Therefore, China's talent-attracting programs only have partially succeeded in bringing back the academics at
the high end.

The sixth chapter extends theoretical and empirical interests in
understanding the role of the Chinese government through its organization of mission-oriented mega-R&D programs (MMRDs). In particular, this chapter proposes a theoretical framework with a particular
focus on such programs' three contextual characteristics – technical
goal of the mission, dominant actor, and end-user. We then apply
the framework to ten cases across different historical periods and sectors in different countries to test its validity. The finding suggests that
exploitative R&D programs with a clear and singular technical goal
whose performer and end-user are public actors entails government
to adopt MMRDs, while in doing so government also should take
into consideration such factors as economic efficiency, national security, and public interests. In the case of China, the state-led innovation
model favors to concentrate resources on initiating MMRDs.

Our final chapter concludes the book by summarizing the findings
from our studies of the political economy of science, technology, and
innovation in China, discussing tensions faced by China through
the perspective of the political economy in the studies of science,
technology, and innovation in China, and drawing some governance
implications for the political economic study of China's science,
technology, and innovation in general.

1 | Studying Science, Technology, and Innovation
Bringing the State In

As indicated in the Introduction, China's impressive progress in science, technology, and innovation in the past several decades could be attributed to various factors, among which is the inarguable role of the Chinese state. A variety of theories have advanced scholarly understanding of the role of the state in innovation. In this book, we focus on one that is based on political economy, which typically refers to the study of the process through which politics affects the economy, and the economy in turn shapes politics.

As a rather elusive term, political economy has a long and rich history. While its application to the study of science, technology, and innovation is quite recent, "How are the states getting rich?" has been a lingering question. For Adam Smith (1776 [1999]), the division of labor is the key. Friedrich List (1841 [2005]) introduced political economy to inquire about how a nation can obtain prosperity, civilization, and power. Inspired by List, Joseph Schumpeter was the first who tried to answer the question by using the concept of innovation (Knell, 2018). Karl Marx also viewed science as a fundamental factor in explaining the exceptional growth in productivity and humanity's capacity to drive progress (Perelman, 1978).

Especially for Schumpeter (1939), innovation, as essentially an economic concept, is an enterprise's behavior, through which the enterprise dominates the market by creating temporary monopolies ("first-mover advantage"). Such monopolistic status in turn affords the enterprise abnormal profits that would soon be competed away by rivals and imitators, as well as incentivizing it to develop new innovative and commanding products and processes. In a word, entrepreneurial activities and accompanying innovation-originated market power provide enterprises with better results than the "invisible hand" and competition.

To the extent that it is an economic concept, innovation also is subject to political decisions. Indeed, innovation is more than an enterprise's behavior *per se*. For innovation to happen and sustain requires an environment that encourages the enterprise to be innovative. In this regard, government can make a huge difference, according to List (1841 [2005]: vol. 2: 94) by formulating a set of "institutions, regulations, laws, and conditions on which the economy of the individual subjects of a State is dependent, and by which it is regulated." It is the joint effort of market's "invisible hand" and the government's "visible hand" that levels the playing field for innovative enterprises and eventually makes some of the nations rich technologically and economically. While Smith (1776 [1999]) rejected government interference in market activities, John Maynard Keynes believed it necessary for government to stimulate the economy by investing in infrastructure, education, and other areas for their "public goods" nature (1936 [1973]).

This chapter visits the theories that have been developed to explain the role of the state in innovation and economic growth. Our focus is the literature on the political economy of science, technology, and innovation, starting with and extending from the neoclassical economics and the national innovation system (NIS) approach. We will especially highlight the literature's relevance to China and to our book. Doing so will help acquaint our reader with the knowledge of how political economy is useful in advancing our understanding of science, technology, and innovation in general and that in China in particular. We will end up with discussions of how our book contributes to the literature.

The Roles of Science, Technology, and Innovation in National Economic Growth

Theoretical approaches regarding conceptualization and theorization of the national economy and economic growth did not consider factors other than labor and capital. Nor did they capture why there exist relatively huge differences among countries with similar levels of economic development. It is neoclassical economists who viewed technology as a key element of production that drives economic growth and impacts national economies.

In particular, Solow (1956) defined productivity growth as rising output with constant input of capital and labor. However, part of the growth is not accountable when capital is accumulated and labor increased. The so-called Solow residual, or the unaccounted-for part in his growth model, measures productivity gain through technological progress, which in turn is associated with research and development (R&D); human capital development through education, on-the-job training, and healthcare; institutionalization of technology; technical competence; institutional/organizational restructuring and management; and production methods. For Helpman (1998), in addition to the importance of physical and human capital accumulation, economic activities are organized around the effects of technological factors on the rate of this accumulation; the process of knowledge creation and its influence on productivity; the interdependence of the growth rates of different countries; and, finally, the role of economic and political institutions in encouraging knowledge accumulation, innovation, and technological changes. That is, both Solow and Helpman imply explicitly that state is a prime player in a nation's technological changes and economic development.

Indeed, the introduction of changes in technology has become a major factor in explaining the economic growth and development of a country (Nelson, 1959; Romer, 1990, 2000). And the neoclassical economic doctrine had dominated the global narrative for quite some time and had been practiced in some developed and developing countries (Aghion *et al.*, 2008).

National Innovation System

Over time, the scholarly community has reached a consensus that innovation is an essential factor of economic growth. Economists and innovation scholars have gained increased knowledge of innovation systems and technology adoption in developed and more recently developing countries.

The application of political economy to the study of science, technology, and innovation probably dates back to List, who is credited with the genesis of the NIS approach (Freeman & Perez, 1988; Freeman, 1995; Soete *et al.*, 2010). In his seminal work, *National System of Political Economy*, List (1841 [2005]) critiqued the free-market doctrine and suggested that the government should be responsible for nurturing the productive resources of its country. For List, a true political economy study should start from the point of view of the interests of nations (Knell, 2018). As such, the Listian political economy means to provide the economic rationale for using industrial policy measures such as infant industry protection, export subsidies, and others to promote technological progress, or to provide the economic rationale for the state's role in its relations with technical change and technological learning (Levi-Faur, 1997; Knell, 2018).

In the 1980s, Japan's growth model with its developmental state features – strong government intervention and industrial policy – attracted tremendous international attentions (Johnson, 1982). In the process of studying Japan's economic miracle, innovation scholars found that firms do not normally innovate in isolation, but rather through collaboration and by means of interdependence with other organizations, thus helping to shape the notion of an innovation system (Freeman, 1987). Indeed, since the early 1990s, national innovation studies have rapidly gained their prominence, of which one systematic approach toward comprehending the evolution of innovation – the NIS – stood out (Freeman, 1987; Lundvall, 1992; Nelson, 1993).

The NIS approach, or an analytical model or framework, if not a theory, stresses that the flows of technology and information among people, enterprises, and institutions are key to the innovative process (Sun & Grimes, 2016). It attempts to understand innovation activities and processes from a system's perspective, emphasizing learning and interactions between innovative actors as well as the pivotal role of government policy in promoting and strengthening these connections. Innovation and technological development not only involve various actors – enterprises, universities, research institutes, and other organizations – but also result from a complex set of relationships among these actors in the system (OECD, 1997). The NIS also emphasizes the policy framework that can provide policymakers with mechanisms and instruments necessary to design and implement various innovation policies. As a kind of institutional arrangement covering a wide spectrum of R&D and related activities, innovation policies are critical in remedying market failures, building innovation networks, creating a fertile innovation environment, and improving overall innovation capacity (Lundvall & Borrás, 2005). As policymakers began paying more attention to innovation, the scholarly discourse has been centered on the conundrum of how the state develops and enhances national indigenous innovation capacity. In this case, the relationship between the state and market in the innovation system becomes a crucial issue.

The NIS approach was initially built on the case studies of developed countries, where the innovation system operates in the context of a market-oriented economy (Nelson, 1993). When it was first proposed, enterprises were already leading innovation systems in these developed countries. Now, the approach has been applied to the study of innovation in developing countries, of which China's NIS is probably among the most studied (Liu & White, 2001; Sun & Liu, 2010; Fu *et al.*, 2021).

The Political Economy of Science, Technology, and Innovation

The political economy of science, technology, and innovation concerns "How are the nations getting innovation?" or "Why are some countries more technologically innovative than others?" (Taylor, 2016). It covers the historical roots of issues such as the function of science in technological innovation and economic growth, technological development, the generation of new products and processes, and the climate for innovation in industry (Martin & Nightingale, 2000). Nevertheless, there really is no consensus in the political economy of science, technology, and innovation, as every new theory that acquired the "mainstream" status has put forward a new theory concerning the main factor (driving force) of economic development and rejected a previous theory (Bazhal, 2017). In his book, *The Political Economy of Innovation Development*, for example, Bazhal (2017) proposed a conceptual framework of the political economy of innovation by introducing Schumpeter's theory of economic development in which innovation is a separate key factor of economic growth. With a particular focus on the work of Ukrainian economists, Tugan-Batanobvsky and Vernadsky, the book seeks to explain the extent to which innovation has become dominant in economic development in recent decades and why its role will become even more dominant in the future. According to Bazhal, genuine economic growth – especially in transitioning and developing countries – is only possible with innovation.

Despite not focusing on the politics of innovation *per se*, most of the literature of the political economy of science, technology, and innovation does offer a number of insights about the relationship between enterprise activities such as innovation and the political and social environment in many countries. The literature pays particular attention to government's role in the allocation of resources among different R&D pursuits and assurance of a socially desirable direction of R&D activities through proper administration or regulation of science (Clark, 1985). Studies also examine innovation at enterprises than in identifying the important institutional features of the central state, although nations also derive their comparative advantages from their institutional infrastructures. In general, the varieties of capitalism – laissez-faire economies such as the USA and the UK, coordinated market economies of Europe, and communitarian Japan – may lead to varieties of innovation and NISs with respective comparative advantages (see, e.g., Ibata-Arens, 2003).[1]

In fact, the national-level institutions and policies influence the technological innovation outcomes across nations. Such institutions, according to Taylor (2016), include intellectual property rights, R&D subsidies, education, trade policy, democracy, federalism, international networks, clusters, and technological standards. Nevertheless, countries may excel despite "bad" institutions, while countries with "good" institutions might fail to flourish. In fact, building a national technological infrastructure and a strong national knowledge base was essential to the American system of innovation (Knell, 2018). Japan and other East Asian economies since the middle of the twentieth century also had been successful examples of Listian political economy. According to White and Wade (1988:1), in order to harness national interests, East Asian "states have played a strategic role in taming domestic and international market forces." Specifically, in China, a consensus seems to have been reached that development is "a national endeavour guided by a strong and pervasive state" (White & Wade, 1988: 26). This also implies the intertwined and inseparable relationship between developmental state and interventionist state.

Toward the end of the twentieth century, technological change had radically altered economic development and become ever more important to understand the sources, nature, and consequences of innovation. Meanwhile, globalization had brought benefits to both developed and developing countries, which had increasingly integrated innovation policies into their economic development strategies. Consequently, governments had stipulated increasing support for R&D activities and high-tech development. Through foreign direct

---

[1] For Zhang and Whitley (2013), Japan is considered a networked capitalism from the 1970s to the 2000s.

investment, developed countries had transferred technology and production know-how to developing countries and turned countries such as China into the "factory of the world." Governments in developing countries also had become more proactive in steering their efforts toward nurturing and strengthening indigenous innovation capability.

Indeed, the NIS approach currently still dominates the literature on how to intensify interactions between actors – enterprises, universities, research institutions, intermediaries, and others – in the system of innovation. It politicizes the question of innovation system's reform, thus moving away from the analysis that focuses on the knowledge and fund flows involved in the production, trade, and consumption of knowledge, as well as from models that focus on the structure of enterprises, universities, and research institutions in the innovation system and innovation performance (Sun & Liu, 2010). Meanwhile, the political economy of science, technology, and innovation mainly explains a nation's innovation from the perspective of politics, institutions, and state and international relationships (Taylor, 2016). It is silent about the question of agencies in the state and treats "systems" within the state as a "black box," and the institutional framework as a given rather than as constructed and as the result of particular path dependencies or conflicts. Nevertheless, Taylor (2016) intends to answer whether decentralized states are better at technological innovation than centralized states.

The State in Innovation: From Function to Structure

Institutions are surely important. In reality, each of the institutions, relationships, roles, and norms that together constitute a state serves a particular function, and each is indispensable for the continued existence of the others and of the state as a whole (Breznitz, 2007). Regarding science, technology, and innovation, out of the concerns for public goods and market failure, the state should support basic research where payoffs are uncertain and invest in public goods such as health, environmental protection, and national defense, among other areas (Stephan, 2012).

The state invests in S&T for the sake of national prestige as scientists are perceived to participate in a global competition for discoveries and new knowledge. The state also invests in education for the sake of turning out the next generation of scientists and engineers who shoulder responsibility in S&T and economic activities (Stephan, 2012). The role of the state is also critical in formulating laws and regulations to protect intellectual property rights, to prevent and punish monopolistic behaviors, and to support and stimulate new and emergent technological development through government procurement (Rockett, 2010). And an "entrepreneurial state" makes the high-risk investments before the private sector finds the courage to invest (Mazzucato, 2013).

These functions of the state aside, political economy pays increasing attention to agencies within the state, power relationships between agencies, and the institutional framework within which agencies operate and through which they interact with each other. It also explores whether the relations of agencies behind policy or set of policies are responsible for the impacts and if so how. In other words, in performing their respective functions, government agencies not only have to play their own roles but also make efforts to get connected structurally.

In the domain of science, technology, and innovation, while diving deep into the role of the state or government agencies, political economy also concerns about the structural relations of the state and especially agencies with different interests in playing their roles. For example, by identifying and analyzing main stakeholders in China's innovation policy framework, Huang *et al.* (2004) propose that innovation policies have been formulated by a combination of government agencies' macroeconomic and structural actions, as well as the mutual support among those actors. Breznitz (2007) argues that the industrial development agencies of Israel, headed by the Office of the Chief Scientist in the Ministry of Trade and Industry, spurred a series of changes in the NIS, influencing both supply and demand for R&D, as well as nurturing R&D prowess and capabilities. Anadón (2012) argues that approaches of the USA, the UK, and China for accelerating energy innovation have been shaped by the ability of their respective governments' supporting ways, such as Energy Innovation Hubs and ARPA-E (Advanced Research Projects Agency–Energy) in the USA, the Carbon Trust in the UK, and National S&T Programs in China.

The Role of the State in China's Science, Technology, and Innovation Development

Scholarly research has covered a wide range of China's approach toward science, technology, and innovation development. The topics studied include reform of S&T system and the construction of the NIS; innovation policy and indigenous innovation strategy; and national innovation capability at the macro level, territorial distribution of innovation, Zhongguancun Science Park in particular, and technological learning and catching up in industry at the meso level, to the determinants of enterprises' innovation and performance, enterprises' indigenous innovation, and university's spin-offs and venturing at the micro level (Sun & Cao, 2020). Studying science, technology, and innovation in China has drawn the interests of scholars from social science disciplines such as political science, sociology (including science, technology, and society), public and business administration, China studies, and others.

Political economy is one of the focal points and approaches. For example, Dolla (2015) discusses three main components of the Chinese S&T system – the state, society, and the international system. For him, the organizational structure represents the state; the research system, or the scientific community society; and technology acquisition through the international system with each having serious implications for China. Again, the role of the state in science, technology, and innovation is prominent. Contextualizing China's innovation-driven economic growth in light of high-level structured uncertainty and low-level institutionalization, Breznitz and Murphree (2011) argue that within the current, globally fragmented production system, China has been sustaining its run of rapid economic growth, the world's longest, by innovating in many stages of production. Contrary to conventional wisdom, they conclude, cutting-edge innovation is not a prerequisite for sustained economic vitality with China a perfect case in point. Through analyzing its social conditions, industrial characteristics, and economic impacts in China's transition to an innovation-oriented nation, Zhou *et al.* (2016) observe a continued co-evolution of state policy, market demand, and technology development. According to them, foreign firms and, particularly, local governments have played more notable roles in bringing technological dynamism into China's innovation system, and Chinese firms have managed to catch up with international levels of production, although they have yet to develop an indigenous innovation capacity to reach the cutting edge. Similarly, for Fuller (2016), hybrid firms – those firms with both ethnic Chinese management know-how and foreign financing power – are the "hidden dragons" driving China's technological development, whereas China's domestic firms are merely technological "paper tigers." He also argues that the state's efforts to build local innovation clusters and create national champions have not managed to transform these firms into drivers of technological development.

Appelbaum *et al.*'s (2018) study is probably the most critical of China's state-led model to technology and innovation. By assessing the model's successes and failures from the perspectives of S&T policy, innovation at enterprises, international S&T relations, and high-tech development, they found that in recent decades, China has seen huge investments in high-tech parks, a surge in home-grown top-ranked global companies, and a significant increase in scientific publications and patents. However, the state-led model might not yield the same level of progress going forward if China does not address fundamental and serious institutional, organizational, and cultural challenges that the model entails. The major issues at stake for China's technological leapfrogging, according to Dai and Taube (2019), include not only the role of top-down politics but more importantly the role of bottom-up entrepreneurship. They found that successful innovation relies on the favorable interplay between business, politics, and society. While it needs to create its own path for innovation, China still has to learn from the Western paradigm of successful innovation regimes.

While touching upon some aspects of China's state-led approach toward science, technology, and innovation development, by and large, the literature does not offer a comprehensive analysis of the state's operation in China's science, technology, and innovation, nor does it focus on achieving an understanding of the central role of the state in China's science, technology, and innovation. The questions to be answered are centered on: How do we understand the role of the state in a state-led S&T system? What did the state do to lead the enterprise of science, technology, and innovation?

Government Agencies in Science, Technology, and Innovation in China

Indeed, in China, as in Europe, the USA, or Japan, both the state and the market are very important for science, technology, and innovation development. As both government and market mechanisms could fail to some extent, the key lies in neither total dependence on government nor total dependence on the market, but in identifying the precise division of labor or maintaining a delicate balance between the two mechanisms, and in making institutional arrangements for resource allocation and coordination of economic and social activities so as to achieve complementary effects (Mowery & Nelson, 1999: 13–15 and 375–381). In other words, there is the need to determine a "proper" role for the state and policy in driving innovation.

While in general, decentralized, market responsive approaches are far more successful, the state-led innovation probably is more suitable for some countries, especially in their catch-up stage. China is such a country. Given its national, state-directed innovation policies that have been so extensive that its mixed institutional approach, which also integrates the market into intervention, has been gradually extended from the economy to the management of science, technology, and innovation activities. Zheng and Huang (2018) argue that state (political) principles are dominant over market (economic) principles in China's economy. The role of the Chinese state in a state-led innovation system is more impactful than that of the state in the enterprise-centered innovation system of developed countries. Therefore, there is the necessity to better understand or interpret the role of the Chinese state in innovation.

It is worth noting that the state functions as a "black box" in political economy terms (Zheng & Huang, 2018). As such, to understand China's state-led approach to innovation is to open the "black box" (Appelbaum *et al.*, 2018). By paying attention to Chinese state's behavior and competence in exploring various facets of S&T policymaking, scholars were oblivious to the internal structure and operation of the state. Investigation into the structure of the state, along with functions, is critical to understanding China's model of science, technology, and innovation. So, we intend to transform the study from the role of the state in science, technology, and innovation (functions) to the exploration of what is inside the state related to science, technology, and innovation (structure), or examine the structure of the state through investigating what government agencies do and how they establish their relations with each other. For example, science, technology, and innovation policy making and implementation often involve one or more government agencies with similar functions. The integration of the functions and structure determines the making of China's evolving science, technology, and innovation policy, especially at the central government level, and its impacts on China's science, technology, and innovation trajectory. Let us start with an introduction of government agencies and organizations in the domain of science, technology, and innovation.

It is well known that China has a sophisticated bureaucratic system in place to make and implement policies related to the economy, national defense, and so on (Lieberthal & Oksenberg, 1988). There is no exception in the domain of S&T, where policy is formulated by the interaction of scientific and political institutions, involving players from the legislature, government, advisory bodies, performing organizations, funding agencies, and others (Huang *et al.*, 2004). The National People's Congress (NPC) has the authority to draft, enact, and amend an S&T-related law, which usually is drafted by a specific government ministry. Technically speaking, the NPC also monitors the implementation of such laws and approves state budget on S&T. Members of the National Committee of Chinese People's Political Consultative Conference (CPPCC), a highest-level advisory body, many being non-Communist Party of China (CPC) member scientists and engineers, also voice their expert opinions and comments.

Of the constituting ministries of the State Council, China's cabinet, the Ministry of Science and Technology (MOST), which succeeded the State Science and Technology Commission in 1998, is a principal participant in China's S&T enterprise. The MOST administers China's national S&T programs, ranging from basic and applied research and development to downstream commercialization of S&T achievements, supports innovation within enterprises (along with the National Development and Reform Commission, NDRC), and manages and promotes science parks and incubators. After the 2018 reform of the party and government institutions, the MOST absorbed the State Administration of Foreign Experts Affairs (SAFEA), which was previously under the Ministry of Human Resources and Social Security (MHRSS). Placing the SAFEA under the MOST was aimed to boost the recruitment of foreign scientists. The MOST also took over the country's leading basic-research funder, the National Natural Science Foundation of China (NSFC), previously an independent entity. The NSFC mainly supports basic research and mission-oriented research projects through competitive and peer-review processes. The merger was supposed to consolidate the role of the ministry in administering China's national S&T programs.

However, the 2023 reform of the party and government institutions intends to restructure China's S&T system again. First, the new

MOST will become an office of the Central Science and Technology Commission (CSTC), a party organization to be set up, focusing on top-level design, unified planning, and interagency coordination with its responsibility for S&T strategy and policy formulation related to specific sectors being redistributed to mission-oriented and other agencies, such as the Ministry of Agriculture and Rural Affairs (MOARA), the Ministry of Industry and Information Technology (MOIIT), the National Health Commission (NHC), the Ministry of Ecology and Environment (MOEE) and the NDRC. Second, the restructuring will move the SAFEA from the MOST back to the MOHRSS.

The MOST also is expected to exercise an important power with regard to the design and implementation of science, technology, and innovation policies in conjunction with the Ministry of Education (MOE), MOARA, and MOIIT, the former Commission of Science, Technology, and Industry for National Defense, which was merged into the MOIIT in 2008, and the NHC, which was previously the Ministry of Health, the Population, and Family Planning Commission, and then the Health and Family Planning Commission. Indeed, the MOST assists these government agencies to formulate and execute policies related to their respective missions in S&T. The Ministry of Finance has become increasingly important in the formulation of innovation policies, especially in scrutinizing ministerial budget, allocating monies for particular programs and initiatives, and monitoring the usage of the funds.

The role of NDRC deserves special attention given its continued direct involvement in innovation policymaking to ensure China's technological advance from an economic perspective. In 2003, the NDRC succeeded the State Development and Planning Commission (SDPC) as well as the State Economic and Trading Commission. Both commissions were formed in 1998, with the former based on the State Planning Commission (SPC), established in 1952, as the most important government body overseeing economic development planning, while the latter had its roots in the State Economic Commission and the State Council Office of Economic System Reform. One of NDRC's responsibilities is to formulate policies related to innovation and high technology in Chinese economic and social development. The NDRC also manages and implements major S&T programs such as the State Major S&T Achievement Industrialization Program, the State Key Industrial Testing Program, and the National Engineering Research Center Program, which date back to the SPC and the SDPC.

The Chinese Academy of Sciences, an entity with multiple functions in research, high-tech development, technology transfer, and training, also plays a significant advisory role in S&T policymaking through its honorific academicians (*yuanshi*), who, along with academicians (*yuanshi*) of the Chinese Academy of Engineering, a high-level advisory institution, provide services to support decision-making pertaining to the nation's engineering and technological sciences.

Nevertheless, it is the CPC that has final say in innovation policy-making, as it does virtually in all matters in China. Although its direct involvement in the S&T affair has diminished from the early periods of the People's Republic, the heyday of the Cultural Revolution, and even since the 1980s, the party has never conceded altogether from its "overly pervasive pattern of directive state intervention" (White & Wade, 1988: 18). Now, not only does the CPC's Central Committee (CPC CC) stipulate innovation policies directly, it also inserts influence through the so-called leading group mechanism. A leading group usu-ally is set up within the State Council to tackle issues involving more than one government agency and usually is chaired by the premier or a vice premier who is likely to be a member of CPC CC Politburo or even its Standing Committee, China's *de facto* governing body, so as to mobilize resources and coordinate efforts across the bureaucracy. In our case, the S&T affair is administered by the CSTC of the CPC CC, a party organization with the MOST as its office. In a word, while it does not enact laws directly, the party exercises influence and power in policymaking through a variety of indirect means that still provide it lots of clout. Indeed, all major initiatives are reviewed by senior party officials before they are sent forth to the NPC for legislation consider-ation or the State Council and associated ministries for specification and implementation.

The state is not an entity or a whole, but a collection or network of departments or government agencies. Each department has its own functions and interests, and there are some functional overlaps between agencies, which is characterized by cooperation and competi-tion. Each department also represents the state, although it is not the state itself. In China, it is more complicated. In 2018 and in 2023 again, the CPC CC introduced new initiatives to deepen the reform of party and state institutions, including CPC CC institutions, NPC insti-tutions, State Council institutions, the CPPCC, the administrative law enforcement system, military-civilian system, and mass organizations such as the China Association for Science and Technology. That is, what China considers as state or government is not only departments under the State Council but also party departments and public institutions subordinate to the government, or all of the government and public agencies. It is in this sense that the government's or the party-state's "unlimited power" also characterizes China's innovation system (Fang, 2010).

However, the powers of these institutions are unequal. On the top of the policymaking hierarchy is the CPC CC. Then, there is the NPC as the highest organ of state power and lawmaker. The ministries and agencies under the State Council are principal participants in policymaking and policy implementation in their respective areas. Such a structure inherently determines the underlying strength and weakness of China's science, technology, and innovation strategy and development. In this book, we focus on the structure and the changing role of government agencies and their relations behind the function of government in making science, technology, and innovation policies and promoting science, technology, and innovation development.

Our Approach: Focusing on Institutional Structure behind Four Functions

In general, the state is embodied in policies or institutions or exerts its influence through policies or institutions. There is a rich connotation of policies. In addition to laws, regulations, plans, and programs that are common in other settings, central policy documents, leaders' speeches, departmental rules, and even notices are paramount in the Chinese case. The broader scope of policies not only is unique but also sets the parameters for the operation of the S&T system. Of particular interests for our purpose are institutional structure behind four functions of the central government – policymaking, funding, talent-attracting, and organization (PFTO), each representing state's important and nuanced role in both enabling and constraining the nurturing of institutional environments for innovation. These functions involve actors such as enterprises, universities, research institutions, and governments, and so on, as well as their interactions that generate mobility of knowledge, funding, talent, and others. Within China's S&T institutions, government agencies, as actors or policymakers, interact to cooperate and compete with each other. The state improves the innovation system through reforming the S&T system to raise the system's efficiency and effectiveness.

In fact, China's state has done much to reform and strengthen its innovation system, focusing on reconstructing innovation actors and their interactions. For example, the reform has made institutional transformation of public research institutions, part of which have become enterprises; the reform has restructured state-owned enterprises (SOEs); the reform has led to the strengthening of research-oriented universities; the reform has encouraged the rise of small- and medium-sized S&T enterprises; and the reform has seen the coming of age of technology markets. These continuous reforms of China's NIS have been reflected in the nation's policymaking process. In particular, as an institutional interlock between the innovation and political systems, **policymaking** is an important process of making policies to improve the performance in science, technology, and innovation, while also showing the inside operation of S&T institutions through the structure of government agencies. At the same time, China's state also has been constantly reforming and improving government agencies, as mentioned, with the most recent one involving the reform of party and state institutions in 2023.

The innovation system also represents a process of generating, spreading, using, and valuing knowledge (Buesa *et al.*, 2006). Empirical studies of knowledge production uncover the existence of a high correlation between innovation inputs – such as R&D costs – and outputs, such as the number of patents (Griliches, 1990). Apparently, **funding** or expenditure for R&D activities and **talent** are basic inputs. The budgeting mechanism of fiscal investment in S&T and R&D is one of the most important tools for the state to influence the innovation system. In fact, China's reform of the S&T system started from the reform of the fiscal S&T budgeting process. Meanwhile, science, technology, and innovation entail activities of knowledge generation and application, to which the high-quality talents are a fundamental input. Attracting overseas talents, especially those at the high-end, has always been an integral part of China's innovation policy.

In addition to funding research and attracting talents, the state also directly **organizes** science, technology, and innovation activities through certain ways. China's state-led innovation is characterized by its "whole-of-the-nation system" (*juguo tizhi*), featuring mobilizing and concentrating resources – material, human, and financial – to accomplish essential national goals. China's strategic weapons pro-grams (*liangdan yixing*) in the mid- and late-twentieth century exem-plify the positive side of the "whole-of-the-nation system," which Chinese policymakers subsequently have adopted time and again to intervene directly in science, technology, and innovation through organizing and implementing mega-engineering programs and mega-science programs.

Altogether, we try to explore the operational aspects of China's sci-ence, technology, and innovation system, to which the scholarly lit-erature of science, technology, and innovation in China has yet to pay sufficient attention. As such, our approach is believed to be unique and insightful.

Contributions of the Book

In this book, we put on the lens of political economy to decode the story of China's development in science, technology, and innovation during the country's reform and open-door era. In particular, we examine how the state has played its role in making innovation poli-cies, allocating funding for R&D, making efforts to allure talent, and organizing critical S&T activities. Such a study has resulted from our more-than-a-decade systematic and comprehensive research under-taking. Compared with other book-length studies of China's science, technology, and innovation, as mentioned, ours is significant and unique in at least the following aspects.

First, the book contributes to the literature of China's science, technology, and innovation studies from the perspective of political economy, which is the first of its kind to our knowledge. Most of the existing studies achieve an understanding of the development and evolution of China's science, technology, and innovation through the NIS approach, which in fact also is political economy in essence, as discussed (Chang & Shih, 2004; OECD, 2008; Sun & Liu, 2010; Cao *et al.*, 2013; Cao & Suttmeier, 2017). Indeed, the interactions among enterprises, universities, and research institutions, or key actors of the NIS, are critical to the innovative process, whereas the govern-ment promotes such interactions through policies and allocation of resources. In other words, the existing studies pay more attention to the elements of the NIS including enterprises, universities, research institutions, science parks, and so on.

However, the NIS approach emphasizes more the function of the state in the NIS than the innovation system's institutional structure, especially specific actors inside the state. Indeed, the political economy perspective is interested in not only actors and power relationships between actors but also the institutional framework within which actors operate and through which they interact (De Schutter, 2019). Such a perspective starts by moving from the function of the state to the structure of the state related to science, technology, and innovation development. We specifically focus our analysis on state's four critical functions in the S&T system – policymaking, funding, talent-attraction, and organization – so as to provoke novel insights and shed new lights on the structure of the state related to science, technology, and innovation development in China.

Second, the book is data driven and evidence based. We introduce new sets of data and analyze the data to provide new evidence for exploring internal structures of the state, thus contributing to the literature of science, technology, and innovation studies. Previous studies on science, technology, and innovation mainly used data to analyze inputs and especially "productivity" of science, technology, and innovation development, such as R&D expenditure, papers, patents, technology trade, new products, and so on. However, the studies on "production relations" behind the productivity, especially the relations between government agencies, and the relation between productivity and production relations, are mainly qualitative in nature as it is difficult to obtain the data underlying the relations between government agencies and assess the effects of governments' policies.

We will introduce new sets of data and explore new data sources and methods of data quantification. The book will apply the quantitative research methodology to study policy documents, and draw the data on collaboration between government agencies based on their co-sponsoring of the formulation of policy documents. The book will introduce the funding data of central government agencies based on Departmental Annual Reports on Final Accounts by various Chinese government agencies, which reflects the power relationships between central agencies. The book will assess the effects the talent-attracting program quantitatively at the micro level by constructing the talents data based on their CVs and public information. That is, all of our analyses are based on objective data and information and our findings are scientifically replicable. As such, the book itself represents an effort to triangulate information from different sources and is both inductive and deductive.

Third, our findings from the Chinese case may shed new lights on the global science, technology, and innovation governance and thus contribute to the literature of science, technology, and innovation governance. Our book is China focused and takes science, technology, and innovation in China as the research topic but our findings go beyond China. As the coordination and cooperation between different government agencies are challenges facing all countries in the world, the empirical findings from the Chinese practice are of enlightened values to other countries.

For example, in industrialized countries, self-organization of government agencies around policy issues related to innovation is central to policy network's governance (Berardo & Scholz, 2010). In China, in addition to self-organization, there is evidence that the policy network for innovation has been sustained through the intervention of policy agenda. Brain drain is a prominent challenge for emerging countries. Our study of the Chinese case shows that the country's talent-attracting programs have partially succeeded in bringing back some academics at the high-end, in which government policy does matter. This book also examines particular tensions between the state and other actors in the S&T system, including those between government agencies related to the S&T enterprise, facing China as a latecomer country whose institutions still are in the process of improvement. Therefore, the findings will have implications for policymakers of emerging economies in making policies, distributing resources, attracting and utilizing talents, and organizing programs critical to the mission of the state in science, technology, and innovation.

2 | *Innovation Policies*
Institutional Structure and Evolution

With the critical role of science and technology (S&T) in economic development fully appreciated after World War II, there has been a shift of focus in science, technology, and innovation "from universities and technological sectors … toward all parts of the economy that have an impact on innovation process" (Lundvall & Borrás, 2005:614–615). This has led to the formulation of specific policies to harness the benefits of S&T, initially in developed economies, and later, albeit more slowly and gradually, in developing countries (Sagasti, 1989). Over time, both the technical and policy communities have recognized that simple allocation of resources to research and promotion of S&T is not enough to enhance the competitiveness of a firm or a nation. Innovation policies thus were introduced, aiming at stimulating the creation and commercialization of new or improved products, processes, or services.

Since the late 1970s, the Chinese government has issued a slew of S&T policies to reform the S&T system, to increase investment in research and development (R&D) and S&T, to develop human resources, to establish high-tech parks, to encourage venture capital investment, to protect intellectual property, and lately to build an innovation-oriented nation. Meanwhile, the government has introduced an industrial policy that supports the development of high-tech sectors, aiming at strengthening industrial competitiveness, encouraging investment in innovation, and promoting high-tech trades. Innovation financing, preferential tax treatment, and better management of S&T, R&D, and innovation funds also have become important. Taken together, S&T, industrial, financial, tax, and fiscal policies have comprised a more coherent package of innovation policies in China as the state's tool to intervene or stimulate the country's S&T development.

Although such measures as tax incentives, R&D subsidies, and restrictions or promotion on high-tech trade usually are treated as industrial policy (Okimoto, 1989), China's Ministry of Science and Technology (MOST), the government agency in charge of the country's science, technology, and innovation policymaking, has leaned toward including it into "innovation policies," and defined as such.[1] In fact, this broader and somewhat loose definition allows us to systematically examine the evolution, institutional structure, and trajectory of China's innovation policies in the reform and open-door era. Broadly speaking, these policies can be defined as "a set of policy actions, measures, and tools intended to raise the quantity and efficiency of innovative activities and enhance the innovative capability" (European Commission, 2000:9). Just as "crossing the river by touching stones" has been the rule of thumb of China's economic reform, the country's innovation policy framework still is a work in progress, involving "historical reflection, grass-roots experimentation, top-down trial and error in designing and revising policy" as well as gradually learning, digesting, utilizing, and adopting innovation practice from developed countries and making adjustment and adaptation to the Chinese situation (OECD, 2008:392; see also Naughton, 2021).

The current understanding of China's innovation policymakers is as follows (Research Department of the MOST General Office and CASTED, 2006). S&T policy is the starting point of innovation policies, aiming at establishing and nurturing an institutional arrangement that facilitates S&T progress and innovation. It includes laws, regulations, guidelines, and codes of conduct for S&T activities as well as strategies, plans, and programs. In the context of a country's innovation policies, industrial policy promotes technological progress in industry, regulates industrial structure, leads the direction of industrial development, and enhances industrial competitiveness by providing subsidies and support to specific industries. Fiscal policy provides support, subsidies, and guidance to technological innovation activities through fiscal input; tax policy reduces R&D costs and innovation investment risks, and increases expected revenue of R&D by providing various preferential tax treatment to enterprises or levying special taxes; and financial policy aims at perfecting financing environment

---

[1] There could be other ways to categorize China's innovation policies, such as those fostering an innovation culture (human resources development), establishing a framework conducive to innovation (including competition, IP protection, innovation financing, taxation), and gearing research to innovation (fiscal policy) (Huang *et al.*, 2004).

and channels through which innovation actors reduce, avoid, and mitigate innovation risks by way of financial markets, intermediaries, and financial tools.

Apparently, there are overlaps between S&T and industrial policies on the one hand, and between S&T and fiscal, tax, and financial policies on the other. In general, S&T and industrial policies take effects by themselves and play direct roles in promoting innovation as they usually have substances, while fiscal, tax, and financial policies are policy tools that governments use to promote the construction of an environment conducive to innovation or facilitate innovation activities. However, if innovation is the desired end, the components of innovation policies – regardless of which category they fall into – are all means to the end.

The Chinese case offers a rare and unprecedented opportunity to examine state-led innovation as few other countries have intervened so systematically and invasively in their national innovation system. Indeed, the existing literature already has assessed the effectiveness of China's innovation policies and the obstacles that innovation in China has encountered (see, e.g., OECD, 2008). This chapter takes a different approach by quantifying all the policies formulated at the national level to reflect the reality that China remains largely a centrally controlled system with most policies formulated and executed top down. Our approach is unique in that we are less concerned about the exact content of a particular policy. Rather, by paying attention to the multiple dimensions of China's broad array of innovation policies, we try to describe, also from a novel angle, the evolution of these policies – from narrowly defined S&T policy at the onset of the reform and open-door initiative in the late 1970s to a broader and more comprehensive package of innovation policies in the first 20 years of the twenty-first century. In other words, instead of directly measuring the impact of China's innovation policies as other studies have shown, we indirectly evaluate their respective types and issuing agencies. In this way, we attempt to achieve the goals of describing and assessing the evolution and institutional structure of China's innovation policies and projecting China's innovation trajectory.

Method and Data

Innovation policies have been studied qualitatively by way of narratives and case studies (see, e.g., Nelson, 1993). This is understandable as these policies are not in a large number and not many government agencies are involved in the policymaking process, which is not only lengthy but also not systematic. For example, although it is significant in promoting technology transfer and innovation in the USA, the *Bayh–Dole Act* is only one piece of legislation, which had been debated for many years before its passage. But qualitative studies sacrifice the quantitative dimensions of the policies. On the other hand, text mining, one of the quantitative approaches of policy analysis, counts the frequency of keywords in a policy with the underlying hypothesis that the more frequently a keyword appears, the more important the relevant policy is. But the method ignores the differences between the types and effectiveness of different policies and their interactions (Kayser & Blind, 2017).

We adopt a different and multidimensional, quantitative approach. China's adoption of a more sophisticated, yet nuanced mixture of innovation policies in significant numbers permits such an analysis that innovation scholars have long envisioned. We directly count the number of policies in particular dimensions and issued by particular government agencies based on the assumption that the more the policies in a certain dimension and issued by a particular ministry, the greater the efficacy of these types of policies or these types of government agencies, although doing so may overlook the differences between specific policies in certain dimensions.

According to our understanding of the workings of the Chinese policymaking apparatus, as mentioned in Chapter 1, a Communist Party of China's Central Committee (CPC CC) document is the most authoritative and supposedly most influential, impactful, and effective, followed by a law enacted by the National People's Congress (NPC), an administrative statute formulated by the State Council, and a regulation issued by the respective ministries under the State Council. In other words, regardless of the content of a specific policy, the political weight and stature of a CPC CC document (Grade A policy) is greater than that of a law (Grade B policy), which, in turn, is greater than that of a State Council administrative statute (Grade C policy), and that of a ministerial regulation (Grade D policy). Our comparison of the impact and influence of various policies by grade, or the initiator of policies, is necessarily ordinal as it is hard to establish an exact interval relationship between them. In general, a high-grade policy guides the macro and strategic direction, while a policy with a low grade largely is focused on the interpretation of specific issues and the operational mechanisms associated with the macro policy.

We have used two sets of data for our purpose. The first is an existing compilation of national innovation policies issued between 1980 and 2005 (Research Department of the MOST General Office and CASTED, 2006). These policies, issued by the CPC CC, the NPC, the State Council, and assorted government ministries, took the form of decisions, laws, administrative statues, regulations, announcements, opinions, implementation measures, and so on. They were categorized into five innovation policy types – S&T, industrial, financial, tax, and fiscal – as defined and based on the scope of their respective impacts. Of course, not all were formulated for science, technology, and innovation *per se*.[2] Altogether, a total of 289 policies were scrutinized to exclude redundant ones, to correct categorical errors, and to ensure that the relevant policy-issuing agencies were aligned with their current names.[3] Therefore, the list ended up containing 287 policies.

The second data set is composed of 343 innovation policies formulated by ministries under the State Council between 2006 and 2019.[4] The data set includes all the policy documents formulated between 2006 and 2008 to implement the *Medium and Long-Term Plan for the*

---

[2] For example, in general, China's five-year plan is not about science, technology, and innovation *per se*. But the compilation lists the *Seventh Five-Year Plan for the National Economy and Social Development (1986–1990)* but not other five-year plans; presumably, this particular five-year plan had more to do with the science, technology, and innovation theme.

[3] In the transformation of the Chinese economy from planning into market orientation, the State Council has gone through a series of – seven, to be exact – administrative reshuffles in 1982, 1988, 1993, 1998, 2003, 2008, 2018, and 2023. Each restructuring brought about shifts in missions, functions, roles, and sometimes even the names of the ministries (OECD, 2005:14–15). We attributed a policy to a current ministry, with the exception of Commission of Science, Technology and Industry for National Defense (COSTIND), but use the name of the ministry at the time when it issued the policy in discussion. While sacrificing certain information, doing so makes the analysis succinct and consistent. The National Natural Science Foundation of China (NSFC) and the Administration of Foreign Experts are merged into MOST in 2018. However, the NSFC still operates independently, so it is still considered an independent agency.

[4] The policy issuers also include the China Development Bank, a share-holding company; the China Association for Science and Technology, a nongovernment organization; the National Commission on the Management and Coordination of Post-Doctoral Scientific Research Stations, a quasi-government agency; and the Department of General Logistics of the People's Liberation Army. They are not exactly ministry-level agencies but have been treated as such in the analysis.

Development of Science and Technology (2006–2020) (MLP) (MOST, 2009; Liu *et al.*, 2011), and all innovation policies formulated between 2009 and 2019 to mitigate the effects of the global financial crisis, and implement the strategy of innovation-driven development (Sun & Liu, 2014). They fall into the following policy topics – S&T investment, tax stimulus, financial support, government procurement, talent, intellectual property right (IPR) creation and protection, education, and S&T popularization, building of bases and platforms for science, technology, and innovation, coordination, and so on but have been re-coded corresponding to the categorizations used in the first data set. It is possible that one document is re-coded corresponding to two categorizations. As a whole, China's innovation policies under study in this chapter and the following one consist of a total of 556 innovation policy documents issued by various central government agencies and 74 innovation policy documents issued by CPC CC, NPC, the State Council a span of some 40 years.

Evolution of China's Innovation Policies

From the perspective of innovation policies, China's post-1978 era can be divided into five periods, marked by five significant national S&T conferences, held in 1978, 1985, 1995, 1999, and 2006, respectively, during which strategic decisions were made to reshape and recast many policies and initiatives (OECD, 2008: 381–393) (Tables 2.1 and 2.2). For our purpose, however, we divided the 40 years into four periods instead, using 1985, 1995, and 2006 as key demarcation years when three national S&T-related conferences were held and three important pieces of new policy originated around the time of these conferences.

In March 1985, while holding a national S&T working conference, the CPC CC issued the *Decision on the Reform of S&T System*, initiating the reform of S&T management system to ensure close alignment of research with the economy. Ten years later, in May 1995, CPC CC, along with the State Council this time, formulated the *Decision on Accelerating the Progress of Science and Technology*, putting "revitalizing the nation through science, technology, and education" (*kejiao xingguo*) on top of the agenda of the national development and erecting innovation as China's new "religion." The release of the MLP in 2006 was a new milestone in China's innovation drive. By committing to the promotion of stronger capabilities for "indigenous innovation" (*zizhu chuangxin*) and to leapfrogging into leading positions in

Table 2.1 *China's national science and technology conferences*

Time	Name	Significance
March 1978	National Science Conference	Deng Xiaoping brought forward the famous thesis that S&T is a productive force, intellectuals are part of the working class, and S&T is the key to China's Four Modernizations drive.
March 1985	National Science and Technology Working Conference	Deng Xiaoping made an important speech on the "Reform of the S&T System Is to Liberate the Productive Force." The CPC CC issued the *Decision on the Reform of the S&T System*. Afterward, China pulled off the reform prologue of the S&T system and set the main task to enhance the economic orientation of the S&T system.
May 1995	National Science and Technology Conference	The strategy of "revitalizing the nation through the science, technology and education" (*kejiao xingguo*) was put forward and the CPC CC issued the *Decision on Accelerating the Progress of Science and Technology*, advocating that economic development should rely on the progress of S&T.
August 1999	National conference on technological innovation	The CPC CC and the State Council issued the *Decision on Strengthening the Technological Innovation, Developing the High Technology and Realizing Industrialization*, calling for the construction of a national innovation system and speeding up of the industrialization of the S&T achievements.
January 2006	National Science and Technology Conference	The CPC CC and the State Council issued *Medium- and Long-Term Plan for the Development of Science and Technology (2006–2020)* (MLP) to turn China into an "innovation-oriented country" by 2020 through enhancing an indigenous innovation capability.

Source: OECD, 2008: 381–393.

Table 2.2 *China's innovation policies by period, agency, grade, and type (1980–2005)*

Period	Agency	Grade of Policy	Policy					Subtotal	% Agency
			S&T	Industrial	Financial	Tax	Fiscal		
1980–1984	CPC CC	A	0	0	0	0	0	0	–
	NPC	B	0	0	0	0	0	0	–
	State Council	C	0	3	2	2	0	7	41.2
	Ministries	D	6	1	2	1	0	10	58.8
	Subtotal		6	4	4	3	0	17	100.0
	% Policy		35.3	23.5	23.5	17.6	0	100.0	
1985–1994	CPC CC	A	2	0	1	0	0	3	4.0
	NPC	B	4	2	1	0	1	8	10.5
	State Council	C	8	6	5	3	0	22	29.0
	Ministries	D	20	17	1	5	0	43	56.6
	Subtotal		34	25	8	8	1	76	100.0
	% Policy		44.7	32.9	10.5	10.5	1.3	100.0	

								Total	%
	CPC CC	A	2	0	0	0	0	2	1.0
	NPC	B	3	1	9	0	1	14	7.2
	State Council	C	5	6	4	2	1	18	9.3
1995–2005	Ministries	D	74	28	22	26	10	160	82.5
	Subtotal		84	35	35	28	12	194	100.0
	% Policy		43.3	18	18	14.4	6.2	100.0	
	CPC CC	A	4	0	1	0	0	5	1.7
	NPC	B	7	3	10	0	2	22	7.7
	State Council	C	13	15	11	7	1	47	16.4
1980–2005	Ministries	D	100	46	25	32	10	213	74.2
	Total		124	64	47	39	13	287	100.0
	% Policy		43.2	22.3	16.4	13.6	4.5	100.0	

Sources: Research Department of the MOST General Office and CASTED, 2006.; MOST, 2009, 2020; Liu *et al.*, 2011; Sun & Liu, 2014.

new science-based industries, China stated its intention to become an "innovation-oriented society" by the year 2020 and a world leader in S&T by 2050. When the MLP was made public, the CPC CC and the State Council unveiled the *Decision on Implementing S&T Plan and Strengthening Indigenous Innovation Capability*.

The years from 2006 to 2020 are critical for two reasons. First, central government agencies under the State Council published 79 innovation policies for the purpose of the MLP implementation between 2006 and 2008. Meanwhile, China also seized the occurrence of the global financial crisis in 2008 to make innovation policies. Second, in 2016, China issued the *National Outline of Innovation-driven Development Strategy*, or a "three-step" strategy, to further emphasize the strategic steps unveiled first in the MLP: China aims to join the ranks of innovation-oriented countries by 2020, advance to the forefront of innovation-oriented countries by 2030, and become a world S&T leader by 2050. The MLP implementation can be further divided into three periods, the first focusing on strengthening indigenous innovation between 2006 and 2008; the second mitigating the impacts of the international financial crisis between 2009 and 2016; and the third moving forward with the innovation-driven development between 2017 and 2019.

Accordingly, we discuss the evolution of China's innovation policies in four periods, namely, the first, the pre-reform period between 1980 and 1984; the second, between 1985 and 1994; the third, between 1995 and 2005; and the fourth, after 2006.

Prelude to the Reform (1980–1984)

The total number of innovation policies issued during this period was fairly small – only 17 – with the majority in the category of S&T policy (6) plus a few industrial (4), financial (4), and tax policies (3); there was no fiscal policy. The period started with an initial revitalization of China's S&T system, which emerged from the Cultural Revolution between 1966 and 1976 severely damaged. The leadership felt compelled to restore the nation's key S&T organizations and industrial technological capabilities. The 1978 National Science Conference was held against such a backdrop, during which Deng Xiaoping, who later would become China's paramount leader, remarked that S&T is the primary productive force and intellectuals are part of the working class, therefore laying the ideological foundation for designing China's new S&T development strategies in years to come. From then on China truly rekindled its commitment to S&T development and innovation activities.

In specific terms, this period is characterized by the initiation of various national S&T programs, including the State Technological Reconstruction Program (1982), the State Key Technologies R&D Program (1982), the State Major Technological Equipment R&D Program (1983), the State Key Technological Development Program (1983), the State Key Laboratory Construction Program (1984), and the State Key Industrial Testing Program (1984). Many of these programs were run by either the State Planning Commission (SPC) or the State Economic Commission (SEC), which would evolve into The State Economic and Trading Commission (SETC) and eventually the National Development and Reform Commission (NDRC), with the State Key Technologies R&D Program also having the participation of the State Science and Technology Commission (SSTC), now the MOST. Apparently, during this early period, it was the SPC and SEC that set the agenda for China's S&T development, controlled and allocated resources for technological development activities, and administered S&T programs while the SSTC was only a player on the sideline.

Initial Reform of the S&T System (1985–1994)

While the total number of innovation policies in this period reached 76, the main focus was on S&T and industrial policies (34 and 25, respectively). Both financial and tax policies increased to eight and the first fiscal policy was issued.

There is no doubt that the most important S&T policy during this period is the 1985 CPC CC decision to reform China's S&T system. In the following years, the State Council introduced a series of S&T policies, from the *Temporary Regulation on Expanding the Autonomy of S&T Research Institutes* (1986), the *Opinions on Furthering the Reform of S&T System* (1987), to the *Decision on Several Issues to Deepen the Reform of S&T System* (1988), interpreting and providing details to the implementation of the CPC CC decision. While these four policies were designed to reform the S&T system to meet the demands of economic development, the *Decision on Some Issues in the Establishment of a Socialist Market Economic System*, issued by

the CPC CC in 1993, was specially aimed at creating a macroeconomic environment more conducive to S&T development. This aspect
also was reflected in the enacting of several laws by the NPC, such as
the *Patent Law* (1985, amended in 1992), the *Law on the Progress
of Science and Technology* (1993), and the *Law on Anti-Unfair
Competition* (1993), to lay out the contours for a new and more competitive business environment.

Thanks to the 1985 decision on S&T system's reform, high-tech
start-ups started to spin off from research institutes and universities
in Beijing's Zhongguancun and other high-tech concentration areas.
Thus, the establishment of high-tech parks became a prominent aspect
of the new S&T push. In 1988, the State Council formally approved
setting up the Beijing Experimental Zone for New Technology and
Industrial Development, now known as the Zhongguancun Science
Park, granting 18 preferential policies on taxes, loans, and personnel mobility and recruitment to support its development. Three years
later, the State Council issued the *Announcement on the Approval
of National High and New-Technology and Industrial Development
Zones and Related Policies and Regulations*, approving another 26
national high-tech parks (as of 2021, China had a total of 168 such
parks at the national level).[5] The document not only defined the quali-
fications for certifying high- and new-tech enterprises operating within
a high-tech park but also stipulated various forms of preferential treatment for supporting their overall development.

It is during this period that the SSTC started to take on a more pronounced role in launching and administering national S&T programs.
The most noticeable example is the State High-Tech R&D Program,
also known as the 863 Program, launched in March 1986, to monitor
the high-tech trends in the world and make efforts to develop China's
own high-tech industries. Other programs run by the SSTC included
the Spark Program to develop the rural economy through S&T (1986),
the Torch Program for high-tech industrialization (1988), the State Key
S&T Achievement Promotion Program (1990), the State Engineering
(Technology) R&D Center Construction Program (1991, jointly with

---

[5] The compilation of innovation policies includes the *Announcement on the
Approval of National High- and New-Tech Industrial Development Zones
and Related Policies and Regulations,* but not the State Council approval of
the *Establishment of the Zhongguancun Science Park*, most likely because the
latter document was treated as a policy at the regional level.

the then SPC), and the Climbing Program for basic research (1992). These programs covered a wide spectrum of the S&T and R&D activities – from basic and applied R&D to commercialization – as well as S&T for rural development. In many ways, this broader and more substantial thrust represented a significant departure from SSTC's original mission in policymaking. The legacy of this transition continues to make itself felt today as all these programs are now mainly under the primary purview of MOST, which from time to time also has sought to initiate new programs to enlarge its turf.

In addition to formulating broad guidelines in 1989 and 1994 and specific sector guidelines for information technology and biotechnology, respectively, the State Council, in 1988, focused on one special issue – accelerating technological progress by importing technology and facilitating its assimilation. It issued the *Regulations on the Encouragement of Technology Importation Contracts* in 1985 and the *Regulations on the Work of Absorbing and Assimilating Imported Technologies* in 1986. The SEC also had twice put up catalogs of key imported technologies for technological innovation at enterprises. Given the mixed experiences of Chinese enterprises and local governments regarding technology imports, there clearly was a need to fix the range of prevailing problems to ensure that scarce foreign exchange dollars were better utilized.

Transition from S&T to Innovation (1995–2005)

This period is marked by the introduction of the concept of "innovation" into China, and thereby the expansion of China's innovation policies beyond S&T and industrial policies. At the same time of having a big jump in the number of S&T policy (from 34 in the second period to 84) and a modest increase in the number of industrial policy (from 25 to 35), this period witnessed the rapid introduction of financial, tax, and fiscal policies (from 8 to 35, 8 to 28, and 1 to 12, respectively).

Innovation policies during this period had the following characteristics. First, the NPC enacted various laws to nurture an environment for business activities in China. In addition to three laws treated as S&T policy – the *Law on the Promotion of S&T Achievement Conversion* (1996), the *Law on Contracts* (1999),[6] and the *Law on*

---

[6] The *Law on Contracts* covers technological contracts.

S&T Popularization (2002) – and one related to industrial policy, the *Law on Promoting Small and Medium-sized Enterprises* (2002), there were an entire new series of laws in the categories of financial and fiscal policies devised to provide greater institutional support for promoting innovation. One law was in the area of fiscal policy, the *Law on Government Procurement* (2002), and nine dealt with financial policy, namely, the *Law on the People's Bank of China* (1995), the *Law on Commercial Banks* (1995, amended in 2003), the *Law on Guaranty* (1995), the *Law on Negotiable Instruments* (1996), the *Securities Law* (1998), the amended *Corporate Law* (1999, originally enacted in 1993), the *Trust Law* (2001), the *Insurance Law* (2002), and the *Law on Securities Investment Funds* (2003). Although these laws were not directly related to science, technology, and innovation, their impacts had been enormous as the reform of China's S&T system had increasingly exposed institutions of learning to business imperatives and subjected their behavior to a new legal environment framed by these laws.

Second, the S&T policy was geared toward stimulating broad institutional reforms at government-affiliated R&D institutions. In 1999, 242 institutes affiliated with the then State Economic and Trading Commission (SETC), on the basis of SPC and the Ministry of Internal Trade, were among the first to be transformed – they were either merged into existing enterprises to become their internal R&D units or converted into technology-oriented enterprises themselves. Other types of R&D institutes, including those in the areas of public goods, went on to be restructured as well, of which the most notable is that the Chinese Academy of Sciences (CAS) launched a Knowledge Innovation Program to revitalize itself. To help these reforms proceed smoothly, the then SSTC, in conjunction with other government ministries, issued a series of financial and tax policies to offer favorable treatment to the newly transformed R&D institute enterprises.

Third, policies specifically focused on the transformation of S&T achievements started to appear. After the NPC enacted the *Law on the Promotion of S&T Achievement Conversion* in 1996, mentioned above, additional related policies were put into effect in 1999. They include the *Decision on Strengthening Technological Innovation, Developing High Technology and Realizing Industrialization* by the CPC CC and the State Council, the *Action Plan for Promoting Trade with S&T* by the SSTC and the then Ministry of Foreign

Trade and Cooperation (MOFTEC), now the Ministry of Commerce (MOFCOM), *Some Regulations on Promoting S&T Achievement Conversion* by the SSTC, the Ministry of Finance (MOF), the General Administration of Customs (GAC), the People's Bank of China (PBOC), the State Administration of Industry and Commerce (SAIC), the then Ministry of Personnel, which became the Ministry of Human Resources and Social Security (MOHRSS) in 2008, and the SEC. On the industrial policy front, in 2003, the State Council approved the *Opinions on Accelerating the Technological Achievement Conversion and Optimizing the Structure of Exports*, proposed by MOFCOM, SSTC, SETC, PBOC, and the State Administration of Taxation (SAT). What is worth noting, in particular, is the introduction of relevant preferential tax policy aimed at the promotion of S&T achievement conversion.

Fourth, support for private S&T enterprises became one of the key foci of innovation policies. To make these enterprises the main engine of innovation, in1996, the Ministry of Agriculture, along with the State Development and Planning Commission (SDPC), SETC, SEC, and SSTC, issued the *Opinions on Accelerating S&T Progress at Village and Township Enterprises*; and in 1999, the SSTC and SETC introduced the *Opinions on Promoting the Development of Private S&T Enterprises* to revise a six-year-old policy. The SSTC and its successor, MOST, also introduced several policies pertaining to the development of national high-tech parks and the support of S&T start-ups within these parks. Finally, in 2002, the NPC enacted the *Law on the Promotion of Small and Medium-sized Enterprises*. Taken together, these policies began to shift the locus of innovation toward firms and away from primary reliance on government-run research institutes.

Fifth, sector-oriented industrial policy was used to promote innovation. The SETC, for example, issued catalogs of technological renovation priorities for guiding technology imports in 1995 and 1996. In 2000, the SETC and SDPC came up with a catalog of key industries, products, and technologies that government should encourage to develop. And in 2001, the SDPC and MOST formulated guidelines on key priorities for high-tech industrialization. Moreover, in 2002, the SETC, MOF, MOST, and SAT introduced a set of policies for deploying high- and new-technology and advanced appropriate technology to renovate traditional industries. Also worth mentioning is a 2000 State Council document that outlined policies on encouraging the development of software and integrated circuit industries. In particular, the new policies covered venture capital mechanisms for supporting the software industry, preferential tax rates for enterprises producing software and integrated circuits, support for fundraising through public listing of qualified software companies, and measures encouraging the establishment of software ventures. There also were provisions allowing higher levels of foreign investment as part of the overall development strategy for these two sectors.

Indigenous Innovation (2006–2008)

The 79 policies for MLP's implementation do not include such high-grade policies as CPC CC documents, laws enacted by NPC, or State Council statutes; all are at Grade D level. This by no means suggests that the MLP is not strategically or politically important, and the number itself is significant. In fact, a new decision by the CPC CC and the State Council anchored the MLP; the State Council, the issuing agency of the plan, also initiated the effort to construct an integrated innovation policy framework. Meanwhile, the NPC moved to amend several laws pertaining to innovation, including the *Law on the Progress of Science and Technology* in 2007 and the *Patent Law* in 2008. One of the most significant revisions of the law on S&T progress were its promotion of innovation and creativity by fostering a "tolerance for failure"; and the patent law, following previous revisions in 1992 and 2000 to build additional momentum, was further aligned with international standards, although the international community still alleged that the revision was a setback in the development of IPRs in China (Suttmeier & Yao, 2011). All this has set the stage for expanding and deepening China's innovation activities in years to come.[7]

Of the policies to implement the MLP, 37 can be placed in the S&T policy category. This suggests that even within the high-profile MLP, one of the key challenges facing China's innovation – the S&T development for driving innovation – has not been resolved. Regarding investment in S&T, a policy called for better management of the funding aspects of the national S&T programs such as the 863 Program, the State Basic Research and Development Program, also known as the 973 Program, initiated in March 1997, and the State Key Technologies

---

[7] Both laws were amended again in 2021.

R&D Program, all under the MOST. Addition to the S&T policy was a new emphasis on talent, including components of attracting high-end talent from overseas, postdoctoral fellowships, continuous education for professionals, the nurturing of practitioners in rural areas, and so on. Closely related to the talent issue was the issue of education, with policies introduced of sending students and scholars abroad using government funds, enhancing research-oriented universities, supporting key disciplines, and opening institutions of learning to society for the purpose of popularization of science. Among the concerns regarding the infrastructure for supporting S&T advance and innovation were national engineering centers and laboratories, nationally certified enterprise engineering centers, certification of university high-tech parks at the national level, and key national laboratories established at transformed R&D institutes.

With 19 items, industrial policy to implement the MLP not only emphasized the building up of an indigenous innovation capability, with special attention given to support for innovation activities within small- and medium-sized enterprises and the formal certification of innovative products, but also encouraged innovation based on the assimilation of imported technology, which largely was reflected in the content of an assortment of industrial policy. There even was a policy that specified which priority technologies to be imported. Industrial policy also targeted the talent issue, especially the shortage of key personnel in the S&T areas of critical importance to the nation, the attraction of talent from overseas, and the evaluation and rewarding of key personnel in central government-controlled R&D institutes, design institutes, and enterprises. It is also interesting to notice that industrial policy contained several key catalogs – from key information technologies and important products in which China possesses indigenous IPRs, key technologies that China should possess indigenous IPRs, key areas for high-tech commercialization, imported products without tax free benefits, to industries for encouraging foreign investment. In addition, industrial policy promoted the transfer of civilian technology for military use and the participation of the emerging Chinese private sector in national defense-related S&T activities.

Both tax and financial policies contained nine separate components. Tax policy covered preferential treatment for imports of equipment for scientific research and teaching, venture capital investment, enterprises engaged in innovation activities, university high-tech parks, incubators for S&T enterprises, and the provision of innovation funds for S&T-oriented SMEs. Financial policy, on the other hand, guided the establishment of innovation funds for S&T-oriented SMEs, supported national key S&T programs, and provided a commitment for the establishment and operation of an active exchange market for intellectual properties.

Finally, fiscal policy still occupied the least significant position as measured by its number – five. However, fiscal policy actually was getting played out under the provision of policies regarding government procurement, especially related to indigenously innovated products – their budget management, contract management, evaluation, procurement of first products, and procurement of imported products. This indicates that growing tensions between China and the foreign business community over the indigenous innovation issue require more than just negotiation with the MOST, and the procurement-related aspects of indigenous innovation policy seems to suggest that both the MOF and the NDRC appeared to be heavily involved as well.

Financial Crisis and Innovation-Driven Development (2009–2019)

The 2008 global financial crisis had disrupted the implementation of the MLP. Since 2009, China had issued a large number of industrial revitalization plans and innovation policies to support industrial development.

After the global financial crisis, the Chinese government further strengthened the role of the government in S&T development. One hundred and nine documents can be placed in the S&T policy category. A direct consequence of the crisis was recession and unemployment across the world. So, S&T policy still included a new emphasis on talent, including employing graduates in research projects, attracting high-end talents from overseas, especially talents in biotechnology and new materials, and others. S&T policy also was included in the 12th and 13th five-year plans on S&T development, as well as special plans for international S&T cooperation, university science parks, and so on.

With 48 items, industrial policy not only emphasized the development of high-tech industries, strategic emerging industries, software and integrated circuits, marine engineering equipment, remanufacturing, agriculture, and so on, but also encouraged innovation based on the assimilation of imported technology, which largely is reflected in the content of an assortment of industrial policy. There even was a policy specifying prioritization of technologies to import.

There were 27 items of tax and financial policies, representing a drop of nearly 10 percent compared with those issued in the previous indigenous innovation period. Tax policy covered preferential treatment for technology transfer, R&D expenditures for enterprises, technology imports for innovation, and the development of high-tech enterprises and SMEs. Few in number and aiming to support for S&T-oriented SMEs, financial policy guided the establishment of equity and dividend incentives for S&T-oriented state-owned enterprises and enterprises in Zhongguancun Science Park, and provided a commitment for private capital entering the field of science, technology, and innovation. Finally, the number of fiscal policies increased to 21, surpassing both tax and financial policies. Fiscal policy mainly focused on the management of fiscal funds on S&T.

With the implementation of the innovation-driven development strategy in 2012, the proportion of S&T policy and industrial policy had further increased to 86.4 percent of the total, while fiscal, tax, and financial policies decreased to less than 15 percent. S&T policy not only was about the reform of the S&T system, such as reform of S&T evaluation, reform of the IPR regime, and reform of research institutions, and so on, but also covered the special plans for 13th five-year plans on international S&T cooperation, the military and civilian integration of S&T, urban science, technology, and innovation, among others. Industrial policy emphasized the S&T development for emerging industries, such as Internet plus medical and health care, new energy vehicles, advanced manufacturing, artificial intelligence, among others. Fiscal, tax, and financial policies continued to cover the previous policy issues, with the fiscal policy particularly focused on the division of labor between central and local governments in the field of S&T and how the central government guides local funds on S&T development.

In a word, over the years, innovation policies had increased in number, variety, and reach. Regarding policy domains, more recognizable S&T and industrial policies dominated the first two periods, while financial, fiscal, and tax policies played a more prominent role in the latter periods. In terms of content, innovation policies during the first two periods focused on the initiation of new national S&T programs but shifted in emphasis to innovation capability building and further to the creation of an innovation-friendly environment through the enhanced management of S&T programs during the period of indigenous innovation. Policies in the later periods, while maintaining the recent trends, were geared toward new developments. The reliance on a single policy to support the implementation of specific S&T programs also had given way to the formation of a rich portfolio of policies in which financial, tax, and fiscal policies had become as strategically important as traditional S&T and industrial policies in promoting innovation. That is, more consideration was given to the alignment and coordination between and across policies of same and different types. For China, whose highly vertically oriented bureaucratic structure often precluded close communication, coordination, and cooperation across ministries and other government organizations, the progress on the S&T front represented a major breakthrough.

Institutional Structure of China's Innovation Policies

Institutional Structure of Innovation Policies from 1980 to 2005

Most of China's innovation policies between 1980 and 2005 were issued by a single agency, which accounted for 72.5 percent of the total number of policies. Innovation policies issued by two agencies accounted for another 20.6 percent and the remaining approximately 7 percent were issued by three or more agencies (Table 2.3). In particular, one single entity introduced 85.1 percent of the financial policies, 80 percent of the industrial policies, 71.8 percent of the S&T policies, and 59 percent of the tax policies. The main exception is in the domain of fiscal policy, where only 38.5 percent involved one ministry. As the CPC CC, the NPC, and the State Council are most likely to issue a policy document by itself, the focus of this section is on the role of ministerial level agencies in the formulation of Grade D policies (Table 2.4).

About one-third of China's S&T policy was issued by more than one agency, with one agency most likely being that in direct charge of S&T affairs. In the early years, that agency was either the SPC or the SEC; then their successor, the SETC, got involved before the SSTC and its successor, the MOST, assumed the specific responsibility. As

Table 2.3 *China's innovation policies by period, type, and number of agencies (1980–2019)*

Period	Policy	Number of agencies			Total	% Policy	% One agency
		1	2	3 or more			
1980–1984	S&T	5	1	0	6	35.3	83.3
	Industrial	4	0	0	4	23.5	100.0
	Financial	4	0	0	4	23.5	100.0
	Tax	2	1	0	3	17.6	66.7
	Fiscal	0	0	0	0	0	–
	Subtotal	15	2	0	17	100	88.2
1985–1994	S&T	30	4	0	34	44.7	88.2
	Industrial	23	0	2	25	32.9	92.0
	Financial	7	1	0	8	10.5	87.5
	Tax	6	2	0	8	10.5	75.0
	Fiscal	1	0	0	1	1.3	100.0
	Subtotal	67	7	2	76	100	88.2
1995–2005	S&T	54	20	10	84	43.3	64.3
	Industrial	24	7	4	35	18.0	68.6
	Financial	29	4	2	35	18.0	82.9
	Tax	15	12	1	28	14.4	53.6
	Fiscal	4	7	1	12	6.2	33.3
	Subtotal	126	50	18	194	100	65.0
1980–2005	S&T	89	25	10	124	43.2	71.8
	Industrial	51	7	6	64	22.3	79.7
	Financial	40	5	2	47	16.4	85.1
	Tax	23	15	1	39	13.6	59.0
	Fiscal	5	7	1	13	4.5	38.5
	Subtotal	208	59	20	287	100	72.5
2006–2008	S&T	16	10	11	37	46.8	43.2
	Industrial	6	2	11	19	24.1	31.6
	Financial	5	3	1	9	11.4	55.6
	Tax	0	6	3	9	11.4	0
	Fiscal	5	0	0	5	6.3	100
	Subtotal	32	21	26	79	100	40.5

Table 2.3 *(cont.)*

Period	Policy	\multicolumn{5}{Number of agencies}

Period	Policy	1	2	3 or more	Total	% Policy	% One agency
2009–2016	S&T	65	17	27	109	53.2	59.6
	Industrial	32	2	14	48	23.4	66.7
	Financial	2	4	1	7	3.4	28.6
	Tax	4	6	10	20	9.8	20.0
	Fiscal	7	13	1	21	10.2	33.3
	Subtotal	110	42	53	205	100.0	53.7
2017–2019	S&T	25	25	14	64	58.2	39.1
	Industrial	16	3	12	31	28.2	51.6
	Financial	1	0	2	3	2.7	33.3
	Tax	2	2	2	6	5.5	33.3
	Fiscal	2	3	1	6	5.5	33.3
	Subtotal	46	33	31	110	100.0	41.8
2006–2019	S&T	106	52	52	210	53.3	50.5
	Industrial	54	7	37	98	24.9	55.1
	Financial	8	7	4	19	4.8	42.1
	Tax	6	14	15	35	8.9	17.1
	Fiscal	14	16	2	32	8.1	43.8
	Subtotal	188	96	110	394	100.0	47.7
1980–2005	% Agency	72.5	20.6	7.0	100.0		
2006–2019	% Agency	47.7	24.4	27.9	100.0		
1980–2019	% Agency	58.1	22.8	19.1	100.0		

Sources: Same as Table 2.2.

a whole, the MOST was involved in the making of a total of 75 S&T policy. Also important in Chinese S&T policy formulation efforts had been three other organizations: the NDRC (24 items of S&T policy including those issued by its predecessors, the SPC, the SEC, and the SETC), the MOF (16), and the MOFCOM (11).

Among the participating agencies involved with 46 Grade D industrial policy, both the MOFCOM and the NDRC stood out as key

Table 2.4 *China's innovation policies issued by ministerial level agencies and type (1980–2005)*

Agency	Policy						Agency's contribution to policy (%)
	S&T	Industrial	Financial	Tax	Fiscal	Total	
MOST	75	6	4	1	4	90	42.3
MOF	16	6	1	18	10	51	23.9
NDRC	24	18	1	0	3	46	21.6
SAT	4	5	1	24	2	36	16.9
MOFCOM	11	19	2	1	1	34	16.0
PBOC	1	2	12	1	0	16	7.5
CSRC	0	0	12	0	0	12	5.6
SAIC	6	2	2	0	1	11	5.2
GAQSIQ	3	6	0	0	1	10	4.7
MOE	6	1	0	0	1	8	3.8
GAC	1	1	0	3	0	5	2.3
MOHRSS	4	0	0	0	1	5	2.3
SCOPSR	2	0	0	0	1	3	1.4
SC GO	1	0	0	1	0	2	0.9
SIPO	1	1	0	0	0	2	0.9
SAFE	0	1	1	0	0	2	0.9
MOIIT	0	0	0	1	1	2	0.9
CAS	1	1	0	0	0	2	0.9
NSFC	2	0	0	0	0	2	0.9
CIBC	0	1	0	0	0	1	0.5
EIBOC	0	1	0	0	0	1	0.5
MOFA	0	1	0	0	0	1	0.5
SAFEA	1	0	0	0	0	1	0.5
CAE	1	0	0	0	0	1	0.5
COSTIND	1	0	0	0	0	1	0.5
CPCCC CEW	0	0	0	0	1	1	0.5
GAPP	0	0	0	1	0	1	0.5
MOMI	0	1	0	0	0	1	0.5
CPCCC DOO	1	0	0	0	0	1	0.5
PLA DGL	1	0	0	0	0	1	0.5
SA	1	0	0	0	0	1	0.5
MOA	1	0	0	0	0	1	0.5
MOCA	1	0	0	0	0	1	0.5
SAA	1	0	0	0	0	1	0.5
SC HMO	0	1	0	0	0	1	0.5
MOWR	0	1	0	0	0	1	0.5
Total number of agencies	167	75	36	51	27	356	

Table 2.4 *(cont.)*

Agency	Policy						Agency's contribution to policy (%)
	S&T	Industrial	Financial	Tax	Fiscal	Total	
Total number of policies	100	46	25	32	10	213	
Number of agencies per policy	1.67	1.63	1.44	1.59	2.70	1.67	
Most important policy maker	MOST	MOFCOM	PBOC, CSRC	SAT	MOF	MOST	
% Most important policy maker	75.0	41.3	48.0	75.0	100.0	42.3	

Sources: Research Department of the MOST General Office and CASTED, 2006.
Notes: CAE – Chinese Academy of Engineering; CAS – Chinese Academy of Sciences; CAST – China Association for Science and Technology; CBRC – China Banking Regulatory Commission; CPC CC CEW – CPC CC Commission on Enterprise Work; CPC CC DOO – CPC CC Department of Organization; CPC CC DOP – CPC CC Department of Propaganda; CDB – China Development Bank; CIBC – Commerce and Industry Bank of China; CIRC – China Insurance Regulatory Commission; COSTIND – Commission of Science, Technology, and Industry for National Defense; CSRC – China Securities Regulatory Commission; EIBOC – Export-Import Bank of China; GAC – General Administration of Customs; GAPP – General Administration of Press and Publication; GAQSIA – General Administration of Quality Supervision, Inspection, and Quarantine; MOA – Ministry of Agriculture; MOCA – Ministry of Civil Affairs; MOE – Ministry of Education; MOF – Ministry of Finance; MOFA – Ministry of Foreign Affairs; MOFCOM – Ministry of Commerce; MOHRSS – Ministry of Human Resources and Social Security; MOHURD – Ministry of Housing and Urban-Rural Development; MOIIT – Ministry of Industry and Information Technology; MOLR – Ministry of Land and Resources; MOMI – Ministry of Mechanical Industry; MOPS – Ministry of Public Security; MOST – Ministry of Science and Technology; MOWR – Ministry of Water Resources; NAC – National Copyright Administration; NBS – National Bureau of Statistics; NCMCPDSRS – National Commission on the Management and Coordination of Post-Doctoral Scientific Research Stations; NDRC – National Development and Reform Commission; NSFC – National Natural Science Foundation of China; PBOC – People's Bank of China; PLA DGL – People's Liberation Army Department of General Logistics; SA – Standardization Administration; SAA – State Archives Administration; SAIC – State Administration of Industry and Commerce; SAFE – State Administration of Foreign Exchange; SAFEA – State Administration of Foreign Experts Affairs; SASAC – State-owned Assets Supervision and Administration Commission; SAT – State Administration of Taxation; SC GO – State Council General Office; SC HMO – State Council Hong Kong and Macau Affairs Office; SC OCAO – State Council Overseas Chinese Affairs Office; SCOPSR – State Commission Office for Public Sector Reform; SIPO – State Intellectual Property Office.

players, making 19 and 18 items, respectively. Other important players include the MOST, the MOF, and the General Administration of Quality Supervision, Inspection, and Quarantine (GAQSIQ) – each participated in six pieces of industrial policy. The PBOC and the China Securities Regulatory Commission (CSRC) had been mainly involved in the formulation of financial policy, each underwriting 12 items. With regard to tax, the SAT was associated with 24 items of policy, accounting for three-quarters of the total. Fiscal policy was clearly the main domain of the MOF, which was involved in all ten policies.

Not surprisingly, with 90 innovation policies, accounting for 42.3 percent of the total, the MOST was the one Chinese ministry that was most deeply and systematically involved in the innovation policymaking between 1980 and 2005 and significantly ahead of the MOF (23.9 percent), the NDRC (21.6 percent), the SAT (16.9 percent), and the MOFCOM (16.0 percent). While the MOST also was involved in six pieces of industrial policy, the MOF was associated with S&T policy (16) and fiscal policy (10) in addition to making tax policy, its main domain; the NDRC with 18 pieces of industrial policy in addition to S&T policy; the SAT also set tax policy, and the MOFCOM was heavily involved in S&T policy (11). Also important in the S&T policymaking were the SAIC (6) and the Ministry of Education (6).

Altogether, a total of 36 ministerial level agencies participated in the formation of a variety of innovation policies between 1980 and 2005. As each separate policy involved as little as 1 or as many as 11 individual agencies, a total of 356 distinct agency efforts were involved in the 213 pieces of policy introduction, which translates into about 1.67 agencies per policy. More agencies were involved in fiscal policy (2.70) than in other types of policy and fewer agencies in financial policy (1.44) and therefore among all the components of innovation policies, fiscal policy was probably the most effective, reflecting the more cross-ministry approach and the existence of greater coordination from the outset in the formulation and implementation processes, and financial policy, lest influential. In other words, early on, innovation did not receive much financial support in China. Overall, given institutional divisions and political cleavages across the Chinese bureaucracy, it is hard for a ministry-centric or ministry-specific Grade D policy to have much influence beyond a single ministerial boundary or for one ministry to carry much weight without bringing other ministries on board for support.

That said, it does not preclude the possibility that some innovation policies did receive support from multiple agencies. When this did happen, the policies had turned out to be highly influential. For example, 11 ministries – including the MOST and the NDRC – adopted a fiscal policy on the institutional transformation of government-affiliated R&D institutes. This policy seemed to work quite well in achieving its intended purpose. A policy on national key new product management and another on the transformation of S&T achievements each had seven sponsors, and one on the adaptation of international standards was signed on by six ministries. In the domain of industrial policy, the establishment of Chinese brand exported goods was proposed by eight ministries. Unfortunately, these tended to be the exception rather than the norm.

In a word, China's innovation policies had been largely issued by a single government agency, and in most instances, this organization had been the MOST, as measured by the overall number of policies with which it had been associated, and whose formal mandate placed it in charge of S&T policy formulation, implementation, and administration. Meanwhile, it needed to be recognized as well that the fulfillment of MOST's core missions "requires close coordination, joint decisions and shared responsibilities with other ministries" (OECD, 2008:77). Therefore, it is not surprising to find that its main domain of impact regarding S&T development had been vertically with S&T bureaus at the provincial and municipal levels while its power and horizontal influence vis-à-vis mobilizing other ministries had been minimal. This suggested that the performance of China's innovation system should be dependent on a combination of both vertical and horizontal communication, coordination, and cooperation. By viewing the processes of innovation policy formulation and implementation through this lens, we can better appreciate the tensions within and across the system as well as both the successes and failures of innovation policy heretofore.

Institutional Structure of Innovation Policies from 2006 to 2019

The formulation of the 394 innovation policies to implement the MLP and mitigate the shock of the global financial crisis reflects not just some of the lessons that China had learned from its post-1978 experiences in innovation policymaking, as discussed. Of them, 79 pieces were a set of polices for MLP's implementation. Such an approach also represents a level of mobilization across multiple ministries that is not often easy to achieve even under the best of circumstances. Moreover, because organizational culture and operating environment within each of the ministries are quite different in some key respects such as organizations' history and size, administrative routine, any mobilization push has to take into account of the high degree of heterogeneity that exists across the Chinese bureaucratic structure.

On average, 47.7 percent of the innovation policies designed for the MLP implementation were issued by one agency, 24.4 percent by two agencies, with the rest involving 3 to 16 agencies (Table 2.3). This shows a significantly different pattern from the innovation policymaking and execution experiences between 1980 and 2005 when almost three-quarters were issued by one agency. In particular, one individual agency issued more than half of the S&T policy and industrial policy, more than two-fifths of the financial and fiscal policy, and less than one-fifth of the tax policy.

Involved in the making of 123 items of S&T policy, the MOST, again, was the important government agency in charge of innovation policymaking. It also had emerged as the new key player in the realm of industrial policy and financial policy, replacing the MOFCOM, the PBOC, and CSRC. As the MOFCOM had reduced its importance, the MOST and the NDRC had seen their respective active presence in China's innovation policymaking efforts – and especially industrial policy – significantly enhanced, which may suggest the necessary interaction between S&T and industrial policies. The MOF remained the most important in making fiscal policy. As expected, the main sponsors of tax policy were the MOF and the SAT, as well as the GAC. The MOE and the MOHRSS also had gained stature in terms of their policymaking power, apparently because the talent issue had become increasingly strategic among China's overall innovation policy package.

Comparing Table 2.5 with Table 2.4, we find that the MOST still is the omnipresent contributor to innovation policies by participating in or being the driver behind 56.7 percent of the new policies. However, MOST's presence in financial policymaking was a very interesting new development. This ministry seemingly did not have ample authority to push forward the national innovation agenda on its own; indeed, it has never secured a high position – in terms of political status and prestige – for itself within the Chinese government hierarchy. The fact

Table 2.5 *Innovation policies to implement MLP by agency and type (2006–2019)*

Agency	Policy						Agency's contribution to policy (%)
	S&T	Industrial	Financial	Tax	Fiscal	Total	
MOST	**123**	**46**	**13**	7	13	202	56.7
MOF	51	23	8	28	26	136	38.2
NDRC	40	35	1	6	3	85	23.9
MOE	45	9	0	1	2	57	16.0
SAT	9	9	0	34	0	52	14.6
MOHRSS	24	7	0	0	0	31	8.7
CAS	24	5	0	0	0	29	8.1
MOIIT	5	19	0	3	0	27	7.6
GAC	7	6	0	12	0	25	7.0
MOFCOM	3	16	0	4	0	23	6.5
SIPO	11	8	1	0	1	21	5.9
SC GO	14	3	1	0	2	20	5.8
NSFC	16	0	0	0	1	17	4.8
MOA	5	10	0	0	0	15	4.2
SASAC	6	6	3	0	0	15	4.2
CAE	13	1	0	0	0	14	3.9
CAST	9	0	0	0	0	9	2.5
CPCCC DOP	8	1	0	0	0	9	2.5
MOLR	3	5	0	0	0	8	2.2
MOPS	5	2	0	0	0	7	2.0
PBOC	4	3	0	0	0	7	2.0
CBRC	2	1	3	0	0	6	1.7
GAPP	4	1	0	1	0	6	1.7
GAQAIA	1	5	0	0	0	6	1.7
MOHURD	3	3	0	0	0	6	1.7
NFGA	1	4	0	0	1	6	1.7
NHC	3	3	0	0	0	6	1.7
PLA GAD	5	1	0	0	0	6	1.7
CSRC	2	1	2	0	0	5	1.4
CPCCC DOO	5	0	0	0	0	5	1.4
COSTIND	1	4	0	0	0	5	1.4
MOFA	2	3	0	0	0	5	1.4
CAC	2	2	0	0	0	4	1.1
CASS	4	0	0	0	0	4	1.1
MOWR	1	3	0	0	0	4	1.1
NBS	1	3	0	0	0	4	1.1
NEA	1	2	0	1	0	4	1.1
SAMR	2	2	0	0	0	4	1.1
CDB	2	0	1	0	0	3	0.8

Table 2.5 *(cont.)*

Agency	S&T	Industrial	Financial	Tax	Fiscal	Total	Agency's contribution to policy (%)
CFDA	1	2	0	0	0	3	0.8
CMC STC	3	0	0	0	0	3	0.8
MEP	1	2	0	0	0	3	0.8
MOT	2	1	0	0	0	3	0.8
SACTM	1	2	0	0	0	3	0.8
SAIC	1	1	1	0	0	3	0.8
SASTIND	3	0	0	0	0	3	0.8
ABOC	0	2	0	0	0	2	0.6
CIRC	1	0	1	0	0	2	0.6
GAS	0	2	0	0	0	2	0.6
MCT	1	1	0	0	0	2	0.6
MEE	0	2	0	0	0	2	0.6
NAC	0	1	1	0	0	2	0.6
NCMCPDSRS	2	0	0	0	0	2	0.6
PLA HDGLD	1	1	0	0	0	2	0.6
SAFE	0	2	0	0	0	2	0.6
SCOPSR	2	0	0	0	0	2	0.6
SPCC	2	0	0	0	0	2	0.6
SPP	2	0	0	0	0	2	0.6
ACFIC	0	1	0	0	0	1	0.3
ACFTU	1	0	0	0	0	1	0.3
ACWF	1	0	0	0	0	1	0.3
CBIRC	0	1	0	0	0	1	0.3
CCCCYL	1	0	0	0	0	1	0.3
CPCCC FAO	1	0	0	0	0	1	0.3
CFPC	1	0	0	0	0	1	0.3
CMA	0	1	0	0	0	1	0.3
MEM	0	1	0	0	0	1	0.3
MOCA	0	0	0	1	0	1	0.3
MOH	1	0	0	0	0	1	0.3
MOJ	0	1	0	0	0	1	0.3
NAO	0	0	1	0	0	1	0.3
NFSRA	0	1	0	0	0	1	0.3
OCMCCSC	1	0	0	0	0	1	0.3
SA	0	1	0	0	0	1	0.3
SAFEA	1	0	0	0	0	1	0.3
SC OCAO	1	0	0	0	0	1	0.3
SC PAD	1	0	0	0	0	1	0.3
SOA	0	1	0	0	0	1	0.3
NASSP	1	0	0	0	0	1	0.3

Table 2.5 *(cont.)*

Agency	Policy						Agency's contribution to policy (%)
	S&T	Industrial	Financial	Tax	Fiscal	Total	
Total number of agencies	501	279	37	98	49	964	
Total number of policies	182	79	18	35	29	343	
Number of agencies per policy	2.8	3.5	2.1	2.8	1.7	2.8	
Most important policy maker	MOST	MOST	MOST	SAT	MOF	MOST	
% Most important policy maker	67.6	58.2	72.2	97.1	89.7	58.9	

Sources: Same as Table 2.2.
Notes: Same as Table 2.4.
ABOC – Agricultural Bank of China; ACFIC – All-China Federation of Industry and Commerce; ACFTU – All-China Federation of Trade Unions; ACWF – All-China Women's Federation; CAC – Office of the Central Cyberspace Affairs Commission; CASS – Chinese Academy of Social Science; CBIRC – China Banking and Insurance Regulatory Commission; CCCCYL – Central Committee of the Chinese Communist Youth League; CPCCC FAO –CPC CC Foreign Affairs Office; CMA – China Meteorological Administration; CMC STC – Science and Technology Committee of the Central Military Commission; GAS – General Administration of Sport; MCT – Ministry of Culture and Tourism; MEE – Ministry of Ecology and Environment; MEM – Ministry of Emergency Management; MNR – Ministry of Natural Resources (Original MOLR); MOJ – Ministry of Justice; MOT – Ministry of Transport; NAO – National Audit Office; NASSP – National Administration of State Secrets Protection; NEA – National Energy Administration; NFGA – National Forestry and Grassland Administration; NFSRA – National Food and Strategic Reserves Administration; NHC – National Health Commission; OCMCCSC – Office of the Central Mental Civilization Construction Steering Committee; PLA GAD – People's Liberation Army General Armament Department; SAMR – State Administration for Market Regulation; SASTIND – State Administration of Science, Technology and Industry for National Defense; SATCM – National Administration of Traditional Chinese Medicine; SC PAD – The State Council Leading Group Office of Poverty Alleviation and Development; SOA – State Oceanic Administration; SPCC – The Supreme People's Court; SPP – The Supreme People's Procuratorate.

that the MOST exerted direct impact over monies, even though it was not the main player, to support innovation activities did broaden its potential role. The main focus of MOST-driven financial policy was the establishment of venture funds for innovation at S&T SMEs, provision of export credit insurance, credit guarantees and soft loans to high-tech enterprises, and operation of IPR exchange markets. Such new "coverages" suggest that an environment in which financial tools are used explicitly to promote innovation was now in place and thus MOST's emphasis can shift, as relevant, to particular areas related to innovation and the implementation of policy in these areas.

But the Ministry of Industry and Information Technology (MOIIT), which oversees China's economic policy and has the potential to become a super-ministry similar to Japan's Ministry of International Trade and Industry (MITI) before its reorganization into the Ministry of Economy, Trade and Industry in 2001 (Naughton, 2009, 2021), almost has been conspicuously low profile and missing in the formulation of even sector-related innovation policies. It remains to be seen whether this will change as more emphasis is being placed on promoting more rapid progress in microelectronics and information technology. Meanwhile, as the new stress on promoting indigenous innovation calls for improvement in the protection of IPRs, especially those generated by domestic inventors, an increase in the position and importance of the State Intellectual Property Office, renamed the China National Intellectual Property Administration (CNIPA) in 2018 and under the State Administration for Market Regulation (SAMR), in policymaking is expected. After the reform in 2023, NIPA became became an directly affiliated institution of the State Council again, out of SAMR.

More than half of the new array of innovation policies involved the participation of two or more agencies, and in six cases, five or more agencies. Overall, every MLP implementation-related innovation policy had 2.8 participating agencies, with industrial policy 3.5 agencies, followed by S&T policy and tax policy's 2.8, financial policy's 2.1, and fiscal policy's 1.7 agencies. This shows a marked improvement over the previous pattern (see Table 2.4) and perhaps helps to explain why there had been some appreciable progress over the last several years.

In particular, 55 of the 123 items, or almost 45 percent, of S&T policy involving the MOST were jointly issued with the MOF, the NDRC, or the SAT. In comparison, between 1980 and 2005, the MOST issued 75 items of S&T policy, but only 22 or 29.3 percent were

Table 2.6 *Innovation policies formulated by MOST and others by agency and type*

Innovation policies issued between 1980 and 2005

Agency	Policy					
	S&T	Industrial	Financial	Tax	Fiscal	Total
MOST	75	6	4	1	4	90
MOST with MOF or NDRC or SAT	22	4	1	1	4	28
% MOST with MOF or NDRC or SAT	29.3	66.7	25.0	100.0	100.0	31.1

Innovation policies issued to implement MLP between 2006 and 2019

Agency	Policy					
	S&T	Industrial	Financial	Tax	Fiscal	Total
MOST	123	46	13	7	13	202
MOST with MOF or NDRC or SAT	55	26	7	7	12	129
% MOST with MOF or NDRC or SAT	44.7	56.5	53.8	100.0	92.3	63.86

Sources: Same as Table 2.2.
Notes: Same as Table 2.4.

co-developed with the more economic-oriented agencies (Table 2.6). And of the 202 MLP implementation policies having MOST's participation, 129 or more than three-fifths were economic-oriented agencies. These developments suggest that some aspects of the cross-ministry coordination challenges have been tackled and the new combination of agencies involved in the innovation policymaking may lead to more effective coordination in their implementation. At this time, while the quantitative metrics usually associated with the progress on the innovation front show visible achievements, such as rising number of publications and patents, the results on the qualitative side seem to raise continued questions about the efficacy of current policies as well as the policymaking process. That is, the lessons regarding multi-ministry support and cross-ministerial coordination have not been fully digested.

Summary and Discussions

Based on our analysis of Chinese innovation policies during the past 40 years from the perspectives of policy categories and issuing agencies, this chapter tries to shed some new light on the evolution and trajectory of innovation in China. Even though the overall number of CPC CC decisions, laws enacted by the NPC, and State Council statues has been relatively low, in general, their impacts have been most pronounced. Their greater degree of effectiveness derives from the fact that these high-grade policies have been tied explicitly to the power position of these organizations in Chinese politics and bureaucracy – the most strategically important initiatives related to science, technology, and innovation have all been launched by party's Central Committee. Meanwhile, among policy types, those falling to the S&T policy category have continued to occupy a dominant position, followed by those in the industrial policy domain. As policy instruments to promote and stimulate innovation, financial, tax, and fiscal policies have become increasingly significant, reflecting the growing sophistication of the innovation policymaking apparatus in China.

During the early years of the reform and opening, policies – S&T as well as others – tended to be formulated by a single government ministry – the MOST for S&T policy, the MOFCOM for industrial policy, and so on. Because of or as results of the division of labor, no ministry wanted to relinquish to others for their specific prerogatives. Obviously, this reflected a great deal of parochialism on the part of these ministries – a challenge that still has not been totally tackled with the passing of time. Moreover, with S&T issues largely being handled by the MOST, which is comparatively speaking a lower-ranking ministry in terms of overall clout and resources, at least in the early periods, and given the fact that many other ministerial leaders, preoccupied with other matters, have not treated S&T advance as an urgent priority, the status of the innovation issue left it to lie on the margins of the policy agenda across larger numbers of State Council organizations and their local level counterparts. For example, governors and mayors are evaluated primarily by how much local GDP grows during their watch rather than the quality or even quantity of innovation results.

These factors and mode of thinking have frequently made inter-agency coordination in policy formulation and implementation particularly difficult, if not impossible. Indeed, the problems of poor coordination are not simply found in the science, technology, and innovation realm but are much more generic inside of the Chinese bureaucratic system as a whole. Despite sustained efforts of reform and restructuring (*tizhi gaige*), the overall institutional structure of the Chinese government still has many lingering problems regarding the types of inherent cleavages that drive behavior. There has been serious fragmentation of decision-making responsibilities and co-existence of institutions, old and new, with seemingly conflicting roles and mandates. In particular, lack of coordination between closely related organizations has led to pronounced efficiency losses; lack of coordination between organizations with apparent overlapping mandates often has affected the salience of public policy; and the hierarchical structure across the bureaucracy has resulted in behaviors that are inconsistent with the formal mandates of various organizations (OECD, 2005:23).

Our analysis, however, especially with respect to those policies introduced after the release of MLP and the associated policy formulation and implementation processes involved, also suggests that some improvement has been taking place in terms of the nature and extent of collaboration. The MLP was issued as a State Council document, accompanied by a joint decision by the CPC CC and the State Council. The State Council also assigned implementation policy tasks to relevant ministries and individuals and mobilized substantial resources. In this specific case, the State Council, in particular, was willing and able to exercise its top-down authority in a direct fashion – informing all government agencies of their accountability for their respective roles in the nation's innovation drive. Nonetheless, the MLP seemed to have propelled the Chinese bureaucracy forward in a way not readily seen before in the domain of innovation policies, although it is still too early to say that the problem has been fully resolved.

To make up for the lack of the concentration of ample policy resources in a single Chinese ministry, perhaps equivalent to the role of Japan's MITI during its catch-up stage, the MOST formed a series of working alliances with the NDRC and the MOF – the two most critical players in the Chinese economy. MOST's decision to no longer attempt to pursue a "lone ranger" approach stands in sharp contrast to past practices. This more collaborative approach has made it possible to work more smoothly across ministerial boundaries and thus created the conditions for more effective policy impact. In addition, with the existence of the leading group and the newly introduced inter-ministerial joint conference mechanism at the State Council level, and on top of these, the Central Financial and Economic Commission of the CPC CC and now the Central Science and Technology Commission (CSTC) of the CPC CC, another new and very important party organization, the party and government seem to have institutional mechanisms to coordinate efforts in an area between ministries, especially when inter-ministry conflict arises. This also suggests that China has been on a steep learning curve in pursuing state-led innovation and with continuous restructuring efforts, we are seeing the institutionalization of a more systemic understanding of innovation. This in turn has reinforced additional positive-sum behaviors that have yielded a more coherent portfolio of policies formulated by multiple ministries. While it is clear that much more work needs to be done to foment sustainable and effective inter-agency coordination, a step has been taken in the right direction. Of course, this is just a "baby step" in what needs to become a full-fledged change in the value and norms across the Chinese bureaucracy for innovation policies. The future course of innovation in China still will depend a great deal on the continued efficacy of highly brokered collation building and alliance formation for any particular set of issues.

This may explain why in the midst of the ample progress discussed above, the S&T system's rather incremental nature remains a source of great concern among senior leaders in China. To their way of thinking, the pronounced increase in critical inputs devoted to innovation progress – money, equipment, and talent – should have yielded more substantial results across the board. Yet, the continued admonition by high-level party and government leaders to strengthen indigenous innovation efforts and outcomes suggests that the level and pace of progress are lacking in terms of both their expectations and the actual results. For those internal advocates who have argued for greater resources, independence, and flexibility for China's S&T community, this may be a sobering reality that is responsible for the huge level of pressure that exists across the Chinese system for more substantial innovation results. While further fine-tuning of the system will continue to yield some additional improvements, there also will continue to be an ongoing debate as to whether a major overhaul is truly required to enable the system to perform at much higher levels. China's various S&T leading apparatuses at the State Council and the CPC CC, as mentioned, are not permanent institutions, and the MOST is constrained by its coordination power. There has long been discussion on the setting up of a Prime Minister's Office of Science and Technology Policy (OSTP) integrating the current functions related to science, technology, and innovation policymaking in the MOST, the NDRC, the MOIIT, and other agencies. Similar to the White House OSTP in the USA and the Office for Science and Technology Strategy in the UK, China's OSTP is to maximize the role of S&T in advancing health, agriculture, national security, environmental protection, and other domains for the country. The 2023 reform has mandated to establishment of a CSTC under the CPC CC, higher than the one suggested set with the State Council. However, it remains to be seen what kind of role such an organization will mitigate the problems confronting China's S&T system going forward.

3 | Innovation Policies
Policy Network and Policymaking Process

In Chapter 2, we discussed China's evolving innovation policy as well as analyzing the involvement of various government agencies in or the institutional structure of making innovation policy. In this chapter, we will continue our exploration of China's innovation policymaking from the perspective of a policy network. Particularly, we would like to investigate how three mechanisms underlying the evolution of inter-government agency relations – policy agenda, power concentration, and heterogeneity dependence – are applicable to the Chinese case.

As is known, being an institutional arrangement, innovation policy plays a critical role in remedying market failure, creating a fertile environment for innovation, helping build innovation networks, and improving innovation capacity in organizations, especially enterprises (Lundvall & Borrás, 2005). Research on innovation policy is problem-oriented rather than theory- or paradigm-driven (Morlacchi & Martin, 2009). Specifically, a country's innovation policy is designed to help spur its economic competitiveness and increase its aggregate social welfare (Kuhlmann, 2001; Lanahan & Feldman, 2015). International experience suggests that structural relations between government agencies, public and private organizations, and other stakeholders are central to making innovation policy, solving practical problems, and improving competitiveness (Hall & Taylor, 1996). However, as we discussed in Chapter 2, division of labor between government agencies makes it almost impossible for one agency to dominate the policymaking process and in turn calls for joint efforts. Therefore, coordination, which entails mutual adjustment between stakeholders and between the stakeholders and the environment against which policy is made, also affects the overall effectiveness and performance of the innovation policy mix (Flanagan *et al.*, 2011).

Policy network has emerged as an approach that embraces the "structuralism" implicitly by emphasizing the structural relations in or the coordinated nature of policymaking. Such an approach has

diverse disciplinary origins from political science, organizational studies, public policy studies, sociology to social network studies (Klijn,
1996; Sørensen & Torfing, 2007), whose different knowledge back-
grounds have resulted in different understanding and applications.
There also has been little agreement as to whether a policy network
is a metaphor, a theoretical construct, or a method to describe and
understand the policymaking process. But it is clear that the policy
is formulated through interactions of government agencies, or primary participants of policymaking, who collaborate and negotiate,
and exchange resources so as to orient the policy toward their respective interests. As such, policy network describes a shadow structure of
interests (Dowding, 1995; Lewis, 2011).

Empirically, scholars have turned policy network into a real network by focusing on the interests of relations between policymakers in the network. Consequently, policy network can be perceived
as a "network" consisting of "nodes," or policymaking participants
whose interactions around specific policy issues generate "structural
relations" between them for the purpose of policymaking (Berardo
& Scholz, 2010; Lee *et al.*, 2012). Therefore, how to understand the
construction and especially the evolution of such relations through
resource exchange, collaboration, and interdependency becomes crucial for understanding the governance in policymaking (Compston,
2009; Rhodes, 2013).

Finally, policy network is situated in a nation's political context.
In industrialized countries such as the UK, the USA, Germany, and
France where the policy network approach has been developed, self-
organization of government agencies around policy issues, including
those related to innovation, is central to policy network's governance
(Berardo & Scholz, 2010). Now, with their continental-sized economies and ambitions, BRICS countries – Brazil, Russia, India, China,
and South Africa – are emerging as new actors of global governance
(OECD, 2013). Of them, China is particularly positioning itself to
assert a global leadership in science, technology, and innovation in the
coming decades with sources of competitive advantage for its ascent
coming from its centralized power, state-sponsored policy, and government support (Appelbaum *et al.*, 2012; Huang & Sharif, 2016). In
China, most policies are proposed by and negotiated between government agencies, as discussed. Thus, it is of significance to explore the
possibility of applying the policy network approach to the study of

inter-agency relations in China, bearing in mind that its political context of policymaking differs fundamentally from those in industrialized countries (Zheng *et al.*, 2010).

This chapter reveals evolutionary mechanisms of the relations between government agencies in innovation policymaking in China. We are interested in not only the relational structure of innovation policymaking agencies but more specifically how such structure has evolved in the country's reform and open-door era (Klijn & Koppenjan, 2012). We first propose three hypotheses – policy agenda, power concentration, and heterogeneity dependence – regarding policy network's evolution. Then, we extract the structural relations between government agencies involved in policymaking from China's innovation policy documents and use social network analysis (SNA) to analyze such relations by quantifying how China's innovation policy network has evolved. In doing so, theoretically, we aim to enrich the literature of innovation policy and policy network through pinpointing the evolutionary mechanisms in the innovation policy network, particularly how policy network's characteristics have structurally influenced the evolution of the relations between government agencies in innovation policymaking. We also examine China's innovation policy network by performing SNA on data extracted from policy documents, thus expanding the policy network approach empirically and methodologically.

Theoretical Background and Hypotheses

Theoretical Background

To understand policy network's evolutionary mechanism is to reveal the evolving relations of the policy network. In fact, policy network's evolution is a process in which government agencies and other stakeholders create, maintain, or terminate relations with each other (Snijders *et al.*, 2010). Evolutionary mechanisms of a network come from basic factors that drive or shape the network's formation, persistence, dissolution, and content of ties between the network's members (Ahuja *et al.*, 2012). Several schools of thought have emerged to help understand policy network, especially its evolution.

The new institutionalism school considers policy network as an institutional setting in which public and private policymaking participants interact to make policy (Blom-Hansen, 1997; Rhodes, 2006). Such interactions happen in rather similar ways to reproduce more or less the same sets of rules and to exchange heterogeneous resources, thus regularly shaping the structural characteristics of the policy network (Klijn, 1996). From such a perspective, policy network's evolution is an institutionalization process whereby government agencies produce new rules, which, by sustaining a stable policy network over a period of time, facilitate interaction, reduce transaction costs, and affect network's performance.

The social network school brings new insights to the study of policy network. A participant in an inter-agency policy network possesses two structural attributes, or its behavior can be described in two relational variables. Social selection and network selection represent the participant's attributes and relations, respectively, leading to the formation or dissolution of its relations with other participants in the policy network (Robins *et al.*, 2012). For example, some network participants tend to form more ties with those of higher popularity or through a preferential attachment mechanism (Barabási & Albert, 1999).

The power-dependence school treats policy network as a set of resource-dependent government agencies/organizations. Indeed, a government agency depends on other agencies for resources and must exchange resources with others to accomplish its goal in policymaking (Rhodes, 2006). In doing so, each agency deploys its resources – legal, organizational, financial, political, or informational – to maximize its influence over policy outcomes while trying to avoid becoming dependent on other agencies.

The existing research suggests that policy network's evolution is a complex process driven by several mechanisms, three of which serve our purpose. First, policy agenda, as a kind of institutional setting, determines the change of the policymaking process (Hays & Glick, 1997). Second, from social network school's perspective, policy network evolves following the rules of popularity effect as social selection and those of preferential attachment as network selection (Barabási & Albert, 1999; Lee *et al.*, 2012). And third, organizations in policy network also are resource- or power-dependent (Rhodes, 2006). We will construct our theoretical framework about policy network's evolution around these three mechanisms and generate hypotheses accordingly.

Policy network's evolution could be examined in periods, in each of which participating government agencies create or terminate relations with each other. It is possible to empirically investigate the network's change by comparing these agencies' statuses in its different periods (Snijders *et al.*, 2010). The division of periods also reflects how the network evolves in the policy cycle through the agencies' dynamic statuses in the current and following periods. We will observe policy network's evolution by periods as the network changes in responding to the creation, maintenance, and termination of the relations between government agencies.

Policy Agenda and Policy Network's Evolution

A policy network is embedded in and influenced by a nation's institutional context (Borrás & Edquist, 2013), which in turn shapes intergovernment agency collaboration by dictating which organizational actions to be accepted and supported (Aldrich & Fiol, 1994). Within a specific institutional context, a policy agenda is a set of strategic ideologies, issues, and plans laid out by the top leadership as well as policies that government agencies try to determine current and near-future policy practice. Hays and Glick (1997) demonstrated the importance of agenda setting in reaching a more complete explanation of policymaking; that is, policy agenda can be treated as an independent variable to explain network's evolution.

Emerging economies are remarkable in their experiencing an economic growth that is higher than the world's average. Meanwhile, they particularly want to transform their economic structure from labor-intensive manufacturing to capital- and then knowledge-intensive service (The Center for Knowledge Societies, 2008; Kvint, 2009). Technological capabilities in emerging economies also have been on a sharply rising trajectory to catch up with those of the industrialized countries (Fu *et al.*, 2011).

Meanwhile, the innovation-driven development is an adaptive process in which learning by doing is critical. Setting and implementing new policy agendas makes it necessary to create more policies and involve additional participants. The process is also significant in its mobilization of heterogeneous resources to meet a series of challenges and opportunities (Hall & Clack, 2010). Particularly, innovation policy network integrates the interests of government agencies in charge of economic and S&T affairs while engaging other agencies. With the understanding of innovation evolving and becoming sophisticated, economic bureaucracies become major players in innovation policy-making while those with innovation missions continue to play leading roles, thus jointly helping to nurture an environment conducive to innovation.

As we have shown in Chapter 2, as a consequence of its economic transformation to the innovation-driven development, China has embarked on a "more and more scientific and democratic" policy agenda-setting process (Wang, 2008: 81). The Chinese state has intended to achieve a technological catching-up by introducing the market-oriented reform of its S&T system and the innovation-oriented reform of its economic system. In doing so, the state has expanded its policy agendas from the economic domain to the S&T and other domains, and shifted its innovation policy from the acceleration of technology transfer from laboratories to production to the encouragement of mass innovation and entrepreneurship (Fang, 2010). In particular, China's innovation policy agendas have evolved from acknowledging S&T as a productive force to reforming the S&T system, then to initiating the strategy of "revitalizing the nation through the science and education"; from the construction of a national innovation system (NIS) to the pursuit of enhancing indigenous innovation capability then to the improvement of the NIS (Liu *et al.*, 2011). Most recently, there have been calls for the innovation-driven development. Predictably, China's innovation policy agendas will continue to evolve and further determine the transformation of its policy network.

To understand the rising role of innovation policy network's various participants in setting policy agendas, we propose:

Hypothesis 1a: With policy agendas evolving, participation of the innovation policy network will be diversified to accommodate the interests of an increasing number of government agencies.

Engaging multiple stakeholders from S&T, education, finance and trade, and other government agencies and covering multiple sectors such as agriculture, industry, services, and public health, innovation policy is more complex than the policy for a single and clearly defined domain. However, innovation policy studies systematically underestimate the challenge that such a complexity poses on coordinating policies across bureaucratic lines (Flanagan *et al.*, 2011). Strengthening such coordination, therefore, is of primary importance for all countries and probably more so for emerging economies.

The state consists of government agencies. The "actor-centric" institutionalism stipulates that "policy is the outcome of the interactions of resourceful and boundedly rational actors whose capabilities, preferences, and perceptions are largely, but not completely, shaped by the institutionalized norms within which they interact" (Scharpf, 1997: 195). Accordingly, policymaking can be described as public and private actors and institutions shaping policies by focusing on the organization of activities around a particular purpose at a time. Coordination, though difficult, is worth attempting (Braun, 2008). Formal and informal mechanisms often coexist to promote coordination. Regarding innovation policymaking in China, as mentioned in Chapter 2, there have been specialized coordination organizations such as the Central Financial and Economic Commission of the Communist Party of China's Central Committee. Most recently, an inter-ministerial joint conference mechanism was established, within the State Council, responsible for determining the distribution of research and development (R&D) expenditure and coordinating important S&T issues within the central government. Now, the Central Science and Technology Commission of the CPC CC is expected to be more critical.

Collaboration between government agencies represents a significant approach of coordination. These agencies frequently and directly collaborate in policymaking whilst those involved to a lesser extent are loose participants. Inter-agency relationship as a coordination mechanism determines the content of innovation policy. In China, after issuing the *Medium and Long-Term Plan for the development of S&T* (2006–2020) (MLP), through a special policy document, the State Council assigned government agencies specific tasks of formulating rules and regulations and collaborating their work with other agencies (Sun & Liu, 2014; Sun & Cao, 2015).

Although their level of institutionalization is low, relative to developed countries, emerging economies have been experiencing a rapid economic development and have had the necessity of making policies in a large scope. Consequently, they face greater challenges on policy coordination. In order to facilitate cross-agency communication and coordination so as to improve governance in economic transformation, China's State Council has gone through a series of reshuffles, with each leading to changes in missions, functions, roles, and sometimes even names of some ministries (OECD, 2005: 14–15).

To understand the rising role of innovation policy agendas in terms of relations between government agencies, we also propose:

Hypothesis 1b: With policy agendas evolving, the structure of innovation policy network becomes more coherent to strengthen inter-government agency coordination.

Power Concentration and Policy Network's Evolution

It is possible that in a policy network some government agencies are more powerful due to their attributes or relations, or their having popularity effect or preferential attachment in social network terms. In general, popularity effect plays a main role at the early stage of a network's formation while preferential attachment's influence is more gradual.

Popularity effect in a policy network suggests the tendency that a new government agency tends to connect to an existing key and popular one upon joining the network, rather than making efforts to generate direct ties with others (Lee *et al.*, 2012). An agency becomes popular because it possesses rich public resources, is an important administrative power, has access to abundant information, or performs specific professional functions. A popular agency could attract other government agencies to form a "star" network. This is the mechanism of social selection.

If a policy covers an issue beyond the scope of one government agency, an endorsement from other related agencies becomes necessary for the policy's formulation and especially its effective implementation. Therefore, the collaboration between agencies is extremely common. A new policy often is initiated by a lead agency, and other agencies are mobilized primarily because of the opportunity to accomplish the policy goal efficiently and effectively and also because of the exchange of resources with the lead agency and other participants to realize the lead agency's goal as well as those of theirs (Rhodes, 2006). Participation of more agencies often leads to a situation where these agencies benefit from adopting the most common approach to solve a common problem (Berardo & Scholz, 2010).

Following network's mechanism of social selection, we figure out that a popular lead agency more likely possesses professional skills and performs administrative functions to make a policy, and that the number of polices made by the lead agency determines its position in the policy network. In addition to its attributes, the lead agency may be structurally privileged in the network. Its ability to handle policymaking processes and shape policies reinforces its role in the policy network (Flanagan *et al.*, 2011).

At an earlier stage of the network formation, an agency's attributes are central to attracting other agencies because the lead agency is yet to emerge or there is no core node. As seen in Chapter 2, in China, a popular government agency of innovation policymaking such as the Ministry of Science and Technology (MOST) could be appealing to other agencies with its remarkable popularity endowed simply with its administrative power. Other lead agencies also may occupy core positions of the innovation policy network. Such lead agencies in turn attract others to form a "core–periphery" network.

To understand the popularity effect during the evolution of policy network, we thus propose:

Hypothesis 2a: As a policy network evolves, an agency's network power positively correlates with its frequency as the lead policymaker.

Preferential attachment also is a primary mechanism of network's evolution. The nature of preferential attachment is the phenomenon of "the rich getting richer" or more generally "cumulative advantage" (Barabási & Albert, 1999). Upon entering a policy network, a government agency tends to connect with existing agencies with rich collaborative relations or high degree centrality. Core agencies with more collaborators within the policy network are more advantageous in reducing cost and enjoying more benefits including specific information, professional knowledge, and specialized resources through their relations with other agencies. Examined from the perspective of a whole network, the existence of "star" agencies represents a scenario where only core agencies relate to other agencies to provide the most efficient structure for distributing valuable information centrally (Burt, 2005). Preferential attachment thus shapes a "core–periphery" structure of the policy network.

Path dependence also explains why preferential attachment exists. The evolution of a policy network can be considered as an adaptive rather than an exogenously set process with each government agency operating as an interlinked ego network (Hall & Clack, 2010). Agencies at the center of policy network's evolution have to solve policy problems facing the nation, cope with an unpredictable and changing policy environment, and deal with other participating government agencies. Obviously, this is a continuous process, during which the relations between agencies in the current period could determine their relations in the following period.

Therefore, innovation policy agendas are inherently path dependent (Pierson, 2000). Agencies try to create stable and preferential relationships with existing partners because they need trust and rich information exchange to help mitigate collaboration hazards in solving a similar policy issue (Gulati & Gargiulo, 1999). For example, emerging economies need to attract foreign direct investment (FDI) and foreign technology for product export purposes, thus leading to a possibility of foreign technology dependency. To respond, governments intend to strengthen an indigenous innovation capability for achieving high value addition. That is, governments need to develop follow-up policies that tackle nascent challenges created by previous policies.

Methodologically, Abbasi *et al.* (2012) extended the measurement of preferential attachment from degree centrality to closeness centrality and betweenness centrality, and tested hypotheses through calculating correlations between a policy network's existing nodes' various centrality measures and the numbers of new links in the following period. Examining preferential attachment from the perspective of existing agencies, agencies occupying core positions with more collaborative relations in the network (with high degree centrality) would attract more new links, and agencies acting as brokers or gatekeepers (with high betweenness centrality) would continue to act as brokers in the following period (Sun & Liu, 2016). In this chapter, we will apply such logic to the analysis of preferential attachment.

To understand preferential attachment during the evolution of a policy network, we propose:

Hypothesis 2b: As a policy network evolves, an agency's degree centrality of the current period positively correlates with its degree centrality in the following period.

Hypothesis 2c: As a policy network evolves, an agency's betweenness centrality of the current period positively correlates with its betweenness centrality in the following period.

Heterogeneity Dependence and Policy Network's Evolution

As mentioned, the power-dependence approach treats a policy network as comprising of resource-dependent organizations. That is, an agency depends on other agencies for resources or needs to exchange resources with others to realize its goal in policymaking (Rhodes, 2006). An agency is enabled, shaped, and constrained by the behavior and expectations of other agencies who themselves are shaped by an earlier action (Flanagan *et al.*, 2011). The power- or resource-dependence can be heterogeneity dependent; that is, a government agency depends on others with and for different resources.

Theories of homogeneity predict that similarities in organizational characteristics lead to similar policy preferences, reduce information asymmetry, and predispose organizations to cooperate (Lee *et al.*, 2012). In fact, organizations simultaneously consider transaction cost and resource endowment in choosing best potential partners for collaboration. And collaboration between resource-homogeneous organizations could reduce transaction cost and risks but would have difficulty generating high-valued outcomes through resource recombination (Guan & Yan, 2016).

Following the knowledge-based view of enterprises, we consider that a government agency's possession of specific information, knowledge, skills and budgets also represents its possession of the most important resources available for its policymaking, and its capability of coordinating different agencies and creating and implementing policy is the primary source of its advantages (Amin & Cohendet, 2004). Access to homogeneous resources through only collaborating with agencies with similar functions is not enough for an agency to handle the growing complexity needed for policymaking (Masiello *et al.*, 2015). This explains why an agency also needs to gain access to heterogeneous external knowledge and functions and incorporate them into existing internal knowledge and functions or create new knowledge and functions. Inter-agency interactions happen in rather similar ways to reproduce more or less the same set of rules and exchange heterogeneous resources, thus regularly shaping the structural characteristics of the policy network (Klijn, 1996).

To understand the heterogeneity dependence during the evolution of a policy network, we thus come up with:

Hypothesis 3: As a policy network evolves, government agencies in the network prefer to collaborate with those with different resources and functions to achieve organizational heterogeneity.

In what follows, we test our theoretical hypotheses against the innovation policymaking in China, the country that has been facing challenges of its weak cross-agency communication and coordination given the strongly bureaucratic nature of its S&T system and other institutions (Jakobson, 2007; Cao *et al.*, 2013).

Methodology and Data

The Context for a Policy Network Case Study

We have made efforts to quantify the contributions of lead Chinese government agencies to innovation policymaking in Chapter 2 and R&D budgeting process in the following chapter. Meanwhile, Zheng *et al.* (2010) show qualitatively that the policy network of reforming the urban health insurance system involved ministries under the State Council as main players. In fact, during its economic transition, China has endowed its innovation system with mixed characteristics (Liu & White, 2001; Zhong & Yang, 2007). On the one hand, as its political system and policymaking are top-down and S&T system state-led, policy agendas inevitably and strongly have shaped a policy network different from those in the West, making network governance more instrumental. On the other hand, with China becoming increasingly market oriented, policymaking has started to show a bottom-up and enterprise-centered tendency, involving a variety of stakeholders (Kennedy, 2005), or self-organization characteristics are burgeoning in its policy network's governance. Thus, revealing how China's innovation policy network has evolved is useful for understanding the changing role of the Chinese state in making policy generally.

Indeed, China's "policy ideas" are originated from both the top-level design and the bottom-level initiative (Wang, 2008). For example, in 1999, in response to practical challenges such as private enterprises' weak technological innovation capability, the government responded with specific policy ideas such as *Several Opinions on Accelerating the Development of Private Technology Enterprises*. In April 2006, in pushing the MLP to be a top policy agenda for science, technology, and innovation in the next 15 years, the General Office of the State Council followed up with a document, *A Summary Sheet on Regulations of Some Supporting Policies for Implementing the MLP (the first set)* (Summary Sheet thereafter), assigning relevant government agencies tasks to formulate implementation policies (Serger & Breidne, 2007; Sun & Liu, 2014).

Policy Network Construction

The study of policy network has been built on a strong methodological tradition of case studies, emphasizing network participants' or policymakers' actions and interactions in the policymaking process through discourse analysis, in-depth interviews, and documentary analysis. It does not necessarily concern about the evolving relationship between government agencies participating in the policy network. The quantitative approach, which is emerging, identifies policymakers and their relations through interviews and questionnaire surveys but does not visually map the policy network and examine the evolving structural relations of the participants (Sandström & Carlsson, 2008; Robins *et al.*, 2012).

In this chapter, we analyze relational data of policymaking participants drawn from S&T- and innovation-related policy documents issued by China's central government agencies, and as such our approach is replicable. Such agencies include ministries, commissions, and other constituting agencies under the Communist Party of China Central Committee (CPC CC) and the State Council. We exclude local governments and ad hoc inter-functional coordinating bodies such as the NLGST in our analysis because local governments seldom make policy jointly, neither do coordinators, such as the NLGST, which mainly coordinate efforts across government agencies.

Specifically, as discussed in Chapter 2, a policy document is an important instrument through which the Chinese state governs the country. It is usually drafted by several government agencies, thus giving rise to a common policymaking practice that a policy document often has co-sponsors who inevitably strive for their specific interests to be represented in the document.[1] Bearing names of all co-sponsoring agencies, the document provides evidence for the participation of these agencies in making a particular policy. The first co-sponsors can be regarded as leading the issuing of the document or the making of the

---

[1] The co-sponsoring of agencies on a document has been a conventional practice in the Chinese policymaking for a long time. Each government agency performs its own functions, but it may not achieve its policy goals given its diffused and decentralized administrative power. Therefore, the agency needs to work with others with different functions, thus giving rise to the phenomenon of document co-sponsoring. The agency's document sponsoring also has become a tool to safeguard the agency's interests (Liu *et al.*, 2011).

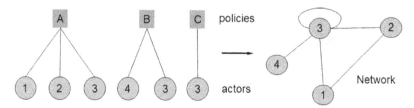

Figure 3.1 A policy network based on co-occurrence of actors in policy documents

Note: A, B, and C denote policy documents; 1, 2, 3, and 4 denote actors.

policy.[2] The data on co-sponsors of all the documents in a particular policy area thus become a useful window to observe the evolution of a particular policy network.

Let us use a hypothetical example to illustrate our approach. Suppose that four government agencies (1, 2, 3, and 4) were involved in the formulation of three policy documents (A, B, and C). Agencies 1, 2, and 3 co-sponsored Document A, agencies 3 and 4 co-sponsored document B, and agency 3 alone also sponsored document C. Thus, four agencies formed four pairs of network ties: 1–2, 1–3, 2–3, and 3–4, and agency 3 also formed a loop (Figure 3.1). By extension, if an innovation policy document has n co-sponsors, each two of whom forms a pair of ties and all these ties form a linked clique. Repeating the same exercise for each policy document in a given year, we could come up with a static policy network for that year. The width of the lines represents the frequency that agencies co-sponsored policy documents or reflects the strength of relations between each pair of agencies in policymaking.

In this way, we construct a valued network whose ties are shown by frequency or strength. The undirected network contains loops and isolated nodes. An isolated node denotes a government agency only formulating a policy on its own and not collaborating with others. And mapping all the innovation policy documents formulated in all years yields a dynamic innovation policy network.

---

[2] For example, in 2006, the General Office of the State Council issued *Summary Sheet*, assigning one government agency as a lead to formulate MLP implementation regulations and coordinate participants in making policies; the agency is the first co-sponsor (Sun & Liu, 2014).

Network Measurements and Hypothesis Testing

For hypothesis testing, we use SNA to study structural attributes of the innovation policy network and use visual graphs to investigate its structure of the innovation policy network (Besussi, 2006; Borgatti *et al.*, 2014).

For testing Hypothesis 1: It is difficult to quantify the influence of a policy agenda on a policy network's evolution. The content analysis of policies is used to study policy agenda-setting in the existing literature (Kayser & Blind, 2017). There are two basic principles in China's innovation policy agendas – the integration of S&T with the economy and inter-agency coordination. Alternatively, we examine the evolution of China's innovation policy network based on these two principles. First, we use network size and ties to measure the numbers of government agencies involved in making collaborative policies, which could reflect the participation of the policy network.

Second, we categorize government agencies into different groups based on their functions in policymaking. The power-dependence approach, the new institutionalism school, and the NIS approach all stress functional differentiation, linkages between organizations, and resource dependency (Kenis & Schneider 1991; Rhodes, 2006; Hekkert *et al.*, 2007). However, none of these idealized functions is mutually exclusive. It is possible that multiple agencies play a similar function, individual agencies play multiple functions simultaneously or play different and multiple functions at different times, whilst different agencies also play a similar function at different times (Flanagan *et al.*, 2011).

Government agencies do play certain roles in policymaking due to their specific functions in an administration. A Chinese agency could be categorized according to its functions endowed by the State Council, and agencies performing similar functions likely possess homogeneous resources with differing quantities. Each of China's government agencies performs its own role as division of labor limits the overwhelming importance of one agency in policymaking (Huang *et al.*, 2004; Liu *et al.*, 2011). Thus, we group agencies involved in innovation policymaking into four according to their administrative functions and roles in innovation (see Appendix Table 3.1). Of them, S&T agencies (Group 1) with members such as the MOST are responsible for S&T administration, R&D funding distribution, and implementation. Members of economic agencies (Group 2) such as the National Development and Reform Commission

(NDRC) are responsible for issues related to planning, fiscal, financial, tax, and trade administration. Mission-oriented agencies (Group 3) include the Ministry of Agriculture (MOA) and its successor, the Ministry of Agriculture and Rural Affairs (MOARA), the Ministry of Industry and Information Technology (MOIIT), and others, which focus on specific sectorial development through integrating S&T and economic resources, performing S&T/economic missions in a particular sector. Sharing some characteristics with the S&T and economic groups, members of this group make policies related to a specific sector rather than overall S&T and economic functions. Finally, agencies that provide support and services for innovation activities but are not directly involved in innovation are named supporting agencies (Group 4). For example, the Ministry of Human Resources and Social Security (MOHRSS) underpins innovation activities related to human resources development.

Third, we use such measures as network density, clustering coefficient (CC), and average path length (PL) to measure policy network's cohesion (Watts & Strogatz, 1998; Uzzi et al., 2007).[3] Network density is the actual collaborative frequency of co-sponsors within an innovation policy network divided by the possible collaborative amount of the network, reflecting the degree of sparseness or denseness in the network. In our case, a policy network's CC is the mean of government agencies' CC while an agency's CC is the density of its co-sponsors' network of collaboration. When an agency has many co-sponsors who themselves also are connected to each other, the network becomes highly clustered or cliqued.

Finally, PL measures the average number of relations along the shortest paths for all possible pairs of policymakers with the length of the path being the number of relations in the network. To measure an agency's PL, we need to find the shortest path from a source agency to all other agencies within the policy network, then count the number of relations in these shortest paths and calculate the average number of relations. A policy network's PL is obtained by calculating the average PL for all agencies. PL represents the efficiency of information that transports within the network.

For testing Hypothesis 2: Along with the number of lead government agencies issuing polices, a policy network's degree-centrality

---

[3] The network cohesion analysis is carried out by UCINET, a software package for the analysis of social network data.

measures quantify an agency's power in the network (Freeman, 1979; Freeman *et al.*, 1989; Kim & Song, 2013). Specifically, degree centrality is the number of the agency's direct ties, reflecting its contribution to the network; betweenness centrality is the number of times when an agency acts as a bridge along the shortest path between two other agencies, reflecting its coordination role in the network.

For testing Hypothesis 3: With the social network approach, the EI index is the number of ties external to the groups minus the number of ties that are internal to the group divided by the total number of ties.

$$EI\ Index = (EL - IL)/(EL + IL)$$

where EL equals the number of external ties that cut across group boundaries and IL equals the number of internal ties that connect agencies within the same group. The EI index ranges between -1 (all linkages are internal to the group) and $+1$ (all linkages are external to the group). We use the EI index to examine whether an agency prefers to connect *homogeneously* with ones within the group (through internal ties) or *heterogeneously* with ones outside the group (through external ties). In other words, the EI index measures the degree of external ties that one group favors to exchange and transact.

Besides the EI index of each agency group, the density matrix of agencies within one group or between two groups donates all actual ties including collaborative frequency divided by the number of possible ties of participating government agencies.

Data

China has many policy documents for innovation that can be used to carry out the proposed line of inquiry. As we described in Chapter 2, the Chinese central government has formulated four sets of innovation policy documents in the post-1978 reform and open-door era. For our purpose, we use the first three sets of documents but not the documents formulated in 2012 and onward, as since 2012, China has launched a new innovation-driven development strategy, and the external environment of the policy network has undergone changes. The policy documents include laws, regulations, guidelines, and codes of conduct as well as strategies, plans, and programs, covering the stages of policy design and policy implementation in the policy cycle. In this chapter, we only focus on those policy documents at the ministerial level but exclude the nation-level S&T and innovation strategies issued by the CPC CC, the National People's Congress (NPC), and the State Council, because these three organizations issue high-profile political and policy documents involving no coordination or collaboration. As such, we perceive the relationship generated from the 463 innovation policy documents China's innovation policy network and study such relationship accordingly.

In order to show institutional changes resulted from government reshuffles, we attribute a document to a current agency if the agency assumed the functions of a previous one that issued the document and attribute a policy to an initial issuing agency whose functions died out. For example, the MOST succeeded the State Science and Technology Commission (SSTC) in 1998, thus all policies issued by the SSTC before 1998 are attributed to the MOST; however, the Ministry of Machine Building (MOMB) no longer existed after 1998, thus all policies involving the ministry are still attributed to it.[4]

In Chapter 2, we divided China's post-1978 innovation policymaking under study into five periods, marked by six significant national science, technology, and innovation conferences, held in 1978, 1985, 1995, 1999, 2006, and 2012, respectively, during which strategic decisions were made to reshape and recast many policies (OECD, 2008: 381–393; Liu *et al.*, 2011). The fifth period (2006–2011) can be further divided into two subperiods (2006–2008 and 2009–2011, respectively), since the Chinese government started to implement the MLP in 2006 and formulated new policies in 2008 to counter the adverse impacts of the global financial crisis. For the purpose of this chapter, however, we divide these 30-plus years into five periods, with the years of 1985, 1995, 2006, and 2009 used as the key demarcation points corresponding to the issuance of three important pieces of high-level policy by the CPC CC and the State Council and the occurrence of the international financial crisis in 2008.

---

[4] The Ministry of Machine Building (MOMB) is significantly important in the history of China's industrial S&T. Between 1952 and 1970, China established seven ministries of machine building responsible for civil machinery (named the First Ministry of Mechanical Industry), nuclear industry (second), aviation (third), electronic industry (fourth), weapons (fifth), shipbuilding (sixth), and aerospace (seventh), respectively. In 1982, these seven ministries changed their names. For example, the First MOMB became the MOMB, the Second MOMB the Ministry of Nuclear Industry, the Sixth MOMB the China Shipbuilding Industry Corporation, and so on. Ministries for machine building no longer existed after the reform of the central government in 1998.

Analyses and Results

China's innovation policy network has been evolving dynamically (Figure 3.2), corresponding to the changes in its characteristics of our interests such as policy agenda, power concentration, and heterogeneity dependence.

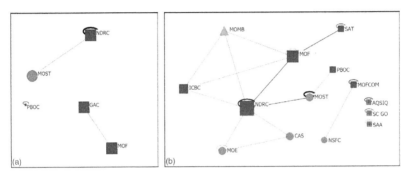

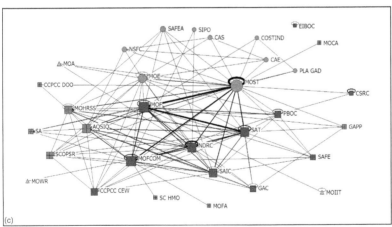

Figure 3.2 China's policy network for innovation (1980–2011): (a) 1980–1984, (b) 1985–1994, (c) 1995–2005, (d) 2006–2008, and (e) 2009–2011
Notes: The circle represents agencies belonging to S&T group, the square represents agencies belonging to the economic group, the triangle represents agencies belonging to mission-oriented group, and the field lattice represents agencies belonging to supporting group. The ring means an agency formulates policies by itself alone. The thickness of ties represents the frequency of connections between policymakers.

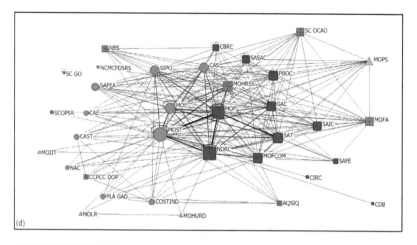

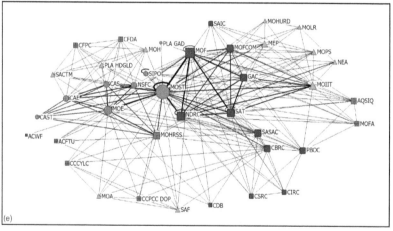

Figure 3.2 (Continued)

Policy Agenda

Along with changes in policy agenda is the evolution of the policy network (Table 3.1). Before the reform, China's S&T system suffered a fundamental structural deficiency of high functional fragmentation and low cross-functional coordination. Only five agencies were involved in the making of innovation policy. The SSTC, the predecessor of the MOST, jointly with the State Planning Commission (SPC), which would become the NDRC in 2003, formulated innovation policies; so did the General Administration of Customs (GAC) jointly with

Table 3.1 *Nodes and ties in China's innovation policy network*

Index	1980–1984	1985–1994	1995–2005	2006–2008	2009–2011
Network size	5	14	32	35	40
Group 1	1 (20%)	4 (28.6%)	9 (28.1%)	11 (31.4%)	8 (20%)
Group 2	4 (80%)	6 (42.9%)	11 (34.4%)	12 (34.3%)	12 (30%)
Group 3		1 (7.1%)	3 (9.4%)	4 (11.4%)	11 (27.5%)
Group 4		3 (21.4%)	9 (28.1%)	8 (22.9%)	9 (22.5%)
Number of policy documents	11	40	154	79	80
Collaborative policy	2 (18.2%)	7 (17.5%)	59 (38.3%)	45 (56.96%)	46 (57.5%)
Network density	0.2	0.1476	0.63	0.7958	0.6051
Clustering coefficient	0	0.533	2.251	1.988	1.607
Average path length	1	1.229	1.8	1.697	1.997

Notes: Group 1 – S&T; Group 2 – Economy; Group 3 – S&T mission-oriented; Group 4 – Supporting.

the Ministry of Finance (MOF); the SPC and People's Bank of China (PBOC) formulated several policies independently.

After the publication of the 1985 *Decision on the Reform of the S&T System*, which set fundamental objectives of the reform as applying results from research to production widely and rapidly, government agencies released more policies to implement the decision. Between 1985 and 1994, while its size increased from 5 to 14, the innovation policy network had only 3 isolated nodes, which was still quite sparse. Then, as the 1995 strategy of "revitalizing the nation through science and education" (*kejiao xingguo*) mobilized more agencies to participate in innovation policymaking, the network enlarged to include some 30 agencies, more than twice the number in the previous decade.

The introduction of the indigenous innovation strategy in 2006 also attracted new agencies to the innovation policy network. Different from the policy network in the Western countries, the Chinese one has seen strong public-sector participation (Zheng *et al.*, 2010;

Klijn & Koppenjan, 2012). In addition to ministries under the State Council, innovation policymakers also included the Export-Import Bank of China (EIBOC), a state-owned bank; the China Association for Science and Technology (CAST) and the National Commission on the Management and Coordination of Post-Doctoral Scientific Research Stations (NCMCPDSRS), both quasi-government organizations; the Department of Organization under the CPC CC (CPC CC DOO), a party organization; the Department of General Logistics of the People's Liberation Army (PLA), among others.

Functionally, economic agencies accounted for 80 percent of all those agencies involved in innovation policymaking before the reform of the S&T system. Afterward, their share decreased to 42.9 percent while the share of S&T and supporting agencies increasing. As discussed in Chapter 2, since 1995, China has changed its S&T policy- and industrial policy-centered innovation strategy to pursue a more coordinated and innovation-oriented economic development by giving increasing attention to a portfolio of policies that include financial, tax, and fiscal measures. Meanwhile, there has been a shift of innovation policymaking from the domination of economic agencies to the diversification of participating government agencies as mission-oriented and supporting agencies also gradually increased their presence in the policy network.

Indeed, more government agencies have joined the innovation policy network. The shift of China's innovation policy agendas – from reforming the S&T system to accelerating S&T progress, and from constructing an NIS to strengthening an indigenous innovation capability – has continuously called for the formulation and implementation of new innovation policies. Meanwhile, the share of collaborative policies was increased from 18.2 percent to 57.5 percent between 1980 and 2011. The visual graph also shows that the policy network was sparse during the first two periods. The years after 1995 had witnessed not only the involvement of more agencies but also more collaboration between them. The network became denser and more cohesive than that in the previous periods.

Regarding network cohesion (see Table 3.1), before 1985, four agencies formed two pairs with other partners (CC = 0). There was one step between the MOST and the NDRC and between GAC and MOF (PL = 1). That is, there was not a real "network" back then because of poor connectivity. But these agencies would have great potential to work together to expand the policy network as network density was only 0.2. Between 1985 and 1994, network density dropped to 0.15 because the number of agencies increased. While formulating innovation policy alone, both the MOST and the NDRC also started to work with others such as the Chinese Academy of Science (CAS), the National Natural Science Foundation of China (NSFC), the Ministry of Commerce (MOFCOM), the Ministry of Education (MOE) and the MOF on new policies, although average density of the network was still low (CC = 0.53). The average number of steps connecting any two agencies increased to 1.229, which means that some agencies did not connect with others directly. After 1995, the network had become more cohesive, not only growing its size but also increasing its density from 0.15 to 0.63. CC increased to 2.25, as the network was better connected to form clusters. The average number of steps to connect any two nodes also increased to 1.8.

Between 2006 and 2008, network density increased to a new high of 0.7958, but the average number of steps to connect any two participating government agencies reduced slightly to facilitate interactions. Since 2006, the State Council's innovation policy *Summary Sheet* had effectively coordinated cross-agency efforts in drafting new policy documents for innovation and helping form a comprehensive policy agenda aimed at enhancing the indigenous innovation capability. Meanwhile, CC reduced to 1.988, as most peripheral government agencies in the policy network also collaborated with the core ones instead of connecting each other. Unfortunately, in 2008, before the State Council issued a new *Summary Sheet* came the global financial crisis, after which the indigenous innovation strategy had neither strengthened the coordination and interactions between government agencies nor transformed the dependency of economic growth on foreign technologies, investment, and exports. The Chinese government saw its primary task as reducing the risk of recession and stabilizing the economic growth, even at the expense of restructuring the economy, thus shifting its attention from coordinating innovation policymaking at different agencies to intervening innovation activities directly. Consequently, all network cohesion indicators deteriorated and interactions between government agencies became less efficient.

The network statistics support *Hypotheses 1a* and *1b*. As policy agendas evolved, government agencies had increasingly entered innovation policy network, whose participation diversified the policy network and moved it away from the domination of economic agencies; the relations between agencies were closer, and the network became more cohesive. That is, the change of policy agendas had greatly facilitated the formation of an innovation policy network. The findings provide quantitative evidence to support the new institutionalism school that evolution of the policy network itself is an institutionalization process (Blom-Hansen, 1997; Rhodes, 2006). Moreover, embedded in its political and economic system, China's innovation policy network had evolved alongside the reform of its economic and S&T systems. As China's "new normal" of much slower but probably steadier and healthier economic growth highlights the urgency for China to transform its labor-, investment-, and resource-intensive economic development models into one that is increasingly dependent upon technology and innovation, it is expected that its central government will come up with new policy documents to guide the changes of the innovation policy agendas.

Power Concentration

Two pieces of key evidence support the existence of a popularity effect (see Table 3.2 and Figure 3.2). One is correlation between an agency's degree centrality in the policy network and the number of policies led by the agency. Between 1985 and 1994, only three agencies – the MOF, the MOST, and the NDRC – led innovation policymaking and contributed to the formation of the network (measured by degree centrality). Then, Spearman correlation coefficient between an agency's degree centrality and the agency as a lead policymaker and the agency's significance were increasing gradually, although there were not many lead agencies. The other evidence is the domination of lead agencies in the network's core positions. Other than the period between 1985 and 1994, lead agencies – the MOST, the MOF, and the MOFCOM between 1995 and 2005, the MOF, the MOST and the NDRC between 2006 and 2008, and the MOST, the MOF and the NDRC between 2009 and 2011 – occupied central nodes of the innovation policy network. Thus, *Hypothesis 2a* is valid; that is, a lead agency is likely to become a core node of a policy network, although this does not mean that the lead agency's degree centrality must be higher than that of other agencies.

Table 3.2 Spearman correlation between lead agencies' policies and degree centrality

No.	1985–1995			1995–2005			2006–2008			2009–2011		
	A	P	D	A	P	D	A	P	D	A	P	D
1	MOF	2	6	CPC CC DOO	1	2	CIRC	1	1	CBRC	1	16
2	MOST	2	3	CSRC	2	3	MOE	2	59	MOF	14	80
3	NDRC	3	8	GAC	1	13	MOF	16	124	MOFCOM	3	42
4				GAQAIA	1	38	MOFCOM	2	40	MOHRSS	1	31
5				MOA	1	3	MOHRSS	5	47	MOHURD	1	7
6				MOF	22	89	MOIIT	1	2	MOST	18	126
7				MOFCOM	10	62	MOST	9	116	NDRC	8	69
8				MOST	15	100	NDRC	8	103			
9				NDRC	3	47	SASAC	1	22			
10				SAT	1	70						
11				SIPO	1	2						
Spearman correlation				0.690*			0.953**			0.964**		

Notes: A – name of agencies; P – number of policies; D – degree centrality. *$p < 0.05$, **$p < 0.01$.

Table 3.3 *Spearman correlation between the agencies' centrality in adjacent period*

Centrality	1985–1995/ 1995–2005	1995–2005/ 2006–2008	2006–2008/ 2009–2011
Degree	0.506	0.605**	0.778**
Closeness	0.615*	0.757**	0.517**
Sample	11	21	26

Notes: $*p < 0.05$, $**p < 0.01$.

An agency's degree- and betweenness-centrality measures in the current period positively and significantly correlate with these two measures in the following period, respectively (Table 3.3). Here, we just consider agencies appearing in the two periods simultaneously. There were only eleven agencies in the first two adjacent periods (1985–1994/1995–2005), and correlation coefficient of their degree centrality is insignificance but that of betweenness centrality is significant at the level of 0.05. Further, their correlation coefficient is significant in the second (1995–2005/2006–2008) and third (2006–2008/2009–2011) adjacent periods at 0.5 or lower. Such evidence supports the existence of a preferential attachment process in policy network's evolution.

In addition, since the reform of the S&T system that started in 1985, more agencies have participated in policymaking, making the policy network increasingly denser and more cohesive (see Figure 3.2). Between 1995 and 2008, the alliance of the MOST, the NDRC, and the MOF formed a "core–periphery" structured network, with the core being the MOST, the MOFCOM and the MOF between 1995 and 2005 and extending to include the NDRC, the MOHRSS, the MOE, the State Administration of Taxation (SAT) and others between 2006 and 2008. The emergence of a "core–periphery" structure indicates that there was a preferential attachment process; or, agencies preferred to collaborate with those who they had had previous connections. "Cumulative advantage" also reinforced the "core–periphery" structure as the network grew. For example, as core nodes of the innovation policy network, the MOST, the MOF, and the NDRC not only continued to connect with existing partners such as the MOE and the

MOFCOM but also attracted other agencies such as the MOHRSS with whom they had had no previous connections. After 2008, the network has shown a "dual core–periphery" structure – one consisting of the MOST, the NSFC, the CAS, the MOE, and the Chinese Academy of Engineering (CAE) and the other the MOF, the NDRC, the SAT, the MOFCOM, and the GAC.

Thus, our results sustain *Hypotheses 2b* and *2c* as well. That is, an agency's degree/betweenness centrality measures within the policy network positively and significantly correlate with its degree/betweenness centrality measures in the following period, thus facilitating the formation of a "core–periphery" structured innovation policy network. Our findings provide evidence for the existence of preferential attachment within a public policy network, like what happened within the network consisted of individuals or private actors (Powell *et al.*, 1996; Wang & Zhu, 2014).

Heterogeneity Dependence

Focusing on the relations between different function groups within the innovation policy network between 1985 and 1994, we find that internal densities for S&T and economic groups in the network were 0.167 and 0.286, respectively, and external densities between these two groups and between the economic and mission-oriented groups were 0.214 and 0.429, respectively (see Table 3.4). Supporting groups did not have internal and external ties with S&T, economic and mission-oriented groups. That is, the economic- and mission-oriented groups generated the most connections. With an EI index of 0.429, the S&T group had more external than internal ties that only existed between the MOE and the CAS. The mission-oriented group had an EI index of 1, as this one-member (MOMB) group had only external ties. The EI index of the entire network for the period was 0.231, indicating that as a whole, government agencies preferred to collaborate with agencies outside their groups in formulating innovation policy.

With more agencies entering the network and establishing more internal ties between 1995 and 2005, the S&T group witnessed its EI index reducing to 0.164. The economic group's EI index was –0.043 and its internal density was the biggest at 1.855, indicating that the group was interested in using economic-related policy to reconstruct

Table 3.4 *Density matrix of four groups and EI index*

1985–1994	1	2	3	4	EI
1	0.167	0.214	0	0	0.429
2	—	0.286	0.429	0	0
3	—	—	0	0	1
4	—	—	—	0	0
Total	—	—	—	—	0.231

1995–2005	1	2	3	4	EI
1	0.5	0.949	0.074	0.333	0.164
2	—	1.855	0.091	0.636	−0.043
3	—	—	0	0	1
4	—	—	—	0.25	0.608
Total	—	—	—	—	0.176

2006–2008	1	2	3	4	EI
1	1.800	0.712	0.886	1.295	0.379
2	—	0.197	0.292	0.469	0.663
3	—	—	1.000	0.844	0.631
4	—	—	—	0.821	0.478
Total	—	—	—	—	0.505

2009–2011	1	2	3	4	EI
1	1.071	0.375	0.364	1.556	0.755
2	—	0.152	0.159	0.676	0.640
3	—	—	0.236	0.747	0.636
4	—	—	—	2.028	0.503
Total	—	—	—	—	0.618

Notes: Authors' calculation using UCINET 6; EI Indexes are all significant ($p < 0.05$). 1 – S&T group; 2 – Economic group; 3 – Mission-oriented group; 4 – Supporting group.

the innovation system. The mission-oriented group, with the EI index of 1, still focused on establishing external ties with S&T and economic groups. The supporting group was busy connecting with economic and S&T groups, as its EI index increased from 0 to 0.608. All groups except the economic one had a larger external than internal density. The EI index of the whole network dropped from 0.231 to 0.176 during the period, suggesting that these agencies increased intra-group collaboration at the expense of inter-group collaboration in making innovation policies.

After 2006, the S&T group had created more external than internal ties, thus seeing its EI index increased to 0.379. Its primary partner shifted from the economic group to the supporting group and the density between the two groups increased from 0.333 to 1.295. The economic group's EI index increased from –0.043 to 0.663, although its ties were most with the S&T group. The mission-oriented group's EI index dropped to 0.631. The supporting group had an EI index of 0.478 while keeping the tightest relations with the S&T group. As a whole, the EI index of the network increased to 0.505 as connections between members of different groups increased significantly and participants with different resources depended more on each other. The relationship of policymaking participating government agencies between 2009 and 2011 was like that between 2006 and 2008. The EI index of the network increased to 0.618, continuing the trend of increasing external collaboration.

Thus, our statistical analyses provide evidence in support of *Hypothesis 3*. That is, an agency prefers to collaborate with agencies performing a different function, which shows the value of organizational heterogeneity rather than homogeneity in inter-agency collaboration. Our findings also provide quantitative evidence to support the power-dependence approach that driven by resource-seeking, government agencies tend to create relations with each other (Rhodes, 2006). The EI index of China's innovation policy network has been greater than zero and increased gradually after 1995, as policymakers had established more inter-group than intra-group linkages in making policies. That is, ministries seemed to depend more on those of the outside groups for heterogeneous resources, pointing to the necessity of improving inter-group coordination and sharing resources between government agencies in achieving their mutual goals. Power dependence of government agencies engaged in innovation policymaking also tended to be organizationally heterogeneous in nature.

Summary and Discussions

Due to its complexity, innovation policymaking often involves more government agencies to increase the exchange of knowledge, information, and resources between these agencies. The relations between agencies are central to the overall effectiveness of the innovation policy mix in both industrialized and emerging economies. This chapter uses the policy network approach to describe and examine the dynamics of the evolving innovation policymaking in China. It especially pays attention to three mechanisms – policy agenda, power concentration, and heterogeneity dependence – related to the evolution of interagency relations in the innovation policy network and apply them to the study of China's innovation policymaking by using SNA to analyze data drawn from policy documents.

In general, China's innovation policy network can be seen as a typical case in which mixed mechanisms of network evolution have been working in tandem. Such a network has been not only sustained through the intervention of policy agendas by way of high-level policy documents but also self-organized due to power concentration and heterogeneity dependence. First, innovation policy agendas have a significant impact on the growth of the network. Embedded in a larger institutional environment, China's innovation policy network has evolved alongside the economic reform and institutionalization process, which in turn have shaped the innovation policymaking. The CPC CC leads and directs policymaking, with inter-organizational units, such as the NLGST, the inter-ministerial joint conference mechanism, and the Central Financial and Economic Committee, steering the network, fostering integration and coordination within and between various participants and most importantly enabling the state to better attain its objectives. Indeed, participating government agencies have been increasing in number and diversified to include non-government, quasi-government, party, and military organizations, and the network is no longer dominated by economic agencies; even business organizations lobby on their own interests (Kennedy, 2005). As coordination of the innovation policy network still is not fully institutionalized in China, the government needs to set institutionalized coordinating agendas, alluded above, rather than merely have a super coordinating body, to ensure and even enforce inter-agency collaboration and networking. In fact, a timetable/summary sheet for China's innovation policymaking could be set within its innovation strategy after assessing existing policies, current challenges, future goals, and innovation requirements to routinize cross-agency collaboration and coordination.

Second, power concentration is a central mechanism for policy network's evolution. A government agency's degree centrality in the policy network positively correlates with the number of policies it leads, thus supporting popularity effect. An agency's degree- and betweenness-centrality measures in the current period positively and significantly correlate with its centrality measures in the following period. Along with the reform, in China, not only has the innovation policy network been gradually formed, the network also has shifted from the domination by one government agency in the network to a "core–periphery" structure with the core being the S&T group, before evolving into a network with a "dual core–periphery" structure around S&T and economic groups. These findings provide new evidence for the existence of preferential attachment within policymakers (Powell *et al.*, 1996). Indeed, Chinese innovation policymakers could take advantage of the popularity effect of lead agencies to strengthen inter-agency collaboration. The lead agencies could govern the network through their core positions and act as intermediaries to increase policy network's operational efficiency. Collaborating with the lead agencies is a better choice for others to access and share the resources and to achieve their respective interests.

Third, heterogeneity dependence also is found in the evolving innovation policy network. A government agency prefers to collaborate with agencies that perform a different function, which shows the importance of organizational heterogeneity rather than homogeneity in inter-agency collaboration. The Chinese case lends empirical support to the power-dependence approach as innovation policymaking participants have become more dependent on others with heterogeneous resources for achieving their goals. A participant brings to the network not only its own characteristics but also its relational resources or position in the network. The implication for policymakers is clear: collaboration between agencies with heterogeneous functions may be a better choice to make a new and more effective policy.

Appendix Table 3.1 *Abbreviation of institutions and their group classification*

Group	Full name	Abb.
	Chinese Academy of Engineering	CAE
	Chinese Academy of Sciences	CAS
	China Association for Science and Technology	CAST
	Commission of Science, Technology, and Industry for National Defense	COSTIND
	Ministry of Education	MOE
	Ministry of Science and Technology	MOST
Group 1 –	National Copyright Administration	NAC
S&T	National Commission on the Management and Coordination of Post-Doctoral Scientific Research Stations	NCMCPDSRS
(12)	National Natural Science Foundation of China	NSFC
	People's Liberation Army General Armament Department	PLA GAD
	State Administration of Foreign Experts Affairs	SAFEA
	State Intellectual Property Office	SIPO
	China Banking Regulatory Commission	CBRC
	CPCCC Commission on Enterprise Work	CPCCC CEW
	China Development Bank	CDB
	China Insurance Regulatory Commission	CIRC
	China Securities Regulatory Commission	CSRC
	Export-Import Bank of China	EIBOC
	General Administration of Customs	GAC
	Ministry of Finance	MOF
Group 2 –	Ministry of Commerce	MOFCOM
Economy	National Development and Reform Commission	NDRC
(16)	People's Bank of China	PBOC
	State Administration of Foreign Exchange	SAFE
	State Administration of Industry and Commerce	SAIC
	State-owned Assets Supervision and Administration Commission	SASAC
	State Administration of Taxation	SAT
	Industrial and Commercial Bank of China	ICBC

Appendix Table 3.1 *(cont.)*

Group	Full name	Abb.
	Ministry of Environmental Protection	MEP
	Ministry of Agriculture	MOA
	Ministry of Heath	MOH
	Ministry of Housing and Urban-Rural Development	MOHURD
	Ministry of Industry and Information Technology	MOIIT
Group 3 –	Ministry of Land and Resources	MOLR
Mission-	Ministry of Machine Building	MOMB
oriented	Ministry of Public Security	MOPS
(13)	Ministry of Water Resources	MOWR
	National Energy Administration	NEA
	People's Liberation Army Health Department of General Logistics Department	PLA HDGLD
	State Administration of Forestry	SAF
	State Administration of Traditional Chinese Medicine	SATCM
	All-China Federation of Trade Unions	ACFTU
	All-China Women's Federation	ACWF
	Central Committee of the Communist Youth League of China	CCCYLC
	CPCCC Department of Organization	CPCCC DOO
	CPCCC Department of Propaganda	CPCCC DOP
	China Food and Drug Administration	CFDA
	China Family Planning Commission	CFPC
Group 4 –	General Administration of Press and Publication	GAPP
Supporting	General Administration of Quality Supervision, Inspection, and Quarantine	AQSIQ
(19)	Ministry of Civil Affairs	MOCA
	Ministry of Foreign Affairs	MOFA
	Ministry of Human Resources and Social Security	MOHRSS
	National Bureau of Statistics	NBS
	Standardization Administration	SA
	State Archives Administration	SAA

Appendix Table 3.1 *(cont.)*

Group	Full name	Abb.
	State Council General Office	SC GO
	State Council Hong Kong and Macau Affairs Office	SC HMO
	State Council Overseas Chinese Affairs Office	SC OCAO
	State Commission Office for Public Sector Reform	SCOPSR

Notes: The Chinese People's Liberation Army (PLA) is the armed forces of the People's Republic of China. The PLA consists of five professional service branches: The Ground Force, Navy, Air Force, Rocket Force, and the Strategic Support Force. On January 11, 2016, the PLA created a joint staff directly attached to the Central Military Commission (CMC), the highest leadership organization in the military. The previous four general headquarters- the Joint staff, the Political Work Department, the Logistic Department, the Armament Department of the PLA were disbanded and completely reformed. They were divided into 15 functional departments including Science and Technology Commission instead – a significant expansion from the domain of the General Office.

4 | Funding
Central Government Expenditure
on Research and Development

China's rapid and sustained growth of research and development (R&D) expenditure should allow the country to make truly outstanding progress in research, which in turn should help develop its national innovative economy and strengthen its economy's international competitiveness. In reality, rampant problems in research funding – some attributable to the science and technology (S&T) system and others culture – have been slowing down China's pace to achieve the goal in science, technology, and innovation (Shi & Rao, 2010). For a long time, due partly to the lack of transparency of China's budgeting process and partly to the lack of understanding of R&D or S&T statistics issued by various government agencies (Simon & Cao, 2012), students of Chinese science, technology, and innovation had to depend upon central government sources for information on China's R&D expenditure.

However, *China Statistical Yearbook on Science and Technology, Annual Report on State Programs for Science and Technology Development, Statistical Bulletin on National S&T Expenditure, China Science and Technology Development Report, China Science and Technology Indicators*, among other sources, only provide fragmented or aggregate information on R&D expenditure without breakdowns on allocation to or spending at relevant government agencies. There was no way to carry out scholarly analysis beyond simple calculations of percentages of the expenditure on basic research, applied research, or experimental development (Meng *et al.*, 2006; Zhu & Gong, 2008; MOST, 2011: 23) and of performers such as universities, research institutes, and enterprises (Hu, 2001; Sun & Liu, 2010; MOST, 2011: 51). While there were anecdotes about the misuse and abuse of R&D expenditure, who spent how much on what was largely a "black box," a mystery, or a puzzle.

The situation seems to be changing, thanks to the enacting of the *Regulations of the People's Republic of China on Open Government Information* by the State Council in 2007. According to Article 9 of the regulations, government agencies should disclose their own information of the vital interests of citizens, legal persons, or other organizations. Then, Article 10 stipulates that governments at the county level and above and their departments should make available statistics on national economic and social development, as well as reports on financial budgets and final accounts (Wen, 2012). In 2010, for the first time, China's central government agencies opened to the public required information such as their Department Annual Reports (DARs) on Financial Budgets and Final Accounts, which contained information on public expenditure on S&T and R&D.[1] Now, most of the government agencies publish their DARs annually. By integrating DARs and other open-source information, this chapter represents a serious attempt to disaggregate China's public S&T and especially R&D expenditure and analyze such expenditure at its key government ministries with missions in S&T.

While putting together various pieces of information on China's public R&D expenditure into a complex but still seemingly incompatible puzzle, our efforts have several caveats. First, by definition, China's R&D statistics (NBS *et al.*, 2012) include the expenditure on basic research, applied research, and experimental development, but budget items disclosed by government ministries do not necessarily align with these R&D statistics. We try our best to match budget items of S&T and R&D expenditure at the ministerial level with the R&D statistics released by the National Bureau of Statistics (NBS), the Ministry of Science and Technology (MOST), and the Ministry of Finance (MOF); nevertheless, there is still a gap. Second, we focus on the R&D expenditure administered by central government agencies without discussing how the money is allocated and spent at scientific research units such as universities, independent R&D institutes, and enterprises under these agencies. Third, we could only solve part of China's gross expenditure on research and development (GERD) puzzle as we only discuss central government's contribution to the GERD. In 2010, for example, enterprises, including those foreign-invested ones, and other sources are reported to contribute 76.26 percent of China's GERD (MOST, 2011). The situation in 2020 was more or less the same in this regard. That is, three-quarters

---

[1] In this chapter, S&T expenditure and R&D expenditure represent the central public finance expenditure on S&T and R&D, respectively, unless indicated otherwise.

of China's GERD, or the amount spent at enterprises, is still unaccountable. Fourth, according to the OECD definition, research on the social sciences is part of the R&D activities (OECD, 2002: 30). In China, such expenditure is supported by related government agencies and indeed is reported in China's own R&D statistics. But the chapter only examines expenditure on the natural sciences and engineering technology.

Fifth, and most important, we only are able to analyze disclosed information. As a whole, government agencies – ministries, commissions, administrations, offices, and public institutions directly affiliated to or under the State Council, and bureaus under the ministries and commissions – as independent units for the budgeting purpose are required to open their final accounts and budgets. Our analysis is based on the 2011 and 2020 data of S&T expenditure at agencies as have been disclosed in DARs. Despite these limitations, we believe that our analysis contributes to sorting out a significant and critical part of China's public R&D expenditure.

Central Government S&T Budget Management

The Evolution of S&T and R&D Budget Categorization

At China's central government level, the MOF holds the main responsibility in budgeting but it is not the only agency having the power for the central budget allocation.[2] In the planning economy period, scientific research was supported by public finance only and the central government appropriated expenditure to S&T activities as it did for others through a typically centralized system. The reform of China's S&T system in 1985 set the reform of government S&T appropriation as one of its priorities (Figure 4.1).

Afterward, the State Science and Technology Commission (SSTC) was given by the State Council the power to administer all operating expenses for civilian science. It and the MOST, which succeeded the SSTC in 1998, distributed basic expense and part of the special project expense, as part of the scientific research funds, to agencies under the State Council and scientific research institutes affiliated

---

[2] We will discuss later in the chapter on the role of the National Development and Reform Commission (NDRC).

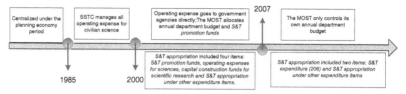

Figure 4.1 The reform of Chinese S&T budget management
Notes: SSTC – State Science and Technology Commission, the predecessor of
the MOST – Ministry of Science and Technology.

to these agencies. The practice was changed after 2000 when these
items were directly channeled to department budgets of the relevant
agencies. Meanwhile, the MOST managed national S&T programs
(NSTPs) and had discretion over the usage of the central S&T promotion funds, operating expenses for sciences,[3] although they were not
included in its department budget (Jia *et al.*, 2006: 34).

An expenditure category system provides a normative framework for
both policymaking and accountability (Allen & Tommasi, 2001: 121).
In China, between 2000 and 2007, S&T appropriation included four
items: S&T promotion funds, operating expenses for sciences,[4] capital
construction funds for scientific research,[5] and S&T appropriation under
other expenditure items (Jia *et al.*, 2006: 34). In 2007, the state started to
reform the budgeting system (MOST, 2009: 52) by shifting revenue and
expenditure categories from economic classification (e.g., compensation
of employees, interest, and social benefits) to functional classification
(e.g., defense, public safety, and health).[6] Under the new classification,
S&T appropriation has only two parts: S&T expenditure (budget item
206), including relevant items under the previous S&T promotion funds
and operating expenses for sciences; and S&T appropriation under other
expenditure items.[7] The budget category of S&T expenditure (item

[3] This includes the S&T expenditure on trial production of new products, pilot
experiment, and subsidy of major scientific research project.
[4] This includes the S&T expenditure on the natural sciences, social sciences, and
popularization of science.
[5] This includes the S&T expenditure on new constriction, reconstruction,
extension, and purchase and capital assets used in scientific research, and
upgrading and major repair of scientific research equipment.
[6] For more information about the expenditure classification system, see Allen
and Tommasi (2001): 121.
[7] Email communications with an official in the finance department of the
Chinese Academy of Sciences (CAS) (February 2013). Before the reform, S&T

206) in turn includes ten sub-budgetary items (see Table 4.1). Under the R&D expenditure are "basic research" (budget item 20602), of which expenditure on the mega-science programs (MSPs) under the *Medium and Long-Term Plan for the Development of Science and Technology (2006–2020)* (MLP) is a part;[8] "applied research" (budget item 20603) and "technology research and development" (budget item 20604).

In addition, mega-engineering programs (MEPs) (budget item 20609), also under the MLP, are an important strategic component of China's R&D activities.[9] According to the *Interim Measures on Fund Management of Civilian Mega-Engineering Programs*, issued by the MOF, the MOST, and the NDRC in 2009, government funds for the MEPs are mainly spent on basic research and research on social and public goods (*shehui gongyi yanjiu*), which, given their precompetitive nature, the market mechanism is unable to support effectively. Thus, the expenditure for the MEPs should be included in R&D expenditure. In sum, R&D expenditure includes four sub-budgetary items – 20602, 20603, 20604, and 20609 – under budget item 206.

The budget category of S&T appropriation under other expenditure items does not have a clear boundary. Specifically, each ministry is an independent budget unit; if it has missions in S&T, its budget includes not only S&T expenditure (item 206) but also S&T appropriation under other expenditure items. For example, the Ministry of Education (MOE) has education expenditure (budget item 205) and the Ministry of Agriculture and Rural Affairs (MOARA)[10] has expenditure on agriculture-, forestry- and water-related affairs (budget item 213). Apparently, part of the latter expenditure items – 205 and 213 – are likely to be spent on S&T activities. In this chapter, however, we only discuss the R&D expenditure under the S&T expenditure (item 206)

promotion funds were included in MOST's department annual budget, but the MOST had considerable discretion in their allocation.

[8] The MLP, released in 2006, selects four mega-science programs (MSPs) – protein research, quantum modulation research, nanoscience and technology, and growth and reproduction (Suttmeier *et al.*, 2006). *The National 12th Five-Year Plan on S&T Development* added two MSPs – stem cells and global change.

[9] The MLP also includes core electronic components, high-end generic chips and basic software, extra-large scale integrated circuits (IC) manufacturing and technique, and others (Suttmeier *et al.*, 2006).

[10] The MOARA was formed in 2018 as the agency superseding the former Ministry of Agriculture (MOA). Some of its additional responsibilities come from the agricultural investment projects of the NDRC, the MOF, the Ministry of Land and Resources, and the Ministry of Water Resources (MOWR).

Table 4.1 *Chinese budget item (206) for fiscal expenditure on S&T*

Sub-budget item	Types	Items name
20601	Non-R&D	S&T affair management
20602	R&D	Basic research
2060201		Operation of institution
2060202		Key basic research programs
2060203		National Natural Science Foundation of China (NSFC)
2060204		Key laboratory and relevant facilities
2060205		Mega-science programs (MSPs)
2062026		Special basic research
2060207		Special technology basic
2060299		Other basic research expenditures
20603	R&D	Applied research
2060301		Operation of institution
2060302		Research on the social and public goods
2060303		High-tech research
2060399		Other applied research
20604	R&D	Technology research and development
2060401		Operation of institution
2060402		Applied technology research and development
2060403		Industrial technology research and development
2060404		Transformation and diffusion of S&T achievements
20605	Non-R&D	Condition and service of S&T
20606	R&D*	Social sciences
20607	Non-R&D	Popularization of S&T
20608	Non-R&D	Exchanges and cooperation of S&T
20609	R&D	Mega-engineering programs (MEPs)
2060601		Special Mega-engineering programs
2060902		Key R&D programs
20699	Non-R&D	Other S&T expenditures
2069901		S&T awards
2069903		Transformed scientific research institutions
2069999		Other S&T expenditures

Sources: MOST, 2011.
Note: The social sciences are part of R&D activities, but are not included in the present study.

because no detailed information is available on other budgets that might also be used for S&T activities (Jia *et al.*, 2006: 34).[11] As such, we may underestimate China's R&D expenditure.

S&T Budgeting Process

Nowadays, China's budgeting process involves two rounds of budget requests and guidelines (Ma & Yu, 2007). Let us use the budgeting process of the MOST as an example. Upon receiving the announcement of budget for the coming year from the MOF, the MOST submits to the MOF a departmental annual budget (first budget request, *yi shang*). The MOF reviews the budget against current year's total budget and final accounts, and issues a restrained budget to the MOST (first budget guideline, *yi xia*). Then, the MOST resubmits an adjusted budget to the MOF by taking into account the restrained budget (second budget request, *er shang*). The MOF puts budget from the MOST along with those of all other government agencies and presents a national budget to the National People's Congress (NPC) Standing Committee for initial examination before it is deliberated and approved at the annual session of the NPC. Finally, the MOF re-issues the budget to the MOST for its implementation (second budget guideline, *er xia*).

For a period, China had decentralized the distribution of its central R&D spending. But the funding system suffered from a lack of top-level design, unified planning, ineffective coordination, and a lack of transparency in fund distribution and accountability in spending the funds (Sun & Cao, 2014). To solve these problems and respond to the call for reform proposed by the scientific community, in 2014, the State Council decided to reorganize NSTPs. A substantial change was to establish the National Key R&D Programs, the largest, by integrating the then Nation's Basic Research Program, also known as the 973 Program, including MSPs under the MLP; the then Nation's High-Tech R&D Program, also known as the 863 Program; and the National Key Technology R&D Program; the Industrial Technology R&D Fund, a policy program that used to be under the NDRC and the Ministry of Industry and Information Technology (MOIIT); and Special Funds for

---

[11] In theory, expenditures on S&T (item 206) and R&D (sub-budgetary items under item 206) come from government's S&T and R&D appropriation and the two are different.

research in public sectors managed by 13 central government agencies, and so on (Cao & Suttmeier, 2017). The budget item for National Key R&D Programs is 2060902 under 20609 – MEPs.

In addition, as mentioned in Chapter 1, in 2018, the CPC CC initiated the reform of the system of party and state institutions. Afterward, the MOST became a super-department by acquiring the independent National Natural Science Foundation of China (NSFC) and absorbing the State Administration of Foreign Experts from the Ministry of Human Resources and Social Security (MOHRSS). The NSFC remains an independent budget agency. The MOF allocates the government appropriation for S&T to the MOST as its department budget, most of which is in turn allocated to scientific research units through NSTPs.[12] Meanwhile, other agencies such as the MOIIT, the NSFC, the MOE, the MOARA, the Chinese Academy of Sciences (CAS), and others also negotiate their respective department budgets, including S&T items, with the MOF separately. In other words, the MOST and other S&T-mission agencies go through the same budgeting process, and get their appropriation from the MOF directly. In 2023, the CPC CC initiated a new reform of the party and state institutions, as mentioned in Chapter 1. However, it is not yet clear how the reform will affect the central government's budget for S&T, although the reorganized MOST may probably have a smaller budget.

An Overview of S&T Appropriation, GERD, and Government R&D Expenditure

According to China's current S&T budget management system, central and local governments manage S&T activities separately and at different levels. In particular, the central government is responsible for important strategic missions with funds consisting of departmental funds managed by agencies under the State Council and their scientific research units (Jia *et al.*, 2006: 34). Based on the statistics released by the central government and data collected from central government agencies, we depict the relationship between government S&T appropriation and GERD, and construct the distribution of China's government S&T expenditure (see Tables 4.2 and 4.3).

---

[12] After the reform of the revenue and expenditure category of budgeting system in 2007, there are no longer S&T promotion funds in the new budgeting system and the MOST only controls its own department annual budgets as many other government ministries do.

Table 4.2 China's structure of public S&T and R&D expenditure in 2011 and 2020 (units: billion RMB and %)

Years	Fiscal S&T appropriation			The central R&D expenditure			GERD		
	Sources	Amount	Share (%)	items	Amount	Share (%)	Sources	Amount	Share (%)
2011	Central S&T expenditure (206)	194.21	39.61	Basic research (20602)	29.43	20.63	Enterprises	642.06	73.91
	Local S&T expenditure (206)	188.59	38.47	Applied research (20603)	97.99	68.67	Governments	188.3	21.68
	S&T appropriation under other items	107.46	21.92	Technology research and development (20604)	8.32	5.83	Other	38.34	4.41
				Mega-engineering programs (20609)	6.95	4.87			
	Total	490.26	100	Total	142.69	100	Total	868.7	100
2020	Central S&T expenditure (206)	321.65	31.86	Basic research (20602)	62.54	23.63	Enterprises	1 889.5	77.46
	Local S&T expenditure (206)	580.19	57.47	Applied research (20603)	152.86	57.73	Governments	482.56	19.78
	S&T appropriation under other items	107.67	10.67	Technology research and development (20604)	−0.02		Other	67.26	2.76
				Mega-engineering programs (20609)	49.36	18.64			
	Total	1 009.5	100	Total	264.74	100	Total	2 439.32	100

Sources: Chinese Central Government's DARs, 2012 and Statistical Bulletin on National S&T Expenditure (2011 and 2020).

Notes: The subitems of the fiscal expenditure on S&T (item 206) in 2011 shown in the table – 20601 and 20609 – only include the fiscal expenditure by 71 agencies because the final accounting sheet of the central government didn't disclose the two items after 2007. According to the share of 20604 accounted for the total fiscal expenditure on S&T in 2007, we estimated the fiscal expenditure on 20604–9.9 billion RMB which is more a little the 8.42 billion RMB spent by 71 agencies. According to the situation in 2010, the expenditure on 20609 by 71 agencies was similar to that by the central government. The subitem-20609 of the fiscal expenditure on S&T (item 206) in 2019 is similar, only includes the fiscal expenditure by 89 agencies. These indicate that the undisclosed part of expenditure on 20604 and 20609 is negligible. The subitem 20604 in 2020 is negative, which is mainly due to the recovery of the surplus funds of the previous year to offset the current year's expenditures during the budget implementation of 2020, and no other item does in the table.

Table 4.3 *China's public R&D expenditure by agencies and fields in 2011 and 2020 (units: billion RMB and %)*

Years	Agency	S&T expenditure (Budget item 206)		R&D expenditure (four budget items)					Share of R&D as S&T (%)
		Amount	Share of Central (%)	20602	20603	20604	20609	Sum	
	MOST	27.28	14.05	4.7	8.81	7.74	0.01	21.26	77.93
	CAS	18.28	9.41	8.21	7.06	0.23	0.71	16.21	88.68
	NSFC	14.04	7.23	14.04				14.04	100
	MOIIT	5.76	2.96	0.17	1.61	0.03	3.87	5.68	98.61
	MOE	3.47	1.78	2.64	0.42	0.1	0.05	3.21	92.51
	MOA	3.12	1.61	0.23	1.93		0.42	2.58	82.69
	MOH	2.17	1.12	0.04	0.55		1.34	1.93	88.94
	CASS	1.58	0.82		0.01			0.01	0.63
2011	MOLR	1.03	0.53		0.92	0.02	0.01	0.95	92.23
	Other agencies	8.52	4.39	0.3	4.51	0.19	0.53	5.53	64.91
	71 agencies	85.25	43.89	30.33	25.82	8.32	6.95	71.42	83.78
				42.47%	36.15%	11.65%	9.73%	100%	
	Central Gov	194.21	100	29.43	97.99			134.67*	
	Local Gov	188.59		3.15	11.81			55.45*	
	GERD			41.18	102.84			868.7	
	GERD by Gov							188.3	

	Col1	Col2	Col3	Col4	Col5	Col6	Col7	Col8
MOST	53.18	16.53	4.82	0.57	2.15	37.52*	45.06	84.73
CAS	37.12	11.54	21.11	11.96	0.22	0.57	33.87	91.23
NSFC	29.79	9.26	29.79				29.79	100
MOIIT	10.35	3.22	0.39	2.76		7.12	10.27	99.23
MOARA	6.85	2.13	0.42	4.13		1.84	6.39	93.27
MOE	4.64	1.44	3.78	0.74		0.07	4.59	98.87
NHC	3.80	1.18	0.05	1.97		1.60	3.62	95.38
NPOPSS	2.57	0.80					0	0
CAST	2.40	0.75					0	0
Other agencies	14.65	4.55	1.02	7.88	0.03	0.64	9.57	65.31
102 agencies	165.35	51.41	61.38	30.01	2.40	49.36	143.15	86.58
	100		42.88%	20.96%	1.68%	34.48%	100%	
Central government	321.65		62.54	152.86	-0.02	223.03*		
Local government	580.19		25.52	33.08	179.81	170.58*		
GERD			146.7	275.72	2 016.89		2 439.32	
GERD by government							482.56	

(Row block labelled: 2020)

Sources: DARs by various government agencies in 2011 and 2019; Statistical bulletin on national S&T expenditures in 2011 and 2020; the reports on financial budgets and final accounts of the central government and the local government released by the MOF in 2011 and 2020; China statistical yearbook on science and technology in 2011 and 2020.

Notes: 1)* – The figures are estimated by the authors. According to the 2000 survey of the government R&D resources, in 1999, R&D expenditure by the central government accounted for 69.34 percent of the central S&T expenditure and R&D expenditure by the local governments accounted for 29.4 percent of the local S&T expenditure (Liu & Li, 2002). In 2011, the central S&T expenditure (item 206) 194.214 billion RMB × 69.34 percent equals to 134.67 billion RMB, and the local S&T expenditure 188.588 billion RMB ×29.4 percent equals to 55.45 billion RMB.

2)* – The figures are predicted by the authors according to the data between 2003 and 2018, because the MOST didn't disclose the number of budget items–20603 and 20609.

3) MOST – Ministry of Science and Technology; CAS – Chinese Academy of Sciences; NSFC – National Natural Science Foundation of China; MOIIT – Ministry of Industry and Information Technology; MOE – Ministry of Education; MOA – Ministry of Agriculture; MOARA – Ministry of Agriculture and Rural Affairs; MOH – Ministry of Health; CASS – Chinese Academy of Social Sciences; MOLR – Ministry of Land and Resources; NHC – National Health Commission; CAST–China Association for Science and Technology; NPOPSS– China National Planning Office of Philosophy and Social Science.

The central government's R&D expenditure is the intersection of S&T appropriation and GERD.

Government R&D Expenditure

There is a gap between government R&D expenditure in S&T appropriation and that in GERD statistics. In 2011, China's GERD was 868.7 billion RMB, of which governments – central and local – contributed 188.3 billion RMB, or 21.68 percent, with the rest, 642.06 billion RMB, or 73.91 percent, coming from enterprises.[13] Nine years later, China's GERD increased 1.8 times to 2,439.31 billion RMB, of which governments' contribution declined by some 2 percent.

In 2011, the Chinese government S&T appropriation was 490.26 billion RMB according to the MOF DAR. Of this amount, 382.8 billion RMB was for the S&T expenditure (item 206), accounting for 78.08 percent of the government S&T appropriation and central and local government's S&T expenditure was 194.21 billion RMB and 188.59 billion RMB or 39.61 percent and 38.47 percent of the government S&T appropriation, respectively (Chinese Central government's DAR, 2012).[14] In 2020, Chinese governments' S&T appropriation increased to 1,009.5 billion RMB, with the S&T expenditure (item 206) accounting for 89.33 percent. This indicates that Chinese governments might move its S&T appropriation from other budget items to item 206 – S&T expenditure, which also became more transparent.

According to *Chinese Science and Technology Indicators 2010*, in 2007, the expenditure on sub-budgetary items 20602, 20603, and 20604 was 12.97 billion RMB, 61.8 billion RMB, and 44.49 billion RMB, respectively, or a total of 119.26 billion RMB (MOST, 2011: 52). The MOF does not provide the data of spending on 20604 after 2007, which is the first year when the new statistical system was introduced. But in the same year, GERD from governments was only 91.4 billion RMB (NBS & MOST, 2009: 10). These indicate that there

---

[13] Back in 2000, the contributions of enterprises, government and other sources to GERD were 57.6 percent, 33.4 percent and 9 percent respectively. Due to the policy push for constructing an enterprise-led innovation system in the last decade, the structure of China's GERD has changed significantly (Sun & Liu, 2014).

[14] In addition, 107.46 billion RMB was under the S&T appropriation under the other expenditure items, accounting for 21.92 percent of the government S&T appropriation, which is not further discussed as indicated.

is a 28-billion-RMB discrepancy between government R&D expenditure reported by the MOF in S&T appropriation and that included in the GERD reported by the MOST, the NBS, and the MOF.

Defense S&T Expenditure

The defense S&T expenditure accounted for about half of the total S&T expenditure. In 2011, 71 agencies' S&T expenditure accounted for 43.89 percent; and in 2020, S&T expenditure of 102 agencies accounted for 51.41 percent of central government's S&T expenditure (see Table 4.3). This implies that the rest of central government's S&T expenditure is most likely to be spent by eight national defense related agencies that did not disclose their budgetary information. Again, with more agencies disclosing their budgets, China's government funding is increasingly transparent.

In 2002, the central S&T expenditure was 51.1 billion RMB, of which defense and civilian S&T expenditures accounted for 52.84 percent (27 billion RMB) and 47.16 percent (24.1 billion RMB), respectively (Jia *et al.*, 2006: 34). Thus, it is possible that most of the unaccounted-for S&T expenditure in our analysis was spent on national defense related S&T activities. The recent progress in China's defense modernization can be explained by government consistently devoting more funds to weapon acquisition from domestic and international sources. In addition, while China has been making defense enterprises more efficient and raising R&D and production capabilities through making enterprises less reliant on state subsidies and the gradual corporatization of some defense R&D institutes, resources are still channeled into these defense R&D institutes (Medeiros *et al.*, 2005: 22; Cheung, 2013: 18). Moreover, as some of the ministries such as the MOIIT do report S&T and R&D expenditure spent by their defense-oriented R&D institutes or state-owned enterprises (SOEs), the question is whether some of the expenditure is double counted.

Central Government's R&D Expenditure

The share of central government's R&D expenditure accounted for less total government's R&D expenditure. R&D expenditure is a part of S&T expenditure in China's statistical system and budget system. According to the 2000 survey of government R&D resources, in 1999, R&D expenditure by the central government accounted for 69.34

percent of the central S&T expenditure, and R&D expenditure by the
local governments 29.4 percent of the local S&T expenditure (Liu &
Li, 2002). Assuming that the same ratios were held for 2011, the central and local government's R&D expenditure might be 134.67 billion
RMB and 55.45 billion RMB, respectively, as the MOF did disclose
central and local S&T expenditure,[15] whose sum (190.1 billion RMB)
is closer to the GERD contributed by governments (188.3 billion
RMB) (NBS *et al.*, 2012). However, in 2020, with local governments
spending more on S&T activities, the central government contributed
some 46.22 percent of government's portion of the R&D expenditure, which is lower than that in 2011, although the absolute amount
(375.82 billion RMB) was almost doubled.

The MOST, the CAS, and the NSFC are the main agencies for
China's central R&D expenditure. In 2020, the nine government agencies listed in Table 4.3 spent some 91.14 percent (90 percent in 2011)
of the S&T expenditure by the 102 agencies and 46.85 percent (51.72
percent in 2011) of the central government's S&T expenditure. R&D
expenditure at these nine agencies is almost identical to their respective
S&T expenditure. In 2011, with more than 10 billion RMB each, the
MOST, the CAS, and the NSFC were three top agencies administering central government's R&D expenditure and their combined R&D
expenditure accounted for 50 percent of that at 71 agencies. In 2020,
four agencies – the MOST, the CAS, the NSFC, and the MOIIT – each
spent more than 10 billion RMB on R&D, with top three' combined
R&D expenditure accounting for 72.63 percent of the total at 102
agencies. That is, China's central R&D budget has become increasingly
concentrated in a few main S&T-mission agencies.

Some S&T-mission agencies such as the MOIIT, despite having
spending on MEPs, are smaller players compared with the MOST and
the CAS. In 2010, MOIIT's S&T expenditure (11.65 billion RMB) was
more than that of NSFC's (10.11 billion RMB), because the MOIIT
spent 9.79 billion RMB on MEPs (item 20609). For unknown reasons,
in 2011, expenditure on the same item reduced to only 3.87 billion
RMB, which changed its position on the list of the R&D expenditure
spenders. After the NSTP reform in 2014, the MOST became the biggest agency funding MEPs (20609) including Key R&D Programs, as·

---

[15] The central S&T expenditure (item 206) 194.214 billion RMB × 69.34 percent
equals to 134.67 billion RMB, and the local S&T expenditure 188.588 billion
RMB × 29.4 percent equals to 55.45 percent billion RMB.

the data of 2020 indicate. The budgeting mechanism of MEPs, to be discussed in the next section, may explain this interesting phenomenon. It is worth noting that the NDRC is not among the top spenders of R&D expenditure in both 2011 and 2020, although it, along with the MOIIT, has been perceived to be one of the super-agencies of China's administration system in science, technology, and innovation as well as other areas (Huang *et al.*, 2004; Jakobson, 2007; Naughton, 2009). As a result of the 2023 reorganization, some of the organizations that used to affiliated to the MOST will move to other government agencies. Therefore, there is likely a change of S&T expenditure that the central government appropriates to its agencies and in turn a possible rising budget at mission-oriented agencies.

The central government spends more on applied research than basic research but does not disclose much information on how the money is distributed to various ministries. In 2020, central government's expenditure on basic research (20602) was 62.54 billion RMB (see Table 4.2), and 102 agencies have reported to spend 61.38 billion RMB on basic research. As a whole, the basic research expense accounted for 42.88 percent of the 102 agencies' R&D expenditure, which is similar to that in 2011.

In 2020, central government's expenditure on applied research (20603) was 152.86 billion RMB. One hundred and two agencies' expenditure on applied research (20603) was 30.01 billion RMB, accounting for 20.96 percent of these agencies' R&D expenditure. Compared with that in 2011, the share of applied research in the central government's R&D expenditure decreased.

In 2020, while 98.15 percent of the central government's expenditure on basic research was spent at 102 agencies, only 19.63 percent of the expenditure on applied research is accountable, indicating that R&D appropriation on applied research is less transparent than that on basic research. Apart from the expenditure on basic and applied research (20602 and 20603), 102 agencies spent 2.40 billion RMB on technology R&D (20604), which only accounted for 1.68 percent of the R&D expenditure at the 102 agencies. The expenditure on MEPs (20609) was 49.36 billion RMB, or 34.48 percent of the R&D expenditure at the 102 agencies.

Within the 102 agencies reporting their S&T expenditure in 2020, which significantly increased from 71 agencies in 2011, the share of the expenditure on applied research and technology R&D decreased, while the share of that on MEPs increased. These figures also indicate that the Chinese central government spent more money on scientific research ("R") than technology development ("D").

Central Government R&D Expenditure by Main Agencies

Above analysis indicates that the MOST, the CAS, the NSFC, and the MOIIT used the larger share of the central government's budget on R&D (Table 4.4). Here, we are going to examine further how much of the central government R&D expenditure was distributed to each of the key science-mission agencies except the NSFC because it funds basic research and mission-oriented basic research solely, which will be discussed in the next section.

We also will discuss why the NDRC, the perceived important agency in China's S&T enterprise, spends so little on R&D. There is a division of labor among the MOST, the CAS, the MOIIT, and the NDRC, whose total S&T expenditure includes not only government S&T appropriation but also revenues from other sources. In both 2011 and 2020, compared with the amount of funding at the MOST, which received about 98 percent of the S&T expenditure from government, nearly half of the S&T funding at the CAS and the MOIIT, and about three-quarters of the S&T budget at the NDRC did not come from government's appropriation.

Ministry of Science and Technology

The MOST is an overarching government agency responsible for China's scientific enterprise. It makes S&T development policies and plans and formulates and organizes NSTPs. Until 1999, the MOST oversaw 12.23 billion RMB, or 34.3 percent, of the central S&T appropriation. In 2001, the government S&T appropriation managed by the MOST reduced to 7.86 billion RMB, or 17.7 percent of the central S&T appropriation (Jia *et al.*, 2006: 34). After the 2000 and 2007 reforms of S&T budget management, other S&T-mission agencies started to compete for government appropriation, mainly through NSTPs, the MEPs under the MLP in particular, thus reducing MOST's weight in the S&T budget. Nowadays, the MOST is no longer in charge of the national S&T budget but its own department budget by administering mainly the funds for NSTPs (Jia *et al.*, 2006: 34). In 2020, the government S&T appropriation managed by the MOST increased to 53.18 billion RMB, which

Table 4.4 *Chinese main central agencies of R&D expenditure by field (units: billion RMB and %)*

Years		2011				2020			
Agency	Budget item	Total expenditure	Government expenditure	Government/Total (%)	Budget item	Total expenditure	Government expenditure	Government/Total (%)
MOST	206 (S&T)	28 094.2	27 673	98.5	206 (S&T)	53 793.78	53 182.51	98.86
	20602	4 693.8	4 693.8	100	20602	4 821.41	4 821.41	100
	2060202	4 493.8	4 493.8	100	2060204	4 293.45	4 293.45	100
	2060204	200	200	100	2060299	527.96	527.96	100
	20603	9 200.7	8 864.4	96.34	20603	783.89	570.36	72.76
	2060301	481.75	145.44	30.19	2060301	416.25	202.73	48.7
	2060302	43.6	43.6	100	2060302	56.20	56.20	100
	2060303	8 618	8 618	100	2060399	311.44	311.43	99.99
	20604	7 755.4	7 755.4	100	20604	2 149.06	2 149.06	100
	2060402	5 525.7	5 525.7	100	2060404	2 149.06	2 149.06	100
	2060404	48.7	48.7	100	–	–	–	–
	20609	16	13.1	82.07	20609	37 523.33*	37 523.33*	100
	R&D Sum	21 665.90	21 326.70	98.43	R&D Sum	45 277.69	45 064.16	99.53
	R&D/S&T (%)	77.12	77.07		R&D/S&T (%)	84.17	84.73	
CAS	206 (S&T)	33 848.3	18 949.6	55.98	206 (S&T)	78 430.11	37 123.88	47.33
	20602	13 041.4	8 301.2	63.65	20602	33 061.27	21 106.90	63.84
	20603	15 103.3	7 457.9	49.38	20603	33 326.65	11 962.75	35.90
	20604	398.8	251.8	63.14	20604	640.64	224.36	35.02
	20609	2 019	424.8	21.04	20609	6 018.78	573.28	9.52
	R&D Sum	30 562.5	16 435.7	53.78	R&D Sum	73 047.35	33 867.29	46.36
	R&D/S&T (%)	90.29	86.73		R&D/S&T (%)	93.14	91.23	

Table 4.4 (cont.)

		2011				2020		
Agency	Budget item	Total expenditure	Government expenditure	Government/Total (%)	Budget item	Total expenditure	Government expenditure	Government/Total (%)
MOIIT	206 (S&T)	11 978.2	6 211.6	51.86	206 (S&T)	25 925.77	10 349.09	39.92
	20602	188	161.1	85.7	20602	396.38	394.10	99.43
	20603	7 377	1 741	23.6	20603	18 271.52	2 755.09	15.08
	20604	32.4	25	77.05	20604	–	–	–
	20609	4 293.5	4 201.4	97.85	20609	7 161.04	7 120.58	99.43
	R&D Sum	11 890.9	6 128.5	51.54	R&D Sum	25 828.93	10 269.77	39.76
	R&D/S&T (%)	99.27	98.66		R&D/S&T (%)	99.63	99.23	
NDRC	206 (S&T)	290.00	73.20	25.25	206 (S&T)	419.08	114.61	27.35
	20603	278.80	62.00	22.23	20603	418.26	114.61	27.4
	20604	4.30	4.30	100.00	20604	–	–	–
	20609	1.40	1.40	100.00	20609	–	–	–
	R&D Sum	284.50	67.70	23.80	R&D Sum	418.26	114.61	27.4
	R&D/S&T (%)	98.10	92.49		R&D/S&T (%)	99.8	100	

Sources: DARs on Final Accounts by various government agencies in 2011 and 2020.

only represented 16.53 percent of the central S&T expenditure (item 206–321.65 billion RMB) but was higher than 14.05 percent in 2011.

In 2011, the MOST spent most of its R&D expenditure on three major programs – the 973 Program including MSPs (4.49 billion RMB, 2060202);[16] the 863 Program (8.62 billion RMB, 2060303); and the National Key Technologies R&D Program (5.53 billion RMB, 2060402). The MOST is the primary organizer and funder of MSPs whose projects were directly performed by scientific research units through competition or direct allocation. In 2020, the situation changed much, as the MOST spent most of its R&D expenditure on MEPs – 70.55 percent of its total S&T expenditure.

Before the most recent round of the reform in 2014, China's NSTPs also included the State Key Laboratory (SKL) Program, the Special Program for S&T Basic Condition Platform, the National Engineering Research Centers Program, the Special Program for S&T Basic Work, the National S&T Infrastructure Program (MOST, 2011: 55), Environment Building for S&T Industries[17] and MEPs. But most of those programs were not funded out of the MOST budget. For example, the MOST was only responsible for macro management of the SKL Program (2060204) in the establishment, evaluation, and dissolution of the SKLs while these labs were based at universities, research institutes, and enterprises. The MOE, the CAS, the State-owned Assets Supervision and Administration Commission of the State Council (SASAC) and local governments oversaw their funding.

In 2020, the central government funded 98.86 percent of the S&T expenditure at the MOST. The expenditure on 20602, 20604, and 20609 all came from government appropriation. The MOST also earned revenues by undertaking R&D projects, providing training and information services, which was under the items of Operation of Institutions (2060301).

Chinese Academy of Sciences

The CAS is China's leading academic institution and comprehensive R&D center in the natural sciences, technological sciences, and

---

[16] MSPs are operated from the Office of the 973 Program at the MOST.
[17] Programs for the environment building for S&T industries include the Spark Program, the Torch Program, the National Key New Product Program, the Innovation Fund for Technology Based Firms, and others (MOST, 2011: 58).

high-tech innovation. It also functions as a nation's high-end scientific think-tank, providing advisory and appraisal services on issues stemming from the national economy, social development, and S&T progress.

In the mid-1980s, the CAS, along with China's other R&D institutes, faced severe financial pressure after China reformed its S&T system in which scientists were required to raise part of the funds for research themselves. In 1995, the policy of "revitalizing the country through science and education" elevated S&T development to a major national priority. In 1997, Lu Yongxiang, the then newly appointed CAS president, submitted an important report, *The Coming of the Knowledge-Based Economy and the Construction of the National Innovation System*, to the central leadership, which approved the report and tasked the CAS to carry out a Knowledge Innovation Program (KIP). The program was seen as a phased "pilot project" of reform, which led to a remade academy by 2010 (Suttmeier *et al.*, 2006). After an assessment of the pilot project in 2010, the government decided to continue to support the CAS with a new program – Knowledge Innovation Program 2020: A Leapfrogging Scheme for Science, Technology, and Innovation, known as KIP 2020, which was expected to generate a series of core intellectual properties and support the construction of the innovation-oriented country (CAS, 2012). Under the new program, the CAS organized and implemented several strategic pioneering science projects, including space science satellites, stem cells, and regenerative medicine research and applications.

In July 2013, the CPC CC Secretary General Xi Jinping visited the CAS and challenged it in taking on a pioneering role by becoming "Four Firsts" – first in achieving leapfrog development of S&T, first in building high ground for cultivating innovative talents, first in establishing a nation's high-level think tank for S&T, and first in becoming a world-class research institution. In 2014, the then president Bai Chunli proposed a Pioneer Initiative as an action in response to Xi's call for deepening the reform of China's S&T system as well as that of the academy. The Pioneer Initiative, has been still going on under Hou Jianguo, who became the president in 2020, albeit different from that under Bai.

In 2020, the CAS operated on an S&T expenditure of 78.43 billion RMB, including 37.12 billion RMB, or 47.33 percent, from government directly. It used most of the government appropriation on basic research (21.11 billion RMB, 20602) and applied research (11.96

billion RMB, 20603). It also spent 224.36 million RMB of the government expenditure on technology R&D (20604) and 573.28 million RMB on MEPs (20609). Clearly, the CAS has placed more emphasis on basic research as the share of basic research in its total S&T expenditure increased to 56.86 percent in 2020 from 44.91 percent in 2011. While CAS received 63.84 percent of its total expenditure on basic research (20602) from government, only 9.52 percent of its total expenditure on MEPs (20609) came from government.

The CAS also allocated most of the nongovernment S&T revenue to basic and applied research. This revenue was from three sources. First, operating revenue was from competitive research funding of the NSTPs and foreign R&D tasks, cooperative projects with universities, enterprises, and local governments. Second, business revenue came from nonindependent accounting business activities by selling research products and providing services. Third, business revenue came from its independent accounting sub-business units. In a word, most of the academy's nongovernment money was research funds obtained from different sources through competition.

The analysis of S&T expenditure at the CAS indicates that the academy not only received support from the central appropriation so as to fulfill government's mandate as an important player of the national innovation system but also competed for funding from NSTPs to perform a significant amount of activities at the research frontier. The academy also received funds from local governments and enterprises through academy–locality cooperation (e.g., co-construction of a research institute, co-construction of a technology transfer center as a platform to promote and facilitate scientific achievement transfer and regional economic development). Indeed, since the KIP implementation, the CAS has been expanding significantly its mission from basic research and strategic high-technology to applied research and technology commercialization (Suttmeier & Shi, 2008). After the Pioneer Initiative's implementation, it has placed more emphasis on basic research as the share of basic research in its total S&T expenditure increased to 56.86 percent in 2020 from 47.8 percent in 2014.

Ministry of Industry and Information Technology

The MOIIT is one of the S&T-mission ministries under the State Council, with its function similar to that of the ministries of agriculture, health, and environmental protection. In particular, the MOIIT is responsible for facilitating R&D in the manufacturing industry of electronic and IT products, the communications and the software industry, and organizing projects to tackle major technical problems and promote the digestion, absorption, and improvement of the imported technologies with a view to applying R&D results to production, and offering support to national industries.

The MOIIT emerged in the 2008 government administration reform as a super-ministry, which is based on the former Ministry of Information Industry but acquired the former State Council Office on Informatization, part of the former Commission of Science, Technology, and Industry for National Defense (COSTIND), and part of the NDRC with the most direct industrial management responsibilities. However, MOIIT's DAR only unveils budget of its administration and affiliated research institutes as well as that of the seven national defense-related universities which used to be under the COSTIND.[18] Despite being a department of the MOIIT, the State Administration of Science, Technology, and Industry for National Defense (SASTIND), or the downgraded COSTIND, remains an independent budget unit and has not disclosed its budget as stipulated by the State Council regulations.

In 2020, the MOIIT spent 25.92 billion RMB on S&T activities, of which 10.35 billion RMB was government S&T expenditure, accounting for 39.92 percent of the total, lower than that in 2011. It spent most of the government appropriation on applied research and MEPs. In 2020, the government S&T expenditure accounted for 15.08 percent of the total S&T expenditure on applied research, and of the total S&T expenditure, 99.43 million RMB was used for MEPs (20609). The MOIIT received most of its nongovernment S&T revenue from three sources – operating revenue, business revenue, and the revenue from affiliated units, and spent this revenue on applied research.

---

[18] They are Beijing University of Aeronautics and Astronautics, Beijing Institute of Technology, Nanjing University of Aeronautics and Astronautics, Nanjing University of Science and Technology, Harbin Institute of Technology, Harbin Engineering University and Northwestern Polytechnic University. These seven universities were administrated by the COSTIND before 2008. Part of the R&D expenditure at these universities is likely to be spent on national defense-related R&D activities.

The R&D expenditure and revenue portfolio at the MOIIT indicates that the ministry, through its public R&D institutes such as China Electronics Standardization Institute, China Electronic Product Reliability, and Environmental Research Institute, and others, are mainly engaged in applied research. Performing important R&D tasks, the seven national defense-related universities presumably may also receive funding from the SASTIND through independent budget, in addition to competing for funds from NSTPs.

National Development and Reform Commission

NDRC's functions in the area of S&T include participating in the formulation of policies with regard to the S&T development; formulating strategies, plans, and major policies for the development of high-tech industries and advancement of industrial technologies; and coordinating and addressing major issues concerning dissemination and application of key technical equipment. The NDRC also is important in the formulation and implementation of public finance, monetary, and land policies, which have implications for science, technology, and innovation.

According to disclosed information (see Table 4.4), in 2020, the NDRC only spent 419.08 million RMB on S&T, of which 114.61 million RMB, or 27.35 percent, was from the government, significantly less than government's S&T appropriation to the MOST. In 2020, the NDRC spent most of the government funds, which was 418.26 million RMB, on applied research (20603). The NDRC mainly used the funds for the enhancement of innovation capability at enterprise technology centers, the National Engineering Research Center Program, and technological innovation of small- and medium-sized enterprises. Research funds were the primary source of its nongovernment revenue, as its Academy of Macroeconomics carried out research for various organizations.

In fact, not just having a small S&T budget, according to its DAR, in 2020, NDRC's whole budget was only 3.85 billion RMB. Other revenue included operating revenue from nonindependent accounting business activities in sub-unit by providing services, training, research and products, other revenue. However, as a comprehensive administration of economic and social development, the NDRC involves in the budgeting process by proposing and allocating the central budget which is not included in its department annual budget so as to possess power in the so-called "secondary budgeting process." In particular, it is in charge of government appropriation for capital construction programs. Although the MOF does not include this item in NDRC's department budget at the beginning of a fiscal year, the money is there for the NDRC to use at its discretion later the year (MOF, 2007).

NDRC's functions and budgets seem to indicate that it participates in formulating China's science, technology, and innovation policies as a major policymaker but does not directly fund S&T activities and distribute large funds. It also funds the construction and operation of big-science research infrastructures such as the Shanghai Synchrotron Radiation Facility, but only a part of such spending is included in its S&T budget (Sun & Cao, 2016). It achieves its roles in formulating important economic regulations and distributing strategic resources through financial resources that are not included in department annual budget but distributed under its discretion, as discussed in the last section.

Central Government R&D Expenditure by Fields

In China as in other countries, the key areas of scientific research financed by government funds are basic research, research on cutting-edge and generic technologies, and research related to the public and social welfare. Under China's S&T budget, the abovementioned activities fall into basic research (20602) and applied research (20603). With prioritized themes targeting national goals, MEPs (20609) support research on major strategic products and key generic technologies as well as major engineering efforts. The government also attempts to induce private sector to support MEPs through its appropriation guidance. The present section discusses the expenditure on basic and applied research (Table 4.5), and Chapter 6 will focus on the organization of MEPs.

Basic Research (20602)

Basic research is government's responsibility, because it takes a long time to gain outcome and it is difficult to capture an immediate return on investment. Moreover, it faces a high losing risk as the outputs – papers – are usually in the public domain, which could be used by others.

Table 4.5 *Chinese main fields of R&D expenditure by agencies (units: billion RMB and %)*

	2011				2020			
	Budget item				Budget item			
Rank	20602	20603	20609	Rank	20602	20603	20609
1	NSFC 14.04	MOST 8.81	MOIIT 3.87	1	NSFC 29.79	CAS 11.96	MOST 37.52+
2	CAS 8.21	CAS 7.06	MOH 1.34	2	CAS 21.11	MOAMR 4.13	MOIIT 7.12
3	MOST 4.7	MOA 1.93	CAS 0.71	3	MOST 4.82	MOIIT 2.76	MOAMR 1.84
4	MOE 2.64	MOIIT 1.61	MOA 0.42	4	MOE 3.78	NHC 1.97	NHC 1.60
5	MOA 0.23	MOLR 0.92	MOEP 0.21	5	MOHRSS 0.93	NFGA 1.03	CAS 0.57
6	MOHRSS 0.19	MOWR 0.61	MOHURD 0.19	6	MOAMR 0.42	MNR 0.85	MOEP 0.46
7	MOIIT 0.17	SFA 0.55	MOWR 0.06	7	MOIIT 0.39	MOWR 0.78	MOHURD 0.14
Total 7 agencies	30.19	21.49	6.79	Total 7 agencies	61.24	23.49	49.25
Total 71 agencies	30.33	25.82	6.95	Total 102 agencies	61.38	30.01	49.36
7/71 (%)	99.52	83.24	97.73	7/102 (%)	99.77	78.27	99.78

Notes: MNR – Ministry of Natural Resources; MOEP – Ministry of Environmental Protection; MOHRSS – Ministry of Human Resources and Social Security; MOHURD – Ministry of Housing and Urban-Rural Development; MOLR – Ministry of Land and Resources; MOWR – Ministry of Water Resources; NEA – National Energy Administration; SFA – State Forestry Administration.

In 1995, China spent 1.81 billion RMB, or 5.19 percent of its total R&D expenditure, on basic research. This ratio had been hovering over 5 percent after 2000 and reached 5.98 percent in 2004. However, between 2007 and 2013, the share of the basic research expenditure as a percentage of GERD had been under 5 percent and even reached 4.59 percent in 2010, the lowest. In 2014, the share of basic research in China reached 5 percent again. The Chinese government has called for spending more on basic research. In 2019, it formulated a five-year plan for the development of basic research to promote its healthy development. In 2020, basic research accounted for 6 percent of the GERD, the highest in the past 20 years. By comparison, most developed countries spend more than 10 percent of their GERD on basic research.

In 2011, China's top seven agencies, including the NSFC, the CAS, the MOE, and the MOST, spent 99.6 percent of the basic research funds (see Table 4.5). Of them, the NSFC and the MOST serve as funding agencies and the CAS and the MOE are both beneficiaries and competitors. The NSFC manages the National Natural Science Foundation Program that supports basic research and mission-oriented basic research. The NSFC is governed by a combination of senior staff connected with government policy evidenced by the fact that the State Council appoints the 25 members of the Foundation's General Assembly and its key officers and the stakeholders through Expert Advisory Committees (NSFC, 2012). In 2018, the NSFC was merged into the MOST while maintaining a separate budget and independent operation. Over time, the NSFC has developed an extensive portfolio of funding instruments to address the needs of different segments of the research community. NSFC programs include funds for projects; funds for talents such as the National Science Fund for Distinguished Young Scholars (Cao & Suttmeier, 2001)[19]; and funds for joint research projects such as the Joint Fund of the NSFC and Hong Kong Research Grant Council. Funds for projects include a general (*mianshang*) program, a key (*zhongdian*) program, a major (*zhongda*) program, major research plans (pilot), and a special program. In 2011, as the major part of NSFC's programs consuming 93.3 percent of its funds, free

---

[19] Other programs included Young Scientists Fund, Joint Research Fund for Overseas Chinese Young Scholars, Joint Research Fund for Hong Kong and Macao Young Scholars, National Science Fund for Fostering Talents in Basic Research, Fund for Innovative Research Groups.

application programs included a general program (8.99 billion RMB), a program for young scientists (3.12 billion RMB), and a program for scientists from underdeveloped regions (999 million RMB). But their share decreased to less than 60 percent in 2020, unhealthy for free inquiry in basic science research. The NSFC uses a peer-review-based project selection process that follows established international practice and has a system of checks and balances in place – including an internal supervision department – to safeguard the quality, independence, and integrity of the process and the interests of the applicants.

In 2011, the MOST managed the basic-research-oriented 973 Program and MSPs as part of its national S&T program portfolio. The 973 Program used to be China's national key basic research program, which was proposed by scientists in March 1997 at the annual session of the NPC and approved by the Chinese government in June 1997. The strategic objectives of the program, which had been organized and implemented by the MOST, included strengthening the original innovations and addressing the important scientific issues concerning the national economic and social development at a deeper level. In accordance with the international practice in the financial management of S&T projects, the 973 Program had implemented the subject management system for funding; namely, the MOST conducted the total fund budgeting by process control and full cost accounting. After the reform in 2014, MOST's funding for basic research dropped significantly with the 973 Program integrated into the Key R&D program under MEPs (20609), which is weird as the 973 Program was for basic research but MEPs were mission-oriented.

As discussed in the last section, the CAS, China's premier R&D institution with basic research as one of its mandates, not only receives funding from the central government for *intramural* research but also actively competes *extramural* funding from the NSFC, the MOST, and other sources. And the MOE has 75 directly affiliated universities that are the key players of basic research. The CAS- and MOE-affiliated universities received funds from the NSFC, respectively, among their multiple funding sources.

Applied Research (20603)

Applied research involves using and extending existing knowledge to solve particular problems rather than generating knowledge for the knowledge's sake (OECD, 2002: 78). Thus, applied research is closer to market than basic research. In 1995, China spent 9.2 billion RMB on applied research, accounting for 26.39 percent of the total R&D expenditure. The share of applied research as a percentage of GERD was decreasing gradually afterward and reached a low of 16.96 percent in 2000. The share started to recover after 2000, and amounted to a high of 20.37 percent in 2004. Then, the share has been on a sharp drop again. In 2020, the share of applied research only was as low as 11.3 percent of GERD at the time when GERD experienced rapid growth and the share of enterprises' contribution to GERD reached a record high, 77.5 percent. By comparison, China's share of applied research is lower than that of the USA and Japan, which was 19.8 percent and 18.7 percent, respectively, in 2017.

In 2020, seven agencies – the CAS, the MOA MR, the MOIIT, the National Health Commission (NHC), the Ministry of Natural Resources (MNR), the MOST, and the Ministry of Water Resources (MOWR) – spent a total of 23.49 billion RMB on applied research, accounting for 78.27 percent of the 102 agencies' expenditures on applied research. Compared with that in the 2011, the size of applied research has not grown much.

In 2011, MOST's government expenditure on applied research (20603) (see Table 4.4) included institution operation (2060301), research on the social and public goods (2060302), and civilian component of the high-tech research or the 863 Program (2060303).[20] The 863 Program, a program funded and administered by the MOST, was intended to stimulate the development of advanced technologies in a wide range of fields from information, biotechnology, agriculture, pharmaceuticals, new materials, advanced manufacturing, environmental protection, and resources and energy development. The ministry's government expenditure on high-tech research was 8.62 billion RMB, or 97.22 percent of its expenditure on applied research. By comparison, in 2020, MOST's government expenditure on applied research (20603) reduced to 783.89 million RMB.[21] Again, the MOST will see its role in fund distribution in some of the above-mentioned

---

[20] The defense component of the 863 Program had been organized and implemented by the People's Liberation Army General Armaments Department and the COSTIND and its successor SASTIND. After the reform of NSTPs in 2014, there is no longer 863 Program.

[21] In 2020, MOST's government expenditure on applied research (20603) only included 2060301, 2060302 and 2060399, but does not include the high-tech

areas declining as its affiliated functions will move to other government agencies as a result of the 2023 reorganization of the MOST.

In addition to funds for applied research that were managed by the MOST available for competition, the CAS, the MOARA, and other mission agencies allocate from their own noncompetitive funds to applied research activities. According to their respective DARs, the CAS spent its funds of applied research mainly on the operation of application-oriented research institutes, research on social and public goods such as the environment, and research on forward-looking high-tech projects; and the MOARA spent its funds of applied research mainly on industrial technologies for modern agriculture, the operation of research institutes under its jurisdiction.

Scientific Research (20602 and 20603)

There is an interesting but discouraging phenomenon that China's share of expenditure on scientific research (basic and applied research), or the "R" in R&D, of GERD, has been declining. In 2020, the share of scientific research as a percentage of GERD was only 17.3 percent in China, compared with the average for the same indicator of over 35 percent in developed countries and newly industrialized economies (MOST, 2011: 43). The low share of scientific research has seriously and negatively influenced the improvement of China's original innovation capability.

According to Jia Nan, then deputy director of the Statistical Division of Social Development, Science and Technology and Culture at the NBS, the low share of scientific research is closely linked with the fact that enterprises hardly carry out basic and applied research (Jia, 2012). In addition to such an official explanation, in reality, the problem also lies in decreasing government efforts. Scientific research is the responsibility of the public sector and should be funded by government while the private sector is responsible for experimental development with funding from enterprises. Although some large innovative enterprises invest in scientific research for their medium- and long-term development prospect, such investment should not be at the expense of government's obligation.

There are several reasons for this Chinese phenomenon. First, the share of government expenditure on scientific research has been

research (2060303) (see Table 4.4), presumably because of the closing of the 863 Program.

declining significantly, albeit the rising absolute value, which has led to the declining share of expenditure on scientific research in GERD. Indeed, almost all funds of China's scientific research are from government. Since 1995, the share of government R&D expenditure as a percentage of GERD has been decreasing despite the rapid growth of GERD. Second, as a result of the reform in 1999, the application-oriented research institutes have been transformed into technology-based enterprises or merged into enterprises and their expenditure is usually counted as expenditure at enterprises, thus leading to de facto decrease of the funds and share of applied research in GERD. Third, applied research follows basic research.[22] If government does not invest enough on basic research, it would not further fund applied research and cannot persuade enterprises to invest in applied research. That is, China's S&T reform for establishing an enterprise-centered national innovation system has an unintended consequence of reducing the share of government R&D expenditure in GERD, while government also has reduced its share of the expenditure on scientific research as the total government expenditure.[23] As shown in Table 4.3, the central agencies' share of basic and applied research expenditure decreased from 78.62 percent in 2011 to 63.84 percent in 2020.

Although the statistics show that enterprises have become the primary funder of R&D expenditure, China has yet to fully establish an enterprise-centered national innovation system (Cao *et al.*, 2009). Enterprises have not undertaken the primary responsibility in innovation. To further discuss this, it is necessary to define "enterprise" in the Chinese context. First, with the corporatization of applied R&D institutes, as mentioned, much of the funding now attributed to "enterprises" is most likely government money supplied to research institutes that used to be registered as companies or as part of existing enterprises (McGregor, 2010). Second, state-owned enterprises (SOEs) including the state-holding enterprises are enterprises in name but government organizations in nature as their assets belong to the government. According to an SASAC report, in 2020, the central SOEs spent 911.5 billion RMB

---

[22] In the business sector, the distinction between basic and applied research is often marked by the creation of a new project to explore promising results of a basic research program (OECD, 2002: 78).

[23] This analysis is based on one crucial precondition, that is, the amount of R&D expenditure contributed by enterprises is as the statistics has claimed; otherwise, China's R&D expenditure would present a completely different picture.

on R&D, which accounted for 48.24 percent and 37.4 percent of R&D expenditure by enterprises and nation's GERD, respectively. As SOEs are major contributors to enterprises' R&D expenditure, their spending on R&D also could be considered that of government's because the SASAC, as a delegate of the state, contributes capital to the central SOEs. In this sense, in 2020, Chinese state's GERD would be increased to some 57 percent and as such the state rather than enterprises still is the primary actor of R&D expenditure.

Summary and Discussions

By integrating the 2011 and 2020 DARs on budget and final accounts of 71 and 102 Chinese government agencies, respectively, and other statistics, this chapter tries to open the "black box" of China's R&D expenditure. Despite not answering all the related questions, it does make one – who spends how much money on what at the central government level – clearer.

In particular, we have found that more than half of the central S&T expenditure is not countable from budget statistics released by 71 or 102 agencies. As none of the key agencies with mission in national defense S&T have disclosed their budgets, this missing portion was likely to be spent at these agencies. The central R&D expenditure is estimated at about 70 percent of government's contribution to the GERD, although we still do not know the exact divisions between the central and local governments. We have found that government's expenditure in GERD as released by the MOST, the NBS, and the MOF is lower than the combined R&D expenditure reported by various S&T-mission agencies and therefore there might be underreporting at these agencies.

The MOST, the CAS, the NSFC, and the MOIIT are key central government agencies in allocating and spending public S&T expenditure. In 2011, the division of labor among these big R&D spenders seems to be clear with the NSFC focusing on basic research, the MOST and the MOIIT on applied research, and the CAS seeing a balance between the two. But the situation was completely different in 2020, with both the NSFC and the CAS focused on basic research, while the MOST and the MOIIT turned their efforts to MEPs. In addition, as important organizers of MEPs, the MOST and the MOIIT seemed to have consumed a large amount of money in a rush, a fact that we will return in Chapter 6.

Since 2000, the role of the MOST in China's national innovation system and S&T budgeting process has been decreasing, due to the reform of S&T budgeting system, the departmental competition, and especially the initiation of MEPs, which have channeled significant amount of central government funds to S&T-mission-oriented ministries other than the MOST or going through it. The reform in 2014 changed the situation. That is, although the amount of the S&T appropriation under the MOST has been increasing, funding diversification may have attributed to its decreasing power while criticism of the MOST for mishandling the government R&D funding may also have accelerated the process. That said, MOST's department S&T budget is still the biggest, which is mainly spent on MEPs, although their share in China's R&D expenditure has been decreasing as well. The MOST's reorganization in 2023 will reposition, and in fact, reduce, the ministry's role in receiving and distributing central government's S&T appropriation.

While the NSFC is transparent in distributing funding to individual scientists and organizations, the MOST, which administers a much large share of the government S&T appropriation, has not made available comparable information on NSTPs under its administration. After the recent government reorganization, the MOST now administers the NSFC by macro-management, coordination, supervision, and evaluation, although the NSFC is still allowed to operate relatively independently. There also is no way to corroborate such funding statistics with that from the CAS or the MOE, both of which presumably have significant part of their research supported by NSTPs.

In addition to the decrease in the share of government-funded R&D expenditure, especially in basic research, the reform to transform application-oriented R&D institutes into enterprises, which started in 1999, also has artificially changed the sources of the R&D expenditure. That is, a significant portion of the R&D expenditure that used to be counted as public finance has been re-categorized as the expenditure by enterprises. Moreover, in 2020, SOEs administered by the central government – some of which are the R&D-institute-turned enterprises – contributed 28.691 billion to the nation's GERD. These SOEs include Datang Telecom Technology & Industry Group, whose predecessor is the Research Institute of Posts and Telecommunications under the now defunct Ministry of Posts and Telecommunications, and the government-agency-turned enterprises such as China National Petroleum Corporation, whose predecessor is the Ministry of Petroleum Industry. Altogether, therefore, government's contribution to China's GERD is much bigger than 20 percent as reported.

The budgeting reform in OECD countries has been from control oriented to policy oriented. That is, according to the standard Government Finance Statistics (GFS) classification established by the International Monetary Fund, aggregate fiscal control requires an economic classification based on clear concepts (e.g., separating borrowing from receipts). However, it should be noted that the GFS focuses only on economic and functional reporting and budget classification also needs to be an instrument of policy formulation, administration of the budget, and accounting (Allen & Tommasi, 2001: 121). In developing countries, however, it is still common that budget decisions are separated from policy decisions and national plans (Cadien, 1980), to which China is no exception.

For example, while the MOF, the MOST, the NDRC, the SAT, and the MOE have since 2006 been important in the formulation of indigenous innovation policy, as discussed in Chapter 2, only the MOST plays a major role in budgeting. Until now, in addition to making S&T policy, the ministry organizes S&T activities and allocates S&T budget while also sharing the policymaking role with the NDRC and the organizational role with the CAS, the NSFC, and other S&T-mission agencies. Meanwhile, the NDRC is responsible for important economic regulations and strategic resources allocation with its role in the area of S&T being confined to making policies related to industrial technology; its role in the S&T budgeting process seems to be very limited. Given its prominence in the Chinese government hierarchy, the NDRC is likely to see its budgeting function and policymaking function further integrated. Similarly, other agencies with a big S&T budget also would participate more in policymaking to harmonize S&T-related policymaking and budgeting.

In fact, China needs an agency like the Office of Management and Budget (OMB) in the USA. Perhaps the single most influential executive branch office in the establishment of scientific priorities, the OMB is mainly to assist the President to prepare the budget, to measure the quality of agency programs, policies, and procedures, and to see if they comply with the President's policies. It also is in partnership with the Office of Science and Technology Policy, which, also under the White House, is tasked with advising the President on the Federal

R&D budget and shaping R&D priorities across those Federal agencies (Neal *et al.*, 2008: 30).

The lack of coordination and transparency in the S&T budgeting and spending process in China has led to problems such as overlapping between NSTPs under the administration of different ministries or even within the same ministry and rush to spend funds in MEPs, thus wasting China's increasing, but still scarce, S&T resources and reducing the efficiency of their spending. To solve these problems and to respond to the demand for reform from the scientific community, in 2014, the State Council decided to reorganize NSTPs (see Chapter 6). As the budget reforms and government reorganizations thus far have not fundamentally resolved the problems, in 2023, the central government introduced another round of government reorganization, targeting especially the MOST, to further streamline its operation. However, it will take time for the government to enjoy the benefits, if any, of the reorganization.

5 | Talent
Talent-Attracting Programs

In the knowledge-economy era, knowledge and skills are the most important resources on which nations rely for their economic development and competitiveness. And highly skilled individuals, recognized as "carriers" of knowledge, are the primary resource that countries all over the world compete for (Pan, 2010; Trippl & Maier, 2010). Therefore, nurturing, attracting, retaining, and utilizing talent always confronts a country's political and scientific leadership. Against the backdrop of globalization, a country also needs to deal with the issues of brain drain, brain gain, and brain circulation as there are significant economic and political consequences, intended or unintended, associated with the migrants themselves, those who remain in the country of origin, and those who straddle between countries of origin or host for business and entrepreneurial purposes (Saxenian, 2005).

Indeed, researchers and policymakers started to discuss the international mobility of talented individuals in as early as the 1960s when a large number of British scholars and professionals migrated to the United States (Baruffaldi & Landoni, 2012). How to attract and retain highly skilled talents has become a critical policy issue for both developed and developing countries (Cervantes & Guellec, 2002). Initially, developing countries such as China and India faced severe challenges of brain drain while making efforts to achieve brain gain and catch up with developed countries in science, technology, and innovation. Developed countries also are increasingly worried about the reverse migration of talents, as the rate of scholars and professionals returning to their home countries has been on the rise since the 1990s (Coe & Bunnell, 2003; Pan, 2010).

In fact, in order to narrow its S&T and the economic gap with developed countries, since the mid-1990s, China has invested a great deal of time, energy, and capital in encouraging overseas academics, entrepreneurs, and other professionals to return (Zweig, 2006) (see Table 5.1). China has gradually established a national financial

131

Table 5.1 *China's select talent-attracting programs*

Program	Year initiated	Agency in charge	Target audience	Budget
One Hundred Talents Program	1994	CAS	Overseas talents under the age of 45	RMB 2 million, including research funds, equipment expenses, and housing subsidies
Distinguished Young Scholars Program	1994	NSFC	Returned young researchers under the age of 45	RMB 4 million per project (2.8 million per project in mathematics and management science)
Chunhui Program	1996	MOE	Outstanding overseas students working short term	Special funds for international travel expenses
Cheung Kong Scholars Program	1998	MOE	Domestic or overseas scholars under the age of 45 (for natural science and engineering) and 55 (for humanities and social sciences)	RMB 200,000 per year for distinguished professors and RMB 30,000 per month for chair professors
Thousand Talents Program	2008	Organization Department of the CPC CC	Overseas tenured full professors or equivalent under the age of 55 (the Young Thousand Talents Program [YTTP] talents under the age of 40)	RMB 1 million (half a million for young thousand talents)

Sources: The authors' research based on Cao (2008) and Hao (2009).
Notes: CAS – Chinese Academy of Sciences; MOE – Ministry of Education; NSFC – National Natural Science Foundation of China.

support system for high-end talents from overseas through programs such as the One Hundred Talents Program at the Chinese Academy of Sciences, the Distinguished Young Scholars Program (DYSP) at the National Natural Science Foundation of China (NSFC), the Chunhui Program and Cheung Kong Scholars Program (CKSP) at the Ministry of Education and the Thousand Talents Program (TTP) sponsored by the Organization Department of the Communist Party of China Central Committee (OD CPC CC) (Simon & Cao, 2009), among others.

The existing research provides two different perspectives toward the policy effects of China's talent-attracting programs. On the one hand, some scholars argued that these programs have brought back a large number of returnees, and the TTP, if successful as designed, even has the potential to infuse Chinese science, technology, and innovation with necessary expertise and knowledge through the return of these high-caliber scholars and professionals (Appelbaum *et al.*, 2016). As a whole, according to Wang and Guo (2012), a total of 818,400 overseas-trained Chinese returned to China between 1978 and 2011. The number was increasing at an average annual rate of 13 percent during the mid-to-late 1990s. "There is more than 1 million overseas-trained Chinese returned to China in 2021," said Wang Zhigang, minister of science and technology, at the 20th China International Talent Exchange Conference in 2022. There is no doubt that talent-attracting programs have been playing an active and positive role (Zweig, 2006). Li *et al.* (2018), for example, showed that those recruited into the Young Thousand Talents Program (YTTP) have significantly contributed to the development of their affiliated institutions by producing compelling publications, extending new research directions, and uplifting domestic academic communities. Cao *et al.* (2020) showed that Chinese returnees published higher impact work and continued to publish more at the international level compared with their domestic counterparts. Shi *et al.* (2023) found that top YTTP returnees outperformed their comparable overseas peers in scientific productivity in the post return era, and this performance gap can be largely attributed to the failure of the current USA (and EU) science funding schemes to support early-stage scientists' pursuit of independent research agenda.

On the other hand, scholars argued that government policies have failed to attract the return of first-rate academics. According to Cao (2008), although we cannot assume all nonreturnee academics of

Chinese-origin to be the best and the brightest, there is little doubt that the best and the brightest have not returned. Tian (2013) finds that China only managed to attract a few emigrant scientists who graduated from the top 200 universities in the world. It is a fact that a majority of returnees did not receive formal foreign doctoral education but acquired overseas experience by short-term working or visiting programs. Meanwhile, Zweig and Wang (2013) provide evidence that 73.5 percent of the candidates of talent-attracting programs did not give up their overseas posts because their talents are sought after globally. Zweig *et al.* (2020)'s new findings also show that among all the returned academics the best are part-timers, and that universities whose presidents nurtured an open institutional culture were able to lure better overseas talents than other universities. Shi *et al.* (2023) lament that compared with non-returned Chinese scientists in the USA, YTTP returnees, as a group, would rank in the top 15th percentile for productivity while the majority (73%) of them worked overseas as postdocs or research fellows. In a word, China is still experiencing a serious shortage of high-end academics and other professionals, which is greatly challenging its efforts to build an innovation-oriented country (Cao & Simon, 2021).

In fact, neither of the perspectives is refined enough to assess the policy effects of these programs. First, it is rather difficult to figure out whether returnees were recruited into talent-attracting programs for their favorable conditions. For example, some of the young returnees receiving offers from the YTTP had planned to return or had returned to China at the time when the YTTP was initiated. It is possible that scholars selected for the program were just the "icing on the cake." Second, the Chinese government's failure to attract high-end academics to return through these programs does not necessarily mean that these programs do not work at all, as existing studies have indicated. Furthermore, the majority of the findings from extant studies were based on qualitative research through observations, in-depth interviews, and case studies with few trying to empirically quantify the policy effects of these programs. Therefore, the question is whether the Chinese government has been able to attract high-quality academics to return through talent-attracting programs, which somehow have helped achieve brain gain.

Taking academic talents as economic agents, this chapter develops a decision matrix of brain gain to provide a new way of thinking to the theoretical debate on how exactly talents' academic ability and individual benefits play their roles in driving brain gain. We use the academic ability to measure returnees' quality, and individual benefits to measure returnees' prospect gains. The decision matrix suggests that overseas academic talents with high academic ability in the host country are less likely to return to the home country than those with low academic ability due to the large benefits – salary plus other perks – they could enjoy in the host country. Thus, to attract the best academics, China's governments and organizations have initiated talent-attracting programs to provide returnees with high salary and excess research funding to fill the benefit gap between China and foreign countries. Consequently, these programs may have been effective in attracting overseas talents with high academic ability. We then use survival analysis to examine the policy effects of the YTTP by taking academic ability into consideration in examining their probability of returning to China or staying abroad.

The Thousand Talents Program: A Background

In December 2008, to further address the brain drain challenge and also take advantage of the global financial crisis that cost some ethnic Chinese scientists, researchers, and professionals jobs abroad, China's Central Leading Group for Coordinating Talent Work, under the OD CPC CC, launched an Attracting Overseas High-End Talents Program, also known as the TTP (Qiu, 2009). This is the first talent-attracting program at the central government level.

Pledging to attract some 2,000 expatriate Chinese scholars to their homeland within 5–10 years, the program initially targeted full professors at well-known foreign institutions of learning, experienced corporate executives, and entrepreneurs with core technologies under 55 years old to support the leapfrogging of China's scientific research, high-tech entrepreneurship, and economic development. In exchange for their permanent return and services, the central government would offer a resettlement subsidy of 1 million RMB tax free and a significant amount of funding for research or entrepreneurship, while local governments and employers would match these incentives with additional funding, housing benefits, and a salary close to the returnees' overseas level.

The TTP has brought back a number of very prominent academics. They include Wang Xiaodong, the first USA-bound mainland Chinese student in the open-door era who was elected as a member of the US National Academy of Sciences (NAS), at age 41, and a Howard Hughes Medical Institute (HHMI) investigator at the University of Texas Southwestern Medical Center; Shi Yigong, a chaired professor and also an HHMI investigator at Princeton University, and now is President of the new Westlake University in Hangzhou; and most recently, Xie Xiaoliang, the first mainland Chinese in the open-door era to hold a tenured full professorship at Harvard University, who also is a fellow of the American Academy of Arts and Sciences and an NAS member, and many others from the world's leading institutions of learning.

However, quite a significant number of awardees have been unable or unwilling to return to China permanently for various reasons, which ran counter to the core objectives and the initial goals of the program (Zweig & Wang, 2013; Zweig *et al.*, 2020). Therefore, the government had to add a component for those who only wanted to commit to a couple of months of part-time work. Given the complicated nature of these part-time arrangements, the government has never made the entire list of TTP awardees public as revealing the broad array of special arrangements would likely cause conflict-of-interest and conflict-of-commitment problems to some of the part-timers.

In December 2010, therefore, the Central Leading Group for Coordinating Talent Work approved adding another component to the TTP and this time, the program was for emerging young scholars. Administered by the NSFC, the YTTP aimed at attracting some 400 promising young talent from overseas annually between 2011 and 2015 and turn them into innovative leaders in academia or high-tech entrepreneurship with moral character, outstanding professional ability, and comprehensive quality. Meanwhile, in 2012 and 2015, the NSFC and the MOE also added components for emerging outstanding young scholars into their respective programs. In 2019, however, the special incentives and provisions used to attract talents – Chinese and foreign – into the TTP became a major political issue in the USA. Through a now defunct "China Initiative," the US Department of Justice targeted quite a number of scholars – both ethnic Chinese and American – because of intellectual property right protection and related national security concerns, as is discussed later in the chapter (Zweig *et al.*, 2020).

Theoretical Background and Hypotheses

Traditional theories on transnational migration have offered ideas and models to explain people's migration from different perspectives. The early studies concentrated on modeling sending countries' labor markets, and later truly dynamic models of brain drain focused on the motivation for human-capital accumulation (Commander *et al.*, 2004). More recent studies suggest that international migration is like a "cycle" more than a one-way flow. According to the "core–periphery" model, only a few core countries receive talents and benefits from migration while more periphery countries send talents and suffer social welfare loss (Meyer *et al.*, 2001; Commander *et al.*, 2004; Ackers, 2005).

Indeed, several factors influence people's decision on cross-border mobility, particularly academics' return migration, such as the education for children and jobs for spouses (Baruffaldi & Landoni, 2012). More important are institutional factors, including but not being limited to political liberalization and freedom in doing research (Cao, 2008), research culture (Cao, 2008; Shi & Rao, 2010), lack of transparency in decision making and a relatively stifling bureaucracy (Zweig & Wang, 2013). The chapter considers two most important factors – returnees' academic ability and individual benefits. On the one hand, talent-attracting programs target returnees with high academic ability. On the other hand, in making decision on returning or staying, academics would consider maximizing their individual benefits. Brain gain happens only if there is a match between an individual's academic ability and benefits that the individual receives from a talent-attracting program.

Academic Ability

International migration as a personal decision responds to the situation where the return to human capital is the highest. Existing studies have observed a strong and positive selectivity in the skilled emigration. The key issue is whether scholars are appraised on their academic merit (Kapur, 2010), and if so, they would always attach importance to acquiring new knowledge (Morano-Foadi, 2005). Some countries are learning centers where scholars can more effectively learn skills, including skills that may be applicable to the home country (Dustmann *et al.*, 2011).

Pursuing a bright career, individuals with a relatively higher endowment of the knowledge and skills that is more highly rewarded in the home country are more likely to stay in the home country, while those with a relatively higher endowment of the knowledge and skills that has a higher value in the host country are more likely to emigrate (Stark *et al.*, 1997; Dustmann *et al.*, 2011). In addition, as more opportunities are available to talents with relatively higher academic ability in international academic markets, there is a positive relationship between the probability of overseas employment and the quality of an individual's education (Tian, 2013).

Individual Benefits

While academic ability enables scholars to have more choices, whether to stay or return also depends on the benefits that migrants can get. A series of classical works depict migrants as economic agents who search for better economic or professional opportunities globally (Gaillard & Gaillard, 1997). Indeed, the economic benefit is a main determinant of migration (Borjas, 1994; Meyer *et al.*, 2001; Baruffaldi & Landoni, 2012). To maximize the economic return of their investments in education, highly skilled talents are likely to migrate if their earnings abroad exceed those at home while they also are likely to remain abroad if the average wage in the foreign country is higher than that in their home country (Becker, 1964; Massey *et al.*, 1993; Stark *et al.*, 1997, 1998; Stark, 2004). Based on a large-scale multi-school revealed-preference survey of job preferences among Chinese science, technology, engineering, and mathematics (STEM) PhD students and postdocs at American universities, Zeithammer and Kellogg (2013) concluded that the reason that Chinese doctoral graduates chose to remain in the USA is ultimately the large salary disparity between the two countries rather than other factors.

In addition to economic benefits, the institutional and academic environment including research infrastructure also is very important for returnees (Busse & Mansfield, 1984; Mahroum, 2000). The opportunity costs in career development are relatively higher for the returnees. Absent for a long time, they need to start again and rebuild professional and social networks that can help and support them (Cao, 2008). Also, migration is more complicated when involving family issues, including schooling for children, employment for spouses, and housing.

A Decision Matrix of Brain Gain

There are two important assumptions in discussing China's case. First, most Chinese students have selected developed countries for education and research, which suggests that overseas PhD students are worth more than domestic PhD students in the academic job market in general. This is reflected in job postings of many Chinese universities. Second, with higher level of economic development in developed countries, the average salary of academics in the overseas host country is higher than that in the home country. For example, according to SalaryList.com (www.salarylist.com/), a leading salary data provider located in Seattle, American professor's average salary is $180,046, median salary is $165,000 with a salary range from $28,800 to $1,000,000. Clearly, a Chinese professor's average or median salary is much lower. In this sense, our assumption is that a Chinese professor is less compensated or valued. Academics, as professionals, are rational economic agents who would pursue greater individual economic benefits.

Indeed, in an academic job market, academics with high academic ability would have numerous options both at home and abroad, and therefore are relatively less likely to return as the benefits at home are low. However, when a PhD graduate tries to get a job in the Chinese academic job market, she may well depend upon whom she knows rather than how she performed in overseas as China is still a *guanxi*-based society (Stark *et al.*, 1998; Cao, 2008; Zweig & Wang, 2013). By contrast, academics with low ability may prefer to return to take advantage of their overseas experiences (Tai & Rory, 2015), especially if they may lose their jobs for their low performance in the overseas job market.

Considering existing theories and China's reality, this chapter addresses the achievement of a brain gain through proposing a decision matrix of academic's return migration or brain gain. In our framework, the migration decision of overseas academics depends on two dimensions – the level of academic ability and the level of academics' individual benefits remaining overseas (see Figure 5.1). Let's take a look at how academics make their decisions on returning to home or remaining abroad.

Indeed, high-caliber academics have stronger competitiveness in both overseas and domestic academic job markets, and especially enjoy a higher salary and academic reputation in the overseas academic job market due to the more mature mechanism of academic evaluation relative to that in their home country. The decision matrix

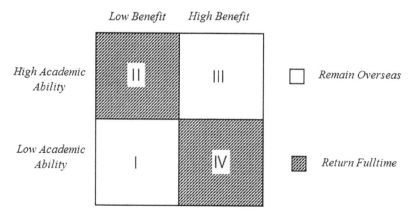

Figure 5.1 The decision matrix of brain gain in China

of brain gain suggest that they would be better off remaining overseas to continue to command high individual benefits (see Quadrant III in Figure 5.1), instead of returning to their home country and losing their benefits in terms of salary and academic opportunity relative to remaining in the host county (see Quadrant II in Figure 5.1).

By contrast, academics with low ability are less competitive in the overseas academic job market and would encounter difficulties getting a tenure-track or permanent position, as well as having a stable life. However, they might enjoy a competitive advantage in the domestic job market because of a big academic gap between overseas and domestic academic organizations. Their overseas PhD training, work experiences, and research outputs would be highly valued at domestic institutions. According to the decision matrix of brain gain, if they chose to remain overseas, they could suffer from low individual benefits relative to returning to the home county (see Quadrant I in Figure 5.1). Therefore, they would rather return to their home country to acquire high individual benefits relative to remaining overseas (see Quadrant IV in Figure 5.1).

The Role of Talent-Attracting Programs in the Decision Matrix

Aiming to boost the country's innovation capability, China is in desperate need of talents, especially those at the high end (Cao, 2008). Specifically, the government wants to provide the best and the brightest talents with a brighter career prospect and compensate them for the benefit disparity. The talent-attracting programs have been organized to guarantee candidates with a relatively higher salary and research funding, which, to some degree, cut the large salary disparity between China and overseas. Consequently, these candidates can expect to gain the very best opportunities and positions given their foreign experiences, advanced knowledge and skills as well as extensive overseas social networks.

According to Cao and Suttmeier (2001), the Distinguished Young Scientist award from the NSFC does help the awardees to navigate the institutional environment for research and find resources and build their research enterprise. However, the effectiveness of China's talent-attracting programs varies by the return decisions of academics with high ability; otherwise, there would be no necessity to render special favors to returnee scientists (Tian, 2013). This chapter is interested in finding whether academics' willingness of returning changed by their levels of academic ability, or whether talent-attracting programs may play their due role in narrowing the benefit gap and in turn bringing back high-end talents.

To summarize, the objective of this chapter is to examine the effects of talent-attracting programs by investigating if the academic ability still is a critical predictor for distinguishing returnees from stayers, or those remaining in overseas. In other words, a particular talent-attracting program worked if it could attract returnees with high academic ability; otherwise, the program is deemed to fail to achieve its originally set goal. In doing so, our study contributes to the existing debate on brain gain by analyzing the role of government's talent-attracting programs in the recruitment of overseas talents, which is critical to understand what motivates academics to migrate across border.

Methods and Data

The Sample

We choose the YTTP as our case. The selection of scholars to the YTTP is a strict process (see Figure 5.2). The organizer calls for applications first, then overseas young scholars choose domestic organizations, or host employers, as their bases for applying for this program. In doing so, applicants presumably accept China's domestic political, economic, and academic environment and have a plan to return.

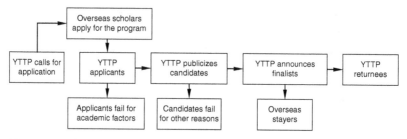

Figure 5.2 The process of YTTP selection

Next, through a rigorous peer-review process, applicants whose academic performance meets the program's requirements become candidates, while others fail. Meanwhile, the program organizer publicizes the list of candidates to solicit public comments on the candidates. Third, most of the candidates would become the finalists of the YTTP and some may fail for reasons such as academic misconduct. Finally, the program organizer announces the list of awardees, most of whom do return to host employers on a fulltime basis, become returnees, while some turn down the offer to become stayers instead. Therefore, the group of YTTP scholars shows not only "who" wanted to return to China but also "who" did return.

Academic criteria for selecting TTP and YTTP candidates mean that the returnees are supposed to help China to achieve a brain gain at the high end. Specifically, the TTP targets the academics at the rank of full professors at well-known overseas universities who are willing to return to China, and the YTTP aims to entice the return of young returnees with academic development potential.

There are several advantages to study YTTP candidates. First, scholars selected into the YTTP are required to return to full-time jobs in China while those for the TTP only need to work six months in China or they are part-timers, although some of them, such as Shi Yigong, as mentioned, did return to a Chinese organization as a full-time professor. As most American universities would not allow tenured principal investigators to work at another institution for more than three months (Hao, 2009), TTP's six-month requirement for fulltime employment is not workable for them. Therefore, some only spent a short period with domestic employers through which they applied for TTP positions, others even have never returned. For policymakers, recruiting full-time young returnees is more meaningful and valuable for China's scientific research prospect.

Second, for a while, the TTP website (www.1000plan.org/) had released basic information on YTTP candidates, which makes an in-depth study of this group possible. By contrast, the government has never made available the names of those selected to the TTP, although many Chinese universities and R&D institutions have publicized their finalists, thus making it difficult, if not impossible, to get the complete information on these returnees and study them.

Third, the majority of TTP finalists had been recruited by previous talent-attracting programs such as the Cheung Kong scholar program at the MOE before becoming TTP finalists, which makes it difficult to differentiate the effect of the new program – the TTP – from that of other programs. But the YTTP recruits a specific group of young academics who other talent-attracting programs had not targeted.

Survival Analysis

Negative binomial regression has been widely adopted in the study of highly skilled international migration (Docquier *et al.*, 2012; Baudassé & Bazillier, 2014). Although this approach suits well for studying migration for which data often involve dummy variables and classified variables at the individual level, its application to the study of YTTP recipients is limited because their information is censored. Specifically, although most of the YTTP recruits had chosen to return fulltime, there still had been stayers, which means that the negative binomial regression is not applicable. However, survival analysis is an appropriate approach to answer our research questions as it enables the analysis of the data involving censored information (Dobrev & Barnett, 2005; Hsu *et al.*, 2007).

Survival analysis is a statistical tool that deals with the analysis of time duration until one or more events, such as international migration, happen (Fang, 2015). In particular, we use Kaplan–Meier analysis and Cox's proportional hazards regression model ("Cox's model" for short) in survival analysis to measure the effect of YTTP recipients' academic ability on their likelihood of returning. We treat return migration of academics as a survival event, defining staying overseas as success or survival or 1, and returning to China failure or 0. And we define the number of years between scholars receiving their PhD degrees and being selected into the YTTP as the time duration or "lifetime" in the survival analysis term.

Academic ability, our primary independent variable, is measured by a scholar's academic position and academic ranking of her last overseas employer. In addition, gender and age are two main independent variables with others being control variables. We present underlying reasons for choosing these variables and their measurement in the following section.

Measures

Academic ability is an important determinant of academics' decision on return to their home country. Scholars with high academic ability would prevail in the overseas academic job market and incline to stay overseas while the YTTP aims and attempts to attract highly academic capable scholars. Specifically, we use a scholar's position before returning and her last employer's academic ranking as proxies of her academic ability.

Generally, a tenure-track position, a tenured position or a permanent position ("a stable position" for short) signals higher academic ability that a scholar acquired through her long-term effort. If she has attained a stable position, including professor, associate professor, and assistant professor at an American university, senior investigator, investigator at an American national lab; lecturer, senior lecturer, reader, professor, or equivalent permanent position at a British university; permanent position in Japan, Singapore, Canada and other countries, her position is defined as 1; other position is defined as 0.

According to Tian (2013), a university's academic ranking reflects the university's educational and academic level, and faculty members at universities with higher ranking are assumed to possess higher academic ability. If an overseas scholar's last employer is ranked in the world's top 100 in a specific subject field on the Academic Ranking of World Universities (ARWU),[1] academic reputation of her last employer is defined as 1; otherwise, the academic ranking is defined as 0.

Obviously, both gender and age are important demographic characteristics of candidates. Gender is a classification variable that is usually expected to account for personal constraints that might affect men

---

[1] The Academic Ranking of World Universities (ARWU), also known as the Shanghai Ranking, is one of the annual publications of world university rankings. Published by China's Shanghai Jiao Tong University first in June 2003, the Shanghai Ranking has been updated on an annual basis. In addition to an overall ranking, the Shanghai Ranking also ranks universities by subject fields.

and women differently (Baruffaldi & Landoni, 2012). Here, male is defined as 1, and female 0. Age is set as a continuous variable, which is defined as the gap between the year of birth and the year when the scholar was selected into the program. Propensities of migrant academics returning increase with the age at entry but decrease with the number of years of residence in a foreign country (Dustmann, 1996). Moreover, we also interacted academic ability with gender and age separately to examine their joint or moderator effects.

Control variables include academic relations, the country in which a returnee received her PhD, the first batch of candidates selected into the YTTP and the classification of host employers.

Academic relations: Academic relations represent a returnee's linkages with the home country, which might increase the probability of overseas talents finding information, opportunities and support (Ackers, 2005). A returnee's academic relations are measured by whether she would return to her alma mater. If an overseas scholar returned to her home country and worked for her alma mater where she received her bachelor's degree or doctor's degree, her academic relations are defined as 1; if not defined as 0.

The classifications of host employers: Within China's education and research system, the CAS differs with the higher education system. Furthermore, the C9 League[2] is an alliance of nine elite universities in mainland China, analogous to the Ivy League in the USA and the Russell Group in the UK. Of them, Peking and Tsinghua universities are on top of the pyramid. The different classifications of host employers may help determine their graduates' job title, salary, work conditions, career development prospect and so on, which would influence academic return migration. In order to examine the attractiveness of different employers, we define host employers as a multiple categorical variable. Specifically, if a returnee's prospective employer is the CAS (including the University of Science and Technology of China [USTC]), her host employer is defined as 0, Peking and Tsinghua are

---

[2] Members of the C9 League are Fudan University, Harbin Institute of Technology, Nanjing University, Peking University, Shanghai Jiao Tong University, Tsinghua University, University of Science and Technology of China (USTC), Xi'an Jiaotong University, and Zhejiang University. In this Chapter, USTC is considered as part of the CAS not part of the C9.

defined as 1, remaining C9 universities are defined as 2, and other universities are defined as 3.

The country in which a returnee received her PhD: The nature of brain drain depends on scholars' education experience and work locations. It is necessary to distinguish the scholars with their PhDs from an overseas institution from those who received domestic PhDs, followed by foreign research experience (Tian, 2013). Altogether, 76.2 percent of the returnees under study received their PhDs from institutions of learning in either mainland China or the USA. Thus, we only consider the country of conferring PhDs as two dummy variables. A scholar who received her PhD in mainland China is defined as 1, else 0; if a scholar received her PhD in the USA, she is assigned a value of 1, else 0.

The first batch of candidates selected into the YTTP: At the beginning, the program was less known and there was a lack of mutual selectivity due to information asymmetry. Consequently, host employers might have difficulty differentiating the skill levels of overseas scholars effectively (Tian, 2013) while overseas scholars also might hesitate to apply for the YTTP, the new program. After the first batch of candidates were selected, the process has become more transparent and routinized. Therefore, if a scholar was selected into the YTTP in the first batch, she is defined as 1, candidates selected in other batches are defined as 0.

In what follows, we examine first whether YTTP candidates' academic ability had a significant impact on China's achieving brain gain at the high end by using Kaplan–Meier analysis and then the Cox's regression model.

Data

The basic data are the first four batches of YTTP candidates selected between 2011 and 2012 with information from the TTP website (www.1000plan.org/), including candidates' name, gender, date of birth, domestic employer, overseas last employer, last job title, discipline, PhD granting institution, and date when PhD was awarded. Furthermore, we built a dataset including the information of YTTP scholars through searching their curriculum vitas (CVs) and other available information such as academic ranking of employers and so on.

CVs can be reliably coded to reflect scholars' valid career constructs and longitudinal records of scientific careers. It is a tradition to use

CVs to study researchers' career transitions (Gaughan & Robin, 2004; Gaughan, 2009). Fortunately, the CVs of most YTTP candidates are accessible on the websites of universities or research institutions where they worked (Hao, 2011). In addition, we also searched Google Scholar, ResearchGate and LinkedIn for information on those candidates whose CVs were unavailable on their employers' websites.

However, there are three caveats. First, there is a little difference between the preliminary list of candidates and the list of final awardees as only few did not become awardees for reasons such as fabrication of academic credentials.[3] We define those who did not become the finalists as failure or stayers. Scholars who received YTTP offers but rejected them because they found new jobs overseas, which partly proves our hypothesis that those highly capable academics tend to not come back. Second, some with YTTP offers did not return to the host institution through which they submitted their applications for the program but to another domestic employer. They also are defined as success or returnees. In such cases, we used the information on their final employers in the analysis. Finally, we were unable to location some candidates' CVs either on the websites of their domestic employers, overseas last employers, or on the Internet. They also were treated as failure or stayers in our analysis.

Consequently, the dataset includes 736 candidates selected into the YTTP between 2011 and 2012.

Results

After collecting, cleaning, and coding the data, we performed Kaplan–Meier analysis and used Cox's model, respectively, to empirically examine how YTTP finalists' academic ability impacted their decision on returned migration.

---

[3] For example, Lu Jun, a professor at the Beijing University of Chemical Technology (BUCT), was recently found to have taken a shortcut of his own. Lu, 39, was hired as a professor by BUCT in November 2011. In March 2002, he was selected into the YTTP. In his online CV, Lu listed seven papers as his key publications. The seven papers were all published in prestigious international academic journals, including two in *Nature*. In fact, it was found that the real author of these papers worked as an assistant professor at Yale University whose name coincidentally shares the same Chinese pinyin spelling as the Lu at the BUCT. Lu also was found to fabricate his doctoral degree from the University of Toronto in Canada and his work experience in an American company. He was deprived of the YTTP position accordingly (Caixin, 2012).

Table 5.2 *The results of Kaplan–Meier analysis*

Variable	Total	Censored	Censored/ Total (%)
Have gained a tenure-track position, a tenure position, or a permanent position	146	32	21.9
Haven't gained a tenure-track position, a tenure position, or a permanent position	590	48	8.1
Academic position Log Rank Sig.		0.000	
Last employer's academic ranking is in world's top 100 in a specific discipline	360	29	8.1
Last employer's academic ranking is out of world's top 100 in a specific discipline	376	51	13.6
Academic ranking top 100 Log Rank Sig.		0.002	

Kaplan–Meier Analysis

Table 5.2 and Figure 5.3 show the differences or gaps of academic ability between returnees and stayers by using Kaplan–Meier analysis.

Of the 736 candidates selected into the first four batches of the YTTP, 146 had a stable position abroad, and 32 did not return to China. Altogether, 21.9 percent of the candidates with stable overseas positions are censored. Of the remaining 590 candidates without a stable overseas position, 8.1 percent are censored. Three hundred and sixty candidates' last employers are academically ranked within the world's top 100, thus the right-censored data account for 8.1 percent. The other 376 whose last employer's academic ranking is out of world's top 100, the rate of right-censored data is 13.6 percent.

Table 5.2 shows that more than 80 percent of the candidates did not have a stable position before being recruited into the YTTP, and about half of them were not with an institution ranked among the world's top 100 at the time of applying for the YTTP. The Log Rank test shows that YTTP candidates' academic position and their last employers' academic ranking significantly impacted these candidates' decision on moving back to China.

Survival curves in Figure 5.3 show how academic position and academic ranking impacted the return of YTTP finalists to China. Cumulative survival function reflects the percentage of finalists who

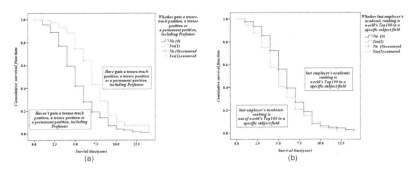

Figure 5.3 The survival curves of returnees selected in YTTP

had not returned after the survival time T. The curves of academic position (see Figure 5.3a) indicate that the percentage of YTTP finalists failed to return. Specifically, the curve above indicates the finalists who had obtained a stable position, while the curve below indicates those who had not. No matter how long the survival time is, the share of finalists with a stable position failing to return is higher than that without a stable position. That is to say, the finalists with a stable overseas position were less likely to return than those without it.

Regarding academic ranking (see Figure 5.3b), the curves intersect twice at 9 years and 10 years, respectively. In the case that the survival time is shorter than 9 years, the share of returnees selected into the YTTP whose last employer's academic ranking in the world's top 100 is rather high. Considering the competition among top universities abroad, it is difficult for young scholars to get or be promoted to a higher position without outstanding research outputs at the early stage of their careers. On the contrary, since there is a serious shortage of academics at the high end in China, returnees with top university working experience would expect a bright academic future after returning.

The average survival time of the scholars in our sample was about 5 years, which means that these scholars returned to China within about 5 years after obtaining their foreign doctoral degrees. When the survival time is between 9 and 10 years, the migration pattern shows an opposite tendency. Compared with young scholars whose last employer's academic subject field rankings are out of the world's top 100, those working in the world's top 100 institutions were less likely to return. Because 10 years are long enough for them to get a stable position but not necessarily to establish a happy family, they may have a comparatively higher chance to return. When the survival time is more than 10 years, the two curves become identical. That is, if a young scholar had stayed overseas for 10 or more years, regardless of where she worked, the institutions whose subject fields are among the world's top 100 or not, she would prefer to stay abroad. The results show that the academic ranking of an overseas-based scholar's last employer did negatively affect an YTTP candidate's decision on returning and in turn China's achievement of an academic brain gain at the high end but the effect was insignificant and changing depending upon the number of years in which she had stayed overseas.

Cox's Model

The results of Kaplan–Meier analysis further suggest that both candidates' academic positions and their last employers' academic ranking had a significant but different effect on China's fulfilment of brain gain at the high end. This section presents the results of statistical analysis of YTTP candidates from an examination of the same relationship (see Table 5.3).

The impact of YTTP candidates' academic position and their last employers' academic ranking on their return were examined, respectively. In model 1, the regression coefficient of academic position is 0.484 and highly significant statistically. In model 2, the regression coefficient of academic ranking is 0.093 but insignificant. When both academic position and academic ranking were added to model 3, the result is consistent with both model 1 and model 2 as the regression coefficient of academic position is 0.478 and still very significant while the regression coefficient of academic ranking becomes –0.064 and insignificant.

Models 4–10 examine the interactive or combined effects between academic ability and gender, age. Regarding the interaction between academic ability and gender, in model 4, both YTTP candidates' academic position and the interaction between academic position and gender are insignificant statistically, so are both YTTP candidates' academic ranking and the interaction between academic ranking and gender, as shown in model 5. When the interaction between YTTP candidates' academic ability and age were added to model 6, the regression coefficients for YTTP candidates' academic position and

Table 5.3 *The results of Cox regression analysis*

Variables	Model 1	Model 2	Model 3	Model 4	Model 5	Model 6	Model 7	Model 8	Model 9	Model 10
Independent variables										
Academic position	0.484**		0.478**	0.310		3.215*		0.273	3.224*	2.973*
Academic ranking		−0.093	−0.064		−0.393		−0.112	−0.365	−0.114	−0.432
Gender	−0.202	−0.173	−0.202	−0.230	−0.344	−0.193	−0.172	−0.407	−0.193	−0.392
Age	−0.327**	−0.331**	−0.325**	−0.327**	−0.332**	−0.340**	−0.331**	−0.326**	−0.341**	−0.341**
Interactions										
Academic position × gender				0.189				0.221	0.259	
Academic ranking × gender					0.330			0.333		0.313
Academic position × age						0.078*			0.078*	0.077*
Academic ranking × age							0.000		−0.002	−0.003

Table 5.3 (*cont.*)

Variables	Model 1	Model 2	Model 3	Model 4	Model 5	Model 6	Model 7	Model 8	Model 9	Model 10
Control variables										
Academic relations	-0.050	-0.047	-0.055	-0.049	-0.046	-0.030	-0.046	-0.052	-0.033	-0.030
Holders of mainland China PhDs	0.612**	0.553**	0.621**	0.608**	0.550**	0.611**	0.553**	0.613**	0.619**	0.610**
Holders of American PhDs	-0.064	-0.110	-0.061	-0.068	-0.109	-0.042	-0.110	-0.066	-0.039	-0.044
The first batch of candidates	0.110	0.178	0.112	0.110	0.179	0.074	0.178	0.115	0.077	0.080
CAS (0)										
Peking and Tsinghua (1)	0.058	0.095	0.057	0.056	0.101	0.070	0.096	0.060	0.070	0.073
Other C9 universities (2)	0.041	0.049	0.031	0.040	0.060	0.042	0.049	0.042	0.032	0.042
Other employers (3)	0.207	0.184	0.198	0.206	0.185	0.202	0.184	0.199	0.195	0.197

Notes: ** $p < 0.01$; * $p < 0.05$.

the interaction between academic position and age become 3.215 and 0.078 and highly significant statistically. In model 7, however, both YTTP candidates' academic ranking and the interaction between academic ranking and gender are insignificant.

Furthermore, all independent variables are added in model 8 and model 9. In model 8, both of the interactions between YTTP candidates' academic position, academic ranking, and gender are insignificant. In model 9, regression results were similar to those in model 6 – the interactions between YTTP candidates' academic position and age and between academic ranking and age are significant. When adding all variables and interactions in model 10, the results show that the interactions between YTTP candidates' academic position, academic ranking, and age are still significant statistically with an impact similar to that in model 6 and model 9.

The results suggest that YTTP candidates' academic position, as a key factor, increased the hazard rate for China to achieve a brain gain. Their academic position had a significant influence on finalists' decision on returning to China. In other words, young scholars with a stable position tended to stay overseas and those stayers also tended to work at the world's top 100 universities. However, academic ranking for YTTP candidates' last employers is not a significant factor for the candidates' decision on returning to China. Interestingly, only the interaction between academic position and age is significant among all the interactions; that is, for overseas scholars with a stable position, the older the higher possibility of staying. Given their stable academic position, a bright career, a happy family, and good social relations, the old scholars would not consider returning.

We also reveal the effects of gender and age in models 1–10. The regression coefficients for gender are between –0.407 and –0.173, and are statistically insignificant. The regression coefficients for age are about –0.3 and highly significant, which indicates that the age decreased the hazard rate of YTTP finalists returning to China with older finalists more likely to return. The impact of age is ambiguous. On the one hand, with longer working experience, the stronger academic ability and more academic achievements a scholar has, the more competitive she becomes in the overseas academic job market. On the other hand, foreign-based scholars have to seriously consider issues such as retirement benefits, children's education, and own career when they got old, and return to the home country may be one of the effective ways to solve all these problems. The result was consistent with Van Noorden (2012)'s report that those who had just obtained their PhDs were more open to an international move than senior scientists, presumably because their career paths were not settled and they were less likely to weigh relationships and families in making their decisions on changing to a new position, even the position is located in a different country.

In addition, YTTP finalists with PhDs from mainland China also saw their hazard rate of academic return increasing as associated regression coefficients are between 0.55 and 0.63 and highly significant. That is, those holding PhDs from mainland China's institutions were less likely to build their careers at home, because their PhDs were most likely to be undervalued in their competition with overseas PhD holders. On the contrary, Chinese students who gained their PhDs from top American universities are more likely to return despite the high-paying overseas jobs (Zeithammer & Kellogg, 2013) as in the Chinese academic market they possess more competitive advantages than those with mainland China's PhDs. But academic relations and other factors have less influence on attracting returnees.

In conclusion, YTTP finalists' overseas academic position has a significant and positive impact on leading finalists to stay overseas, but the effect of academic ranking of their last employers turns out to be insignificant. In general, YTTP finalists' academic ability would lead to China's brain gain at the high end, but their academic position and academic ranking had opposite impacts – having a formal position is important while academic hierarchy of the institution in which the position holder is located is not a major determinant.

Summary and Discussions

In the reform and open door era, China has sent a significant amount of scholars and students to global centers of learning and scientific research while making efforts to attract the return of quite a number of them. Since the mid-1990s, the Chinese government and some Chinese organizations have launched a series of talent-attracting programs to bring some of the best and the brightest back to help develop China's scientific enterprise and economy. But it is rather hard to figure out the effects of these programs on talents' return.

This chapter proposed a decision matrix of academics' transnational migration to explore the talent-sending country's chance of achieving academic brain gain. It should be noted that although we have introduced individual benefits into the decision matrix, we only have assumed that scholars' individual benefits are an important factor in making their decision on returning or staying. Moreover, such an assumption is based on the perceived discrepancy of salary levels between Chinese and American professors without considering fringe benefits associated with employments. As such, we are unable to quantify their impacts empirically. Our focus is on how young scientists' academic ability determined their being bought back by the YTTP or staying abroad so as to assess the program's effectiveness in helping China to achieve brain gain at the high end.

By carrying out Kaplan–Meier analysis and Cox regression of a sample of 736 scientists (the first four cohorts of YTTP finalists from 2011 to 2012), we obtain results that the program was less attractive to academics with higher academic ability – proxied by having stable positions overseas – who in turn were less likely to return, which verifies our hypothesis. These findings provide empirical evidence to highlight the policy effect of the YTTP. First, the results of the Kaplan–Meier analysis show that there was a significant difference of academic ability among those that the YTTP tried to recruit. Obviously, the stayers were more likely to be those with a stable overseas position. That is, overseas scholars with higher academic ability, especially those with a stable position, were more likely to stay overseas. Academic ranking of their last employers has a negative effect on young academics' return and its impact decreased gradually.

Second, the results of Cox's regression analysis also indicate that the YTTP did play its due role in enticing overseas scholars with higher academic ability. To be specific, scholars with a stable overseas position were generally not willing to return, and their willingness to return decreased with age. Some scholars whose last employers' academic disciplinary ranking is among the world's top 100 tended to return from overseas. Thus, considering various factors such as salary disparity and family, remaining abroad was probably the best choice for the scholars with higher academic ability, but talent-attracting programs had partially succeeded in bringing back some good scientists and academics. Meanwhile, age is a significant factor as older scholars opted to stay overseas. Scholars who obtained PhDs in mainland China were more likely to settle in the host country if possible as their degrees are less valued in China.

In addition, our examination of the effect of talent-attracting programs based on the data of YTTP candidates enriches the growing literature that focuses on brain drain and brain gain in China. For example, Zweig and Wang (2013) argued that despite active intervention from the CPC though the TTP, the return of a large number of the very best and the very brightest is still not going to happen so soon. Furthermore, Zweig *et al.* (2020) found that the academics with strongest credentials preferred to be part-time returnees who maintained their foreign permanent positions. However, Shi *et al.* (2023) found that YTTP scientists, compared with their overseas peers, are more productive in terms of journal publications, which can be explained by YTTP scientists' access to larger funding and having a big research teams. These exactly are the benefits and comparative advantages that the program can offer. Our findings also show that the YTTP does play its proper role in attracting young scholars from top overseas universities, thus complementing Zweig's studies on the TTP and Shi *et al.*'s study on the development of the returnees selected into the YTTP after they returned to China.

6 | Organization
Mission-Oriented Mega–Research-and-Development Programs

With resources including funding and talent, science, technology, and innovation policymakers need to consider how to better deploy and utilize such resources for organizing research and development (R&D) activities to meet national and global challenges. Indeed, nowadays, many of the long-term challenges, from public health, food security, climate change, energy, to sustainable development, are not only grand in scale but also global in scope. To tackle such challenges inevitably calls for the introduction of state-led or sponsored measures, including publicly funded mission-oriented mega-R&D programs (MMRDs). The conventional wisdom has it that mission-oriented R&D attempts to generate and exploit radical innovation while the diffusion-oriented R&D concentrates on acquisition, diffusion and assimilation of technology (Ergas, 1987; Chiang, 1991). In fact, in the catching-up stage, countries such as Japan and China also have used mission-oriented R&D programs to concentrate on acquisition and assimilation of technology. Mission-oriented R&D should be a term relative to exploration-oriented or investigator-initiated R&D that is free academic exploration and without specific missions, accordingly, diffusion-oriented R&D relative to creation-oriented R&D concentrating on research, development and creation of new technology (see Figure 6.1). Mega-R&D programs are engineering in nature, using scientific discoveries to produce solutions for grand societal problems, and need a long time to organize. They are technology-oriented, resulting from or using the process of engineering. They also rely on large-scale budgets, staff, facilities, and laboratories. Such programs cover experimental development, applied research, and the user-inspired basic research since these activities often are closely linked (Foray *et al.*, 2012; Sun & Cao, 2014).

In this chapter, we propose a theoretical framework outlining the characteristics under which such programs may be successful. The framework focuses particularly on three contextual

**The purposes of
R&D programs**

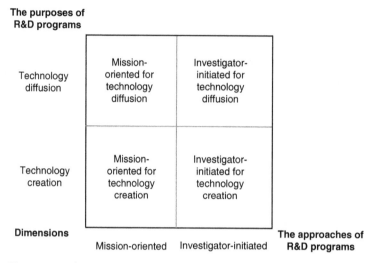

Figure 6.1 The taxonomy of R&D programs

characteristics – technical goal of the mission, dominant actors of the R&D network, and end user of the outcomes. After testing the framework in five cases across different historical periods and sectors in different countries to test its validity, we apply it to the Chinese practice. However, only a few mega-engineering programs (MEPs) under the *Medium and Long-Term Plan for the Development of Science and Technology (2006–2016)* (MLP) are likely to be successful with others probably ending up not achieving their original aims due to obscure and decentralized goals, dislocation of primary actors and ineffective organization.

Mission-Oriented Mega-R&D Programs

The Motivation

As a national strategy, MMRDs need long-term fiscal support and may have long-term consequences. There are several doctrines underlying the evoking of MMRDs. First is the Keynesian government intervention (Mahdjoubi, 1997). The Keynesianism considers that government intervenes in the economy through investing in R&D, especially basic research, because of its "public goods" nature and out of the market failure concern (Mowery, 2009; Stephan, 2011; Wong, 2011).

Second is what Vannevar Bush promoted in his *Science: The Endless Frontier* (OSRD US, 1945). Bush transformed the market failure concern, a theoretical rationale, into a policy practice and a central piece of science and technology policymaking. Third is the "entrepreneurial state," which argues that the state needs to take risk and create a highly networked R&D system for the national good over a medium-to-long-term time horizon (Mazzucato, 2013).

Mega-R&D programs are initiated either as an emergent strategy to counter short-term pressures or as a deliberate strategy to pursue long-term interests (Mintzberg & Waters, 1985). The first and notable MMRDs are the American government-sponsored Manhattan Project and Project Apollo, both of which executed an emergent strategy but made a profound impression.

It is worth noting that there are big differences between Manhattan/Apollo projects and those tackling new global challenges. In Europe, for example, the Maastricht Memorandum has provided a detailed analysis of the differences between old and new mission-oriented projects – the old ones involving defense, nuclear, and aerospace sectors with decision-making for meeting long-term interests coming from grand current pressures; and the new ones being about environmental technologies and societal challenges, which need decision-makers to take into consideration long-term interests but not necessarily grand current pressures. In a special issue of *Research Policy* on mission-oriented public R&D programs, Foray *et al.* (2012) affirmed the view that Manhattan and Apollo projects are not the right models for new programs aimed at the global challenges.

The Cost-Benefit Consideration

In light of above developments, mission-oriented R&D programs have become an important vehicle of government intervention. In most OECD countries, for example, expenditure on such programs accounts for more than 60 percent of the public R&D budget (Ergas, 1987; Chiang, 1991; Mowery, 2009). There are at least three channels – expanding the scientific or engineering knowledge, spinoffs, and public procurement – through which mission-oriented R&D programs affect economy-wide and sector-specific innovation (Mowery, 2009). But the intervention may lead to the misallocation of public support for R&D (Haapanen *et al.*, 2014).

First, even with good intentions, the intervention may not bring the expected benefits. Government's intervention may crowd out the efforts of nonpublic actors, reduce private participation, and generate inefficiency in resource allocation and utilization (David *et al.*, 2000). Second, organization and coordination are critical to the large-scale programs including MMRDs (Datta-Chaudhuri, 1990). As such programs often involve various government agencies or actors, it is conceivable that different actors bring their respective interests to the policymaking process or the implementation of the programs (Krueger, 1990). Third, in order to avoid failures, government also must consider reducing cost, avoiding rent-seeking, and increasing transparency in running MMRDs.

The Context

A range of existing mission-oriented R&D programs can provide useful guidance for the design of new programs aimed at the grand challenges. First, policymakers need to understand the contextual characteristics underlying the mission-oriented or investigator-initiated programs. Sampat (2012) describes a continuing struggle between two perspectives regarding how funds should be allocated at the National Institutes of Health (NIH) in the USA. One views that the allocation of a large share of NIH funds is aimed narrowly at identifying and evaluating promising ways of dealing with diseases. The other thinks that the NIH should largely fund basic research that has promise of eliminating these diseases. In fact, the NIH supports both kinds of work. The question is when an organization should do what and in which way.

Mission-oriented R&D as systemic public policies draws on frontier knowledge to attain specific goals, or "big science deployed to meet big problems," and the need to reinvigorate capacity building, competencies, and expertise within the state is crucial to the implementation of a mission-oriented innovation policy (Mazzucato, 2018). There are cases from different countries such as the USA, France, the UK, and Germany, and in different sectors such as military, health, agriculture, and energy (Foray *et al.*, 2012), from which we can learn experience and lessons. For example, by highlighting the characteristics that distinguish mission-oriented R&D programs in defense-related sectors from those in other sectors, Mowery (2012) argues that the results of the former programs are used by government agencies that also finance such programs, rather than by private firms or individuals, and therefore there is close organizational relationship between the agency or agencies funding and applying the results of R&D programs.

As a kind of government intervention, MMRDs have undoubtful advantages. The question is not whether to intervene but the contextual characteristics for governments to proceed with MMRDs. Case studies indicate that mission-oriented programs differ across sectors and countries because of different institutional environments; however, these case studies mostly do not identify the contextual characteristics for adopting MMRDs where the government could take action. Just as Mowery (2009) argues, the policy debate fails to attend to the characteristics of R&D and market for the results of mission-oriented R&D programs.

Taking into consideration the existing literature and especially its limits, we intend to fill the gap by proposing a theoretical framework that examines and identifies contextual characteristics predictable for the possible smooth outcomes, or analyzing the nature of technological sectors and economic institutions to reveal the prerequisites for government's choices of action. Doing so deepens our understanding of MMRDs across countries and sectors and our understanding of the government–market relationship in general and the role of the state in R&D in particular. We surely do not want to claim that the framework exhausts all *necessary* conditions, nor do we want to assert that these conditions are *sufficient*.

In particular, in order to improve the comprehension of government in R&D governance, the chapter develops a multidimensional framework that enables the analysis of technology goal, effective organization, and end user. We first review the literature of three concepts around technology, organization, and market and then synthesize the findings. The framework is then tested in five cases from the USA, Europe, and Japan, with the aim of evaluating the framework in five Chinese cases whose context differs from those in the developed countries.

Methodology

Empirically, this chapter attempts to explore explicitly the appropriate context for adopting an MMRD so as to propose a theoretical framework. It will then draw preliminary evidence from case studies to test the validity of the framework. The case-study methodology examines details of cases, as well as their related contextual conditions (Yin, 2014). More importantly, it allows us to use a small number of cases to test a general phenomenon or theory (Eisenhardt, 1989).[1] Although government's intervention through the MMRD model under the appropriate context or necessary conditions do not imply that MMRDs should succeed, chance would be higher for the failure of such a program if it does not meet such necessary conditions.

Central to case studies, case selection should consider issues of strategic importance that underlies the research questions. First, as mentioned, our framework attempts for a general theory, which is beyond a specific technological sector and a specific country. Thus, cases should cover as many sectors as possible and innovation models of entrepreneurial, public–private partnership or developmental state. Accordingly, we choose cases from different industries, such as defense, aviation, railway, computing, communications, semiconductor, and health care with different technological characteristics, as well as different countries, such as the USA, Japan, China, and member states of the European Union representing varying national political and economic institutions.

Second, selected cases should include success, failure, and partial success ones. The existing literature prefers to use success cases[2] in the analysis of contrasting roles of government in innovation and the impact of science and technology (S&T) policies on industrial development (Giesecke, 2000; Breznitz, 2007; Vasudeva, 2009). For example, the Manhattan and Apollo projects have been extensively studied, but the Strategic Defense Initiative (SDI, or the Star Wars Program) and the War on Cancer, among others, have been largely ignored. In fact, success is not the only criterion measuring the appropriateness of the government's

---

[1] Case study is effective for generalization using the Karl Popperian falsification, which forms part of critical reflexivity (Popper, 2002). Falsification offers one of the most rigorous tests to which a scientific proposition can be subjected: If just one observation does not fit with the proposition, it is considered invalid generally and must therefore be either revised or rejected. Verification is nearly impossible for a theoretical proposition; however, it is true before falsification.

[2] A simple rule of thumb of the success of an MMRD program is whether the program has achieved its technical goal and completed its R&D mission. If not, the program is considered a failure even if it has advanced knowledge at the frontier. Furthermore, if an MMRD has been launched without a clear and singular goal or mission, the program itself represents a government failure.

intervention. On the one hand, whether a program is successful depends upon complex sets of factors and mechanisms that themselves can fail an R&D program. On the other hand, the consequence of the government's intervention is highly uncertain and often seriously lagged. There is no way to predict a program's result before intervention.[3] Thus, an investigation of both the success and failure cases around the world helps uncover the general precondition of adopting the MMRD model.

Third, most selected cases have been documented or analyzed by scholars or policymakers. Cases from the Manhattan Project in the USA to the core electronic components, high-end generic chips, and basic software program (CHB) in China clearly show that the MMRD model has been a favorite policy instrument of the government and in particular the developmental state. These cases also reflect different phases of technological development (finished or ongoing) so as to allowing us to examine the role of government.

We primarily rely on secondary materials for three reasons. First, because MMRDs may have huge economic and social influences, representing strategies of national defense and industrial development and innovation, it is possible to collect relevant information from open sources. Second, most of our cases are historical in nature. As such, it is difficult, if not impossible, to get firsthand information on these programs. Meanwhile, compared to interviews, published secondary sources are likely to be more objective and comprehensive. Third, published comprehensive secondary materials allow us to achieve data triangulation or verification (Yin, 2014).

In particular, our source materials have been collected through two primary approaches. We have used government's reports on these MMRDs, such as *The Manhattan Project: Making the Atomic Bomb* published by US Department of Energy (Gosling, 2005). We also have depended upon scholarly literature, such as the book, *Sources of Industrial Leadership: Studies of Seven Industries* (Mowery & Nelson, 1999), for information.

---

[3] Some scholars tend to attribute China's rapid economic growth in the reform and opening-up era to appropriate government intervention. However, Coase and Wang (2012) show that it is a series of marginal revolutions rather than radical reform initiatives that have quickly brought market forces back to the Chinese economy. China's state-led reform started in cities, but did not work out, while the successful household responsibility system was initiated in the rural area and later endorsed and promoted by the central government.

Framework Development for the Adoption of the MMRD Model

To engage S&T activities to meet different societal challenges calls for different types of government intervention. In other words, different contextual characteristics, in essence, entail different types of government intervention through initiating R&D programs. Our effort is therefore to contextualize the characteristics of MMRDs. Hitch and McKean (1960) proposed three criteria for evaluating the success of major mission-oriented programs in as early as 1960 – meeting product development goals, finishing the mission within the original limits of time and cost, and achieving objectives for commercial markets. Combining the existing literature (see Table 6.1) and Hitch and McKean's criteria, we propose a useful framework for adopting MMRDs, which considers technology goal, effective organization, and market user (see Figure 6.2).

Technology: A Clearer and Specific Goal

The introduction of an MMRD has to consider issues related to technological differences of a sector in which the program is to be initiated.

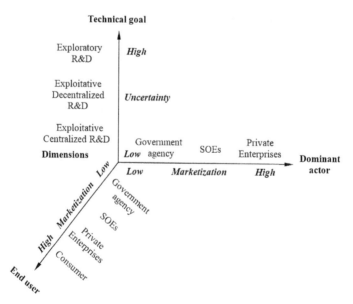

Figure 6.2 A framework on the contextual characteristics of MMRDs

Table 6.1 Key literature review

References	Journal/Book	Type	Technology	Organization	Market	Sample country/sector
Abernathy and Chakravarthy (1979)	Sloan Management Review	Mission R&D program	Funding on the basis of each case's risk/benefit profile, funding only certain prototypes, likely to fulfill desired performance goals			USA/transportation
Ergas (1987)	Technology and Global Industry: Companies and Nations in the World Economy	Mission-oriented policy Diffusion-oriented policy	Radical innovation/clearly set out goals of national importance Incremental adaptation to change	The centralization of decision-making, implementation, and evaluation Decentralization		USA, UK, France/Defense-related Germany, Switzerland, and Sweden/Defense-related
Chiang (1991)	Technovation	Mission-oriented policy Diffusion-oriented policy	Radical innovation/in the early phase of technology life cycle Incremental innovation/Acquisition, diffusion, and assimilation of technology	Trickle-down/Spin-off Trickle-up/Spin-on	More emphasis on performance than on cost Increasing efficiency or entering niche markets	USA/Defense and aerospace related Japan

Table 6.1 (*cont.*)

References	Journal/Book	Type	Technology	Organization	Market	Sample country/sector
Mowery (2012)	Research Policy	Mission-oriented defense-related R&D; Mission-oriented R&D in other fields	Development/well-defined objectives	Loss of link between R&D and procurement	Used by the government agencies; Used by private firms or individual formers	
Sampat (2012)	Research Policy	Mission-oriented biomedical research	Target a specific disease/target specific research	Research centers and contracts		USA/biomedical research in NIH
Anadón (2012)	Research Policy	Missions-oriented RD&D institutions in energy	Whether the implementing institutions focus on single or multiple missions and innovation types	Whether the government's various activities are coordinated or autonomous	Whether the business community is significantly involved in the design and running of the initiatives	USA, UK, and China/energy
Mazzucato (2018)	Mission-Oriented Innovation Policy Challenges and Opportunities	Mission-Oriented Innovation Policy	Tackling specific problems; missions should be well defined. A mission does not comprise a single R&D or innovation project, but a portfolio of such projects.	Reinvigorate capacity building, competencies, and expertise within the state	Address a societal demand or need	

In general, government can tailor different intervention strategies to different sectors, or apply the same or similar intervention strategy to the same or similar sectors, according to respective technological characteristics (Pavitt & Walker, 1976; Dolfsma & Seo, 2013). In reality, various national governments intervened in the same sector with different strategies or intervened in different sectors with a similar strategy without giving too much consideration to technological differences of the sectors (Anadón, 2012; Appelbaum *et al.*, 2012).

Indeed, a great challenge embeds risk and uncertainty of the technologies in the MMRDs, which also is fraught with rising transaction cost (Van Waarden, 2001). Thus, it is useful for policymakers to distinguish the types of R&D programs according to their technical goal which in turn determines their degree of uncertainty. An exploratory R&D program, which is radical and transformative, creates new knowledge or departs from existing knowledge. Such a program does not have a clear technical goal, costs more, and takes longer to get return (Jansen *et al.*, 2006).

An exploitative R&D program, however, is incremental, building on existing knowledge and reinforcing existing skills, processes, and structures, which can be either centralized or decentralized. A centralized R&D program is conducted around a single or multiple clear and specific goals for technological development, generating a technology or product that has a larger and broader impact on subsequent technological innovation (Argyres & Silverman, 2004). By contrast, a decentralized R&D program is conducted with a large number of goals or an obscure goal covering several aspects of technological development.

In presenting their policy framework of government intervention on industrial innovation, Abernathy and Chakravarthy (1979) argue that technology creation actions of mission-oriented R&D programs include leading to a prototype or feasibility model, funding on the basis of each program's risk/benefit profile, and funding only certain prototypes or exploitative R&D. Yet Ergas (1987) and Chiang (1991) argue that mission-oriented programs should focus on radical innovation or the early phase of a technology life cycle, or exploratory R&D. However, Mowery (2012), Sampat (2012), Anadón (2012), and Mazzucato (2018) all emphasized the mission-oriented programs should have well-defined, single or multiple specific missions. It is important to note that the mission that we discuss here is primarily a technical and engineering not a scientific one. Before undertaking an MMRD program, policymakers should ensure if the science and especially the end goal related to the program is well understood. The program is much easier to undertake when the basic science is understood and there is a clear goal.

As mentioned at the onset, because of the market failure consideration, the private sector is likely to refrain from investing in exploratory R&D programs, which usually are government's responsibility to support them at universities or national labs. While usually supporting exploratory R&D by way of investigator-initiated rather than mission-oriented programs, government also favors supporting exploitative research with less risk and uncertainty. Innovation coming from catching-up countries is mostly "new-to-the-country" type (Hobday, 1994; Amsden, 1998; Mathews, 2002; Hu & Mathews, 2005), following leaders who engage in the "new-to-the-world" innovation at the frontier, which has "primary uncertainty" because of no role model to follow (Wong, 2011).

Proposition 1 The MMRD model is suitable for solving challenges with a clearer, well-defined, and more specific technological goal, and R&D programs solving the challenges should be exploitative and centralized.

Organization: Government Dominating the R&D Network

How to organize an MMRD, which is a big system or network, is central to the program's outcome – success or failure. Such a network consists of enterprises, universities, and government agencies as well as individuals such as consumers, government officials, entrepreneurs, and researchers. Interactions between organizations and/ or individuals form an R&D network that constitutes the core of an innovation network. However, who dominates the R&D network differs across economies, and coordination and concerns for property rights and so on are critical to the organization of the network (Abernathy & Chakravarthy, 1979; Johnson, 1982; Henderson & Appelbaum, 1992).

Mega-R&D programs represent government's policy or action, thus the role of the government in MMRDs is an inescapable concern. Ergas (1987) argues that a mission-oriented program entails stages of the centralization of decision making, implementation, and evaluation. Mazzucato (2018) stressed reinvigorated capacity building, competencies, and expertise within the state. Fuchs (2010) suggested the importance of an embedded network governance in which government agencies re-architect social networks among researchers in identifying and influencing new technology directions to achieve an organizational goal.[4] Anadón (2012) also pointed out that whether government's various activities are coordinated or autonomous is an important difference across countries.

Indeed, government not only organizes a strongly centralized or a coordinated governance system for MMRDs but also should dominate the R&D network. The dominant power of the R&D network is a kind of institutional condition, which would change as the economic and political environment changes, depending on how state handles its relationship with the market.[5] Regardless of a country's innovation model, entrepreneurial, public–private partnership, or developmental state, who controls the network influences the way through which MMRDs are organized (Zhang *et al.*, 2011).

The R&D network of MMRDs should be dominated by government agencies, rather than state-owned enterprises (SOEs) and private-owned enterprises (POEs).[6] Mega-R&D programs are launched by governments that command the power of decision-making, funding distribution, R&D implementation, and program evaluation. The role model of MMRDs is American government-sponsored Manhattan or Apollo project, which has demonstration effects and guides current behavior of the state in handling its relationship with the market (Acemoglu *et al.*, 2005: 386–472). When Mowery *et al.* (2010) and

---

[4] Government agencies do not give way to the invisible hand of markets, nor do they step in with top-down bureaucracy to "pick up technology winners." Instead, they are in constant contact with the research community, understanding emerging themes, matching these emerging themes to military needs, betting on the right people, connecting disconnected communities, standing up competing technologies against each other, and maintaining a bird's-eye perspective critical to integrating disparate activities across national innovation ecosystem (Fuchs, 2010).

[5] For example, the British economy became liberal in the nineteenth century; but its nationalization was pervasive only after 1945, followed by the returning of the market mechanism in the 1980s (Foreman-Peck & Federico, 1999). Since 1978, China also has been transforming from a central planning economy to a socialist market-oriented economy.

[6] Private-owned enterprises (POEs) include indigenous invested enterprises (IIEs) and foreign invested enterprises (FIEs); SOEs also are a substantial part of IIEs. In fact, China's indigenous innovation strategy attempts to support SOEs with the hope that they can replace FIEs.

Foray *et al.* (2012) argue that Manhattan and Apollo projects are not the right models for new programs tackling climate change and other global challenges, their underlying reasoning is the difficulty for governments to dominate R&D network for the challenges. This does not mean that government should do nothing; but government just need to adopt the right models.

Proposition 2 *The MMRD model should adapt a government-dominated R&D network.*

Market: Public Actors as End Users

A demand–pull approach toward R&D activities stresses basing such activities upon an identified market need and an identified broader set of market features, including characteristics of the end market and the economy as a whole. Thus, the demand-side policy cannot be neglected for MMRDs.

Mega-R&D programs have to address a societal demand or need (Mazzucato, 2018), so their results should be useable. Chiang (1991) argues that mission-oriented programs emphasize more on performance than on cost, but diffusion-oriented programs should increase efficiency or enter niche markets. However, this does not mean that mission-oriented programs do not have to think about the market or users. Mowery (2012) considered that users of defense mission-oriented R&D should be government agencies but users of mission-oriented R&D in other sectors could be private firms or individual consumers. When R&D addressing a societal demand or need is used by private firms or individual consumers, government should intervene by such policy tools as fiscal subsidies, tax deduction, public procurement, and so on. It must be realized that public procurement is a short-period and early-phase policy of new products used by private firms or individual consumers.

When private firms or individual consumers utilize the outcomes of mission-oriented R&D programs in nondefense sectors, public actors should be the main users at the early stage. From an industrial life-cycle perspective, product development can be divided into "fluid phase," "transition phase," and "specific phase" (Utterback & Abernathy, 1975). A fluid phase is the period from the development of a new product to the emergence of a dominant design, which is the appropriate period for government to intervene.

Proposition 3 MMRDs *should be used by public actors – government agencies or SOEs all the time or at least in the early stage, regardless of the mission being defense- or nondefense-related.*

Decision-Making of MMRDs for Long-Term Interests

According to our framework of technology–organization–market (TOM) (Figure 6.2), the primary condition of adopting MMRDs includes technological goal, effective organization, and market user. In addition, we need to discuss the motivation of decision-making for adopting MMRDs as a strategy.

Mega-R&D programs result from scientific and technological imaginaries for the future and create new technology, new products, new equipment, even new life, and new world. However, just as Verschraegen and Vandermoere (2017:17) argue, "making promissory stories about future scientific and technological developments credible and obtaining enduring support to channel resources into rise projects is a huge challenge." The key is the uncertainty, which the TOM framework needs to address. For the technology part, although we argue that MMRDs could solve challenges with a clearer, well-defined, and specific goal of technology, we do not mean to suggest that these imaginary goals for the future would be realized as expected. There are too many cases in this regard, like the War on Cancer.

For the organization part, governments dominating the R&D network do not necessarily lead to the success of a mission-oriented program. Aiming at overcoming market failure, MMRDs may face two other types of failures – government failure and system failure. As an R&D network or system, an MMRD is inherently risky because of uncertainties associated with the organization and coordination of complementary actors (Adner, 2006). If government dominates an MMRD, its failure in coordinating its agencies with different interests in the MMRD could lead to government failure (Krueger, 1990). If government makes effort to organize and coordinate activities with enterprises, public research institutes, universities, and individuals, either hands-on or hands-off in its interactions with actors in the network, some sort of system failure could occur as well (Woolthuis *et al.*, 2005).

Finally, for the market part, public actors as end users could reduce the uncertainty caused by the market; however, public actors – government agencies or SOEs – also could bring a great deal of uncertainty to

MMRD. Government agencies may face fiscal and budget constraints, and consequently, they may encounter difficulty supporting the public procurement of MMRD without a long-term fiscal planning (Boston & Prebble, 2013). SOEs could meet the demand of an MMRD following the national strategies and policies, but SOEs are enterprises after all, and therefore they need to consider the cost and the benefit of getting involved in the program.

Regarding deep enormous uncertainty that characterizes mega-R&D programs (Lempert *et al.*, 2009), Vink *et al.* (2016) indicate the need to distinguish between two forms of uncertainty – cognitive uncertainty (what is the future) and normative uncertainty (what should the future look like). Mega-R&D programs have both kinds of uncertainty, thus making decisions of adopting MMRDs both important and difficult. Policymakers may try their best to reduce the uncertainty, but they are never able to eliminate the "fundamental uncertainty" of actors' behaviors for their unpredictable and unforeseeable nature (Verschraegen & Vandermoere, 2017). According to Jacobs (2011), a long-term policy is made most likely under the following three conditions in democracies: the degree of electoral safety they enjoy; the expected long-term social returns; and the institutional capacity at their disposal. If one or more of these conditions are not met, long-term decision-making like MMRDs is less likely to occur.

Of Jacobs's (2011) three conditions, two are related to the political regime. For developed countries such as the USA and the EU, it is difficult to initiate the long-term policy due to the political asymmetry, the voting asymmetry, and so on (Boston & Lem: 2011). There is an imbalance of political influence between different actors, and elected governments are primarily concerned with the satisfaction of voters' short-term interests (Congleton, 1992). Consequently, they are likely to suffer from "democratic myopia" or "presentist bias."

By contrast, for a developmental state such as China, the government does not have to worry about electoral pressure and also has a strong institutional capacity, thus the government is able to make long-term policies like MMRDs if these programs are expected to have long-term social returns. For example, in 2006, the Chinese government formulated the 15-year *Medium- and Long-Term Plan for the Development of Science and Technology* (MLP) (Cao *et al.*, 2006). Back in 1987, China's 13th National People's Congress set forth a "three-step" economic development strategy for the next 70 years. Policymakers responsible for making long-term decisions would not eventually benefit from the outcomes of the decisions made long ago; they nonetheless do so for future generations (Boston & Lempp, 2011).

In summary, our theoretical framework suggests that government can intervene on R&D through different ways depending upon contextual characteristics of the R&D activities – a clearer and specific goal, government dominating R&D network, and public actors as end users. But this framework only identifies several *necessary* conditions for the introduction of MMRDs, and such conditions are not *sufficient*. Certainly, as a long-term decision-making, adopting MMRDs also depends on the political regime, in particular policymakers and their political will. There are cases in which government has introduced the MMRD model to exploratory R&D activities and the activities involving the private sector. Unfortunately, most of them have failed to achieve their original goals. This suggests that government failure could occur if it played a role beyond its capacity.

Empirical Application and Findings from the Selected Cases

In order to test the validity and explaining power of our theoretical framework and examine the contextual characteristics for government to adopt the MMRD model, we examine the details of some programs according to their institutional contexts. In particular, we discuss these cases by countries to single out the impacts of political institutions on the proceeding of the programs under study (see Table 6.2).

The American Cases

The USA is a *laissez-faire* market-oriented economy. But it was the American government that launched the Manhattan Project to overcome the world-war stress, which indeed not only opened the door for government's direct intervention on R&D but also created the MMRD model. Subsequently, there were the Apollo Program to land astronauts on the Moon and return them to earth safely and the SDI that attempted to use ground- and space-based systems to protect the

Table 6.2 *Detailed summary of 10 case descriptions*

Name	Country	Time period	Money spent	Technical goal	Dominant actor	End user	Industrial phase	Outcome
Manhattan Project	The USA	1942–1946	$2.2 billion	The creation of a nuclear bomb	Top Policy Group, OSRD, NDRC, USACE	Interim Committee	Fluid	Success
War on Cancer	The USA	1971–	over $105 billion	Finding a cancer cure	NCAB, NIH, NCI	Patients	Fluid	Failure
Airbus 300	EU	1967–1972	—	The creation of a 300-seat airplane	Airbus Industrie	Air France and Lufthansa	Transition	Success
Yun–10	China	1970–1984	RMB350 million	The creation of a large passenger-aircraft	TMOMB, MODSE	CAAC	Transition	Failure
VLSI	Japan	1976–1980	$288 million	Creating integrated circuits by combining thousands of transistors into a single chip	MITI, VLSI-TRA, five major companies	Private companies	Fluid	Success
FGCS	Japan	1980–1988	$400 million	Computers processed knowledge rather than numbers	MITI, ICOT, ten companies, and two MITI's laboratory	Consumer	Fluid	Failure
HSR	China	1999–2008	$13–20 million/km	The creation of high-speed rail system operated with speeds between 200 and 300 km/h	MOR, SOEs	MOR/CRC	Transition	Success

TD–SCDMA	China	1999–2009	RMB200 billion	The creation of 3G wireless communication standards	PTI, Datang, MOIIT	China Mobile	Fluid	Success
CHB	China	2006–2020	RMB 60 billion	Catching up international technological development	MOST, MOIIT, SOEs, and public R&D sectors	Consumer, SOEs and POEs	Specific	On going
AHT	China	2008–	RMB 3.4 billion (2008–2010)	Control and treatment of AIDA, Hepatitis and Tuberculosis	NHFPC, HD-GLD-PLA; hospitals and universities	Patients	Fluid	Ongoing

Sources: Manhattan Project (Hewlett & Anderson, 1962): These costs were adjusted to 2008 dollars using the price index for gross domestic product (GDP), available from the Bureau of Economic Affairs, National Income, and Product Accounts Table webpage, Table 1.1.4, at www.bea.gov/bea/dn/nipaweb/ (assessed April 21, 2017). War on Cancer (Kolata, 2009; Spector, 2010). Airbus 300 (Baldwin & Krugman, 1988) – The size of the subsidy provided to the A300 is a matter of dispute for the simple reason that it is not a directly measurable quantity. Yun-10 (Zhao, 2005; Chen, 2009); VLSI (Sakakibara, 1983); FGCS (Cross, 1989; James, 2008) – At the end of the ten-year period, the project had spent over ¥50 billion (about US$400 million at 1992 exchange rates) and was terminated without having met its goals; HSR (Zhou & Shen, 2011; Bullock *et al.*, 2012) – The construction cost naturally depends on the proportion of such tunnels and structures but typically ranges from RMB 80–120 million per km (US$13–20 million) excluding stations. TD-SCDMA (Gao, 2014; Min, 2014); CHB – The staged achievements of CHB. www.most.gov.cn/kjbgz/201103/t20110324_85613.htm; AHT-news.xinhuanet.com/2011-03/29/c_121243113.htm (assessed April 21, 2017)

Notes: CAAC – The Civil Aviation Administration of China; CRC – China Railway Corporation; HD-GLD-PLA – Health Department, General Logistics Department, People's Liberation Army; ICOT – Institute of New Generation Computer Technology; MITI – Ministry of International Trade and Industry; MODSE – the Ministry of Defense's Sixth Establishment; MOIIT – Ministry of Industry and Information Technology; MOR – Ministry of Railways; MOST – Ministry of Science and Technology; NCAB – National Cancer Advisory Board; NCI – National Cancer Institute; NDRC – National Defense Research Committee; NHFPC – National Health and Family Planning Commission; NIH – National Institutes of Health; OSRD – Office of Scientific Research and Development; PTI – The Post and Telecommunications Institute of the former Ministry of Post and Telecommunications; TMOMB – the Third Ministry of Machine Building; VLSI-TRA – VLSI Technology Research Association.

USA from attack by strategic nuclear ballistic missiles. The Manhattan and Apollo projects have been known for their success, but the SDI was suspended in 1994.[7]

In the organization of the Manhattan Project, the government agency – the US Army Corps of Engineers – dominated the R&D network, which also included universities and newly and purposefully established national labs under the Department of Energy. In May 1945, another government agency – the Interim Committee – was created to advise on wartime and postwar use of nuclear energy. The government functioned as both a supplier of R&D and an end user–demander of the program, thus forming a basic model for either defense-related programs such as the Apollo Program and the SDI (Mowery *et al.*, 2010) or civilian R&D mega-programs such as the Very-High-Speed Integrated Circuits (VHSIC) project that also involved the military early on (OUSD, 1990).

In retrospect, exploitative in nature, the Manhattan Project was set up with a clear and singular technical goal – exploding an atomic bomb. More importantly, before the Manhattan Project started, scientific advances on nuclear reactor technology proved feasible to create a nuclear bomb (Jones, 1985: 35–36). Similarly, the Project Apollo aimed at landing the first humans on the Moon in 1969 to respond to the Soviet effort that flied Yuri Gagarin to space first in 1961. Some twenty years later, however, the SDI was launched with a vague mission of protecting the USA so that the ambitious initiative was widely criticized as unrealistic and even unscientific (Nolan, 2002: 1600). In hindsight, as an exploratory R&D program, the SDI was perceived to be unable to solve a large number of technical problems in a short time. Thus, it is not surprised that the initiative was terminated for high cost and more years of research that would be needed to figure out its feasibility.

Also motivated in part by the success of the Project Apollo, the USA launched the War on Cancer aimed at eradicating cancer as a major cause of death (Sampat, 2012). The NIH had been involved in cancer research since the early twentieth century. The National Cancer Institute (NCI) was founded in 1937 as part of the NIH. The NIH was concerned more with basic medical research behind diseases

---

[7] It does not mean that the SDI was a failure; but the USA did not obtain the expected results at that time.

than finding cures for the diseases. Fighting cancer needs efforts to improve the understanding of cancer biology and develop more effective cancer treatments. The War on Cancer began with the National Cancer Act of 1971, an American federal law. The act stipulated that new cancer research be carried out at the NCI rather than a separate agency, although a National Cancer Advisory Board (NCAB) was created with members appointed by the President. Meanwhile, the NCI also departed from NIH's peer-review process and used funding on a more targeted approach of building cancer centers and contracting out research (Sampat, 2012).

In particular, the Army's breast cancer program, a collaboration between the National Breast Cancer Coalition and the US Department of Defense (DOD), failed due to the lack of money and control needed to coordinate all the players in the network and to hold them accountable for working toward a common goal. Although the DOD had been a successful innovator in fields including digital computer and jet engines, this program provided grants for innovative, high-risk proposals that might not have been funded by the NCI (Sarewitz, 2016). However, cancer treatments turned out to be exploratory in nature, having no concrete technical goals; it also was hard to measure the program's progress, differing with programs such as a digital computer. Thus, it was most suitable to adopt a program dominated by individual investigator-initiated research projects selected through the peer-review mechanism than such a big-push mission-oriented program. Although between 1970 and 1980, the NCI funding had grown nearly three times in real terms, twice the rate of increase for the rest of the NIH over the same period (Sampat, 2012), the program did not achieve its original goal. From this vantage point, Obama's or Biden's Cancer Moonshot to fight cancer, as a new War on Cancer, is less likely to achieve its goal (Obama, 2016).

Reflecting on these programs, we realize the extreme importance of government's long-term strategic initiatives. Sharing the nature of exploratory research, both the SDI and the War on Cancer required long-term fundamental research. The War on Cancer was to respond to a crucial health threat but there was no solution on a short time horizon, although when the program was initiated, scientists were more optimistic. In other words, the goal that the MMRD model set to cure cancers was unrealistic. Comparatively speaking, the sciences that characterized both the Manhattan Project and the Program Apollo were fairly well understood, all needed to do were to work out and test (and retest) numerous technologies and techniques. Similarly, the SDI focused on large-scale systems including computer systems, component miniaturization, sensors, and missile systems whose respective technological goals were largely vague.

In fact, the abovementioned MMRDs, except the War on Cancer, were carried out in different periods to respond to different perceived potential threats from nuclear weapons and the Soviet Union. Much criticism toward the SDI does not mean that MMRD was an inappropriate model, especially given the intense competitive environment of national security. That suggests, however, that the American government was under short-term pressure to start a program aiming for achieving the long-term goal, but the long-term MMRD program required long-term sustained investment and support. When the external pressure was lifted, it is difficult for the government to continue providing funds to the program. Thus, it is inappropriate to simply use cost–benefit analysis to evaluate a long-term program that is initiated to reduce short-term pressure. Under the current political system and institutional arrangements of voting, the USA is less likely to launch and organize new MMRDs with long-term influences that the Manhattan Project and the Program Apollo would have, if there is no great external short-term pressure.

The European Cases

The economy in many continental European countries, from Germany to France, operates on a public–private partnership model (Zhang *et al.*, 2011). This does not prevent governments in these countries from adopting the MMRD model to gain international competitiveness in ways similar to that in the USA. The Airbus A300 Program is one such case.

In 1967, the British, French, and German governments signed a Memorandum of Understanding to launch the Airbus A300 Program to challenge the global dominance of the Boeing Corporation.[8] The program had a clear and singular goal – the creation of a large passenger-aircraft fitted with two engines and having a seating capacity of

---

[8] On April 28, 1967, McDonnell Aircraft and Douglas Aircraft, two independent companies, were merged, to become the McDonnell Douglas Corporation (MDC). MDC would merge with Boeing in August 1997.

250–300 in a twin-aisle configuration. Because of the likelihood of market failure of the newly created European aircraft industry, most notably the tremendous R&D and production costs, governments decided to lend their helping hands (Neven & Seabright, 1995). Not only did the states subsidize this Airbus program, SOEs were the main users at the early stage.[9] In 1970, Airbus Industrie was formally set up as the manufacturer of A300, following an agreement between Aérospatiale,[10] the antecedent of Daimler-Benz's aerospace interests, MTU München,[11] Dornier Flugzeugwerke,[12] and Deutsche Aerospace AG.[13] Product marketing is crucial for the government-launched programs due to their being away from the market, and A300 was no exception. At the early stage, most clients came from European airlines – notably Air France and Lufthansa, both SOEs – that were obliged to support the home-made aircrafts and carve out a market for them.[14] These end user–demanders helped Airbus to get the time and funds for competing with American companies.

Obviously, the situation in Europe is very different from that in the USA. Although politicians in Europe also are largely dependent on elections, leaders may stay in office longer. Germany's Angela Merkel, for example, had served as chancellor for 15 years. But going forward, the question is how the EU member states can reach a consensus on launching long-term MMRDs, given the political asymmetry, the cost–benefit asymmetry, the interest group asymmetry, and so on (Boston & Lempp, 2011).

The Japanese Cases

Different from the *laissez-faire* and coordinated market economies of the USA and European countries, Japan has a state-centric institution, in which the state negotiates with and delegates social and economic

---

[9] Governments around the world have supported and encouraged commercial aircraft production in covert or overt ways (Neven & Seabright, 1995).
[10] A French state-owned aerospace manufacturer.
[11] A German aircraft engine manufacturer, it later became MTU Aero Engines AG.
[12] A German aircraft manufacturer founded in Friedrichshafen.
[13] A Germany state-owned aerospace manufacturer.
[14] Many of the world's airlines are wholly or partially government owned, and aircraft procurement decisions are often made politically as well as commercially.

functions to private organizations (Zhang *et al.*, 2011). As both an initiator and a practitioner of the "big-push" developmental state model, Japan has deliberately and strategically supported large enterprises to strengthen their industrial competitiveness. The very large-scale integration (VLSI) program is such an example.

The program was set up to develop the technology necessary to integrate circuits containing thousands of transistors into a single chip so as to catch up with IBM's technology. In 1976, the then Ministry of International Trade and Industry (MITI) formed a VLSI Technology Research Association (TRA) as the central organization of the cooperative public–private partnership program. The TRA then established a cooperative laboratory consisting of 5 private and competitive enterprises – Fujitsu, Hitachi, Mitsubishi Electric, Nippon Electric, and Toshiba – and 50 additional companies to share both cost and outcome (Sakakibara, 1983). The research outcome would be used in these companies' productions so as to reduce imports of foreign semiconductor production equipment. MITI's role was to communicate with participating companies and coordinate the program in addition to providing 30 percent of the program's funds. Obviously, the ministry acted wisely on the market mechanism, realizing clearly that the semiconductor market was one of free competition. If the Japanese government had organized this program directly instead of depending on the competitive companies, the outcome would likely have been different.

Later in the 1970s, Japan was in the midst of its transition from imitating to creating technology, and the success of the VLSL program motivated and inspired the MITI to start other similar ambitious programs (Cross, 1989; Chiang, 1991). Of them, the Fifth Generation Computer (FGC) Program would supposedly help the Japanese computer industry to produce a new kind of artificial intelligent (AI) computer by 1991 (Nielsen, 1988). The program's architects believed that fifth-generation computers, which processed knowledge rather than numbers through human beings instructing in natural language, would change the world. In fact, the goal of the FGC program was very ambitious by today's standard even with the advent of the Internet, big data, and advanced computing.

The program engaged the similar network actors as those in the VLSI Program with the MITI again implementing the program and adopting the similar mode as the VLSI Program did by establishing an

Institution of New Generation Computer Technology. The difference is that the science of the FGC program was not well understood. One criticism is that the program's entire strategy was only based on one technological approach, ignoring a rival technology creating neural computers with electronics laid out in a similar way to the neurons on the human brain (Cross, 1989). Then, the FGC program's origins were fundamentally flawed. It is true that intelligent machines remain as elusive now as they did then despite advances in AI, especially machine learning.

It is understandable, therefore, that the same mechanism that worked out for the VLSI program did not work out for the FGC program. The Japanese government inappropriately got involved in the program ignoring its striking differences with the VLSI program. The VLSI program was an exploitive development program following the first mover – the USA, with which Japan or Japan Inc. gradually surpassed IBM, the world's leader in the technology, and moved into the first place measured by the technical performance and product cost (Cross, 1989). By contrast, the FGC program's ambition to produce a new class of computer was essentially exploratory in nature. The MITI decided a quite obscure direction for the program based on a misunderstanding of the development trends of the computing technology (Nielsen, 1988; Cross, 1989). It was difficult to change the goal, a critical factor to the program's success, in the middle of the program even if the initially set direction was found infeasible. In hindsight, in choosing AI as the direction of the FGC program, the MITI had missed other opportunities of the next-generation information and communication technology (ICT) such as the Internet, mobile telephony, and mobile Internet.

In addition, contrary to the VLSI program in which enterprises were the major demanders of semiconductors, the primary user of the FGCs was supposedly consumers. The closer the end users to consumers, the closer R&D to the market, and the most suitable for government to adopt policy measures to create an innovation-friendly environment. More than 30 years after the FGC program, despite tremendous progress, research on AI is still exploratory.

As a developmental state, the Japanese government after the World War II was anxious to start future-oriented MMRDs, with both successes and failures. As the degree of marketization continues to increase, including the reform of SOEs, the intervention of the Japanese government in R&D activities has been decreasing. Meanwhile, Japan has since 1995 started to formulate the *Basic Plan of Science and Technology* every five years. The *S&T Basic Plan* is a comprehensive plan prepared by the government in accordance with the *Science and Technology Basic Law* to promote S&T in Japan over a five-year period, based on a 10-year forward outlook. But it remains to be seen whether the Japanese government will initiate new long-term MMRDs in the future.

Evaluation of the Framework against the Chinese Cases

As a latecomer, China has a big gap with in the USA, EU, and Japan in R&D capability and high-tech competitiveness, despite its catching up with these countries alongside its transformation from a centrally planned to a market-oriented economy (see Table 6.2 and Figure 6.2). We profile the MMRDs in these countries is to see how China has done comparatively in organizing such programs and whether histories could tell us any lessons.

Mega-Programs before the MLP

During China's central-planning period, government agencies not only dominated the R&D network but also were the only user of the R&D outcome. One such case of government intervention is that in the early 1970s, it attempted to develop its own large-passenger aircrafts with a capacity of more than 100 seats in a program codenamed 708 or Yun–10.

Suppliers of Yun-10 aircrafts, both the then Third Ministry of Machine Building (TMOMB) and the then Ministry of Defense's Sixth Establishment were government agencies of aviation industry,[15] and the user–demander, the Civil Aviation Administration of China (CAAC) (Chen, 2009), was part of the government. Furthermore, the then State Planning Commission, Shanghai municipal government, and

---

[15] There have been several government agencies related to aviation industry in China. The TMOMB and the Ministry of Defense's Sixth Establishment were central government agencies in charge of the Yun–10 Project. In 1982, the TMOMB was changed to the Ministry of Aviation Industry. The Ministry of Defense's Sixth Establishment (now the Chinese Aeronautical Establishment) was set up in 1961.

other government agencies and local governments also participated in the program. That is, similar to the Airbus A300 Program, the Yun–10 Program had a clear goal to develop a large passenger airplane, and government agencies dominated both R&D activities and the product market. While these contextual characteristics implied the feasibility of applying the MMRD model, at the end, the Yun–10 Program failed to reach the original goal due to many reasons, particularly poor coordination between government agencies. Out of the government's control, the CAAC refused to purchase Yun–10 aircrafts (Chen, 2009). Then, the Ministry of Finance stopped financing the program because it could not see the existence of a potential market. Finally, the top Chinese leadership decided to give up the program for a strategic reason that at that time the government intended to introduce McDonnell Douglas Aerospace's MD-82 (PLRO, 2004: 616). Since the late 1980s when the assembling of MD-82 aircrafts started, the Shanghai Aircraft Manufacturing Factory had produced more than 30.

After a series of reforms between 1982 and 2008, the TMOMB reemerged as the China Aviation Industry Corporation (CAIC), a consortium of Chinese aircraft manufacturers; the CAAC was split into three big state-owned airlines – Air China, China Eastern Airlines, and China Southern Airlines. That is, both the supplier and demander of large passenger airplanes were transformed from government agencies to SOEs. Under these circumstances, the MMRD model was less likely to succeed, not because the program did not have a clear goal but because the government would encounter more difficulties coordinating SOEs than its agencies, although it still resembles the Airbus 300 case.

Given that the capability of manufacturing large passenger-aircrafts was very important to a great power, in 2006, China restarted such a program. In 2008, by employing the similar model of the Airbus A300 Program, China established Commercial Aircraft Corporation of China (Comac), a state-owned aeronautic manufacturer, located in Shanghai, integrating the CAIC, the Aluminum Corporation of China, Baosteel Co., Ltd, and others. It aimed to eventually build large passenger-aircrafts with a capacity of over 150 passengers to reduce the country's dependency on Boeing and Airbus. Our theoretical framework points to a possibility that China could design and build an indigenous large commercial airliner successfully if it well organizes and coordinates its R&D network. Now, Comac has built C919, a planned family of 158–174 seat narrow-body twin-engine jet airliners.

However, inefficient coordination, part of government failure or system failure, could still put the program in trouble.

The development of high-speed rail (HSR) in China illustrates a different scenario. The government was both the end user–demander of the upstream production and the supplier of downstream services, different from the organization and structure of the railway industry in other countries (Amos & Bullock, 2011; Bullock *et al.*, 2012).[16] Until its dissolution in 2013, China's Ministry of Railways (MOR)[17] not only used trains and tracks but also provided service for passengers and enterprises through railway freight transportation such as Shanxi Coal Transportation and Sales Group (Bullock *et al.*, 2012). In particular, the MOR was the end user of the products made by China South Locomotive and Rolling Stock Corporation Limited (CSR) and China North Locomotive and Rolling Stock Industry Corporation (CNR),[18] which, along with China Railway Construction Corporation (CRCC), were all SOEs. The regional rail authorities were a sub-division of the MOR providing freight and passenger services. Now, China Railway Corporation (CRC), also a centrally administered SOE, uses trains and tracks (Amos & Bullock, 2011).

The development and deployment of TD-SCDMA, one of the third-generation (3G) standards for mobile telephony, in China also is different. The standard was developed by Datang Telecom, a Chinese state-owned multinational telecommunications equipment company, along with Siemens in Germany. Datang was founded in September

---

[16] For example, in the USA, the largest number of rail service providers has 23 regional operators, 339 local (or short-line) operators and 194 switching and terminal operators; the most diverse railway country is arguably Japan, where there are six main regionally based service providers (three private and three state-owned), plus 21 large- and medium-sized private companies operating mainly in the suburban or regional passenger railway sector (Amos & Bullock, 2011).

[17] The MOR was a ministry under the State Council of China. The ministry was responsible for passenger services, regulation of the rail industry, development of the rail network and rail infrastructure in mainland China, though in light of recent accidents, there have been calls to institute independent supervision of the rail industry. On March 10, 2013, the government announced that the ministry would be dissolved and its duties taken up by the Ministry of Transport (safety and regulation), State Railways Administration (inspection) and China Railway Corporation (construction and management).

[18] On June 1, 2015, CNR Corporation Limited and CSR Corporation Limited merged into China Railway Rolling Stock Corporation Limited (CRRC), a Chinese state-owned rolling stock manufacturer.

1998 by the China Academy of Telecommunication Technology (CATT), an R&D institute affiliated with the then Ministry of Post and Telecommunication. After the 2003 government reform, the CATT transformed from a national R&D institute into a centrally administered SOE – the Datang Telecom Technology & Industry Group, directly under the State-owned Assets Supervision and Administration Commission of the State Council. Datang developed SCDMA, the basis for TD-SCDMA, in the mid-1990s and played a leading role in developing the indigenous standard. Meanwhile, China's three mobile service providers – China Mobile, China Unicom, and China Telecom – are all SOEs. After TD-SCDMA was approved by the International Telecommunication Union as one of the 3G mobile communication standards in 2000, the Chinese government provided substantial support to further perfect the standard, including allocating frequency spectrum, offering financial support, mandating that China Mobile, the most financially sound service provider, adopt the standard, and helping organizing a TD alliance (Gao, 2014). In 2009, the Chinese government issued 3G licenses to China's three service providers with three different 3G standards after the TD-SCDMA commercialization trials in ten cities and the precommercialization network operation in Beijing during the 2008 Olympic Games, although the government decided to not protect the market for its own TD-SCDMA standard. This indicates that the Chinese government intended to wait for the maturity of the TD-SCDMA standard while balancing the interests between the indigenous and international standards (Kennedy *et al.*, 2008).

MEPs under the MLP

Motivated by the success of the HSR Program and TD-SCDMA Program, in 2006, the Chinese government introduced a series of MEPs under the MLP (Cao *et al.*, 2006; Serger & Breidne, 2007) Following the principle of targeting high-tech development, upgrading traditional industries, solving bottlenecks, improving public health, and safeguarding national defense, the MLP included 16 MEPs in strategic industries such as ICT, biotechnology, new energy, resources and the health as well as in dual-use and national defense technologies.[19]

---

[19] Only information on thirteen programs has been made public and presumably the remaining three are related to national defense science and technology.

According to a MOST official, 690 billion RMB would have been invested in the nine civil MEPs by 2020, of which 200 billion RMB would come from the central government and 100 billion RMB from provincial governments with participating enterprises contributing the rest (Zhou, 2008). In 2020, in terms of funds from government, the top agencies involved in the MEPs were the MOST, the MOIIT, the MOARA, the NHC, whose order was different with the leading agencies – the MOIIT, the MOH, the CAS, and the MOA – in 2011 (see Chapter 4). The MOST and the MOIIT were the primary actors of MEPs, appropriating 37.52 billion RMB and 7.12 billion RMB, respectively, on the MEPs in 2020; however, back in 2011, the MOIIT and the MOH, as the primary actors, only appropriated 3.87 billion RMB and 1.34 billion RMB, respectively.

Funds for the MEPs, which covered basic research, applied research, and technology development, had become an independent budget item (20609), as discussed in Chapter 4, and their impacts on China's S&T/R&D budget were significant. First, their budget was huge. The central government alone had spent some 50 billion RMB on the MEPs from 2008 to 2010 (MOST, 2011, 2012) and probably more in later years. By comparison, during the same period, the NSFC only received some 23 billion RMB from the central government, less than half of the MEPs. In 2010 alone, the central government spent about 22 billion RMB on the MEPs, equal to the sum of funds for the NSFC (9.5 billion RMB), the 973 Program (4.2 billion RMB), and the 863 Program (7.5 billion RMB).

Second, the MEPs had affected the distribution of the central government's R&D appropriation with more funds going to S&T-mission agencies than the MOST. For example, the MOIIT had been the organization unit of three MEPs and the MOH two MEPs. Other S&T-mission agencies such as the MOA, the MOEP, the MOHURD, and the MOWR also had got more appropriations than before, although they still were not as important as the MOST and the NSFC in administering R&D funding and as significant as the CAS in spending R&D funding. More importantly, funding for the MEPs as a new public finance source has not only enhanced the role of the state but also redistributed the resources among government agencies so as to create inter-agency competitions and probably make relevant agencies more accountable. Consequently and probably unintentionally, by channeling funding to other agencies, the MEPs also had weakened

MOST's role in China's national innovation system. Although the National Office of the MEPs (*guojia zhongda zhuanxiang bangong-shi*) is housed at the MOST, its role is limited to making supporting policies, organizing and coordinating the daily operation, collecting related information, and reporting the process of the program to the State Council, rather than allocating resources as an organization unit.

Third, the large amount of money appropriated to the MEPs had been spent in a rush, especially so toward the end of the *11th Five-Year Plan (FYP)(2006–2010)* period in 2010. Operationally, each MEP had been assigned a lead government agency (the organization unit) that received the central government appropriation and then distributed it to participating universities and R&D institutes through competition (Table 6.3). For example, for the Drug Innovation and Development program (MEP-DID), the organization units were the MOH and the Health Department under the General Logistics Department of the People's Liberation Army (HD-GLD-PLA); however, the program's direct organizer is the Office of Implementing and Managing MEP-DID (OIM) under the China National Center for Biotechnology Development (CNCBD).[20]

In August 2008, the OIM issued an application guideline for the first batch of projects for the 11th FYP period to be carried out between 2008 and 2010; in September 2008, it released another application guideline for the second batch of projects to be carried out between 2009 and 2010. These two batches supported 970 projects with a total of 5.3 billion RMB (Sun, 2012), of which some 3 billion RMB was spent on the construction of the large platforms for drug innovation. This amount was matched with supplementary funding of about 20 billion RMB from local governments; for example, more than 3 billion RMB from Hubei province, and more than 2 billion RMB from Tianjin (Ja, 2012). Then, in 2010, the third batch of projects was launched with a total funding of about 1.2 billion RMB (MOST, 2010: 82).

The funding policy for the MEP-DID changed for the 12th FYP period (2011–2015) when in May 2010 the MOH and the HD-GLD-PLA released the 2011 project application guideline. While the research

---

[20] China National Center for Biotechnology Development (CNCBD) is a research center for biotechnology policy and project management for biotechnology and biotech industry under the MOST. After the 2023 reorganization, the center will move from the MOST to the HMC, which succeeded the MOH.

Table 6.3 *Organizations of mega-engineering programs (unit: billion RMB)*

Program	Leading unit	Organization unit	Funding in 11th FYP*	Started time
1 Core electronic components, high-end generic chips, and basic software	MOST	MOIIT	8.50	2008
2 Extra large-scale integrated circuit manufacturing and technique	MOST	Beijing and Shanghai governments	8.56	2009
3 New-generation broadband wireless mobile telecommunications	MOIIT	MOIIT	3.97	2008
4 Advanced numeric-controlled machinery and basic manufacturing technology	MOST	MOIIT	2.19	2009
5 Large-scale oil and gas exploration	NDRC	CNPC and CBM	–	2009
6 Large advance unclear reactors	NDRC	CNPTC	4.58	2008
7 Water pollution control and treatment	MOEP	MOEP and MOHURD	–	2006
8 Genetically modified new-organism variety breeding	MOA	MOA	–	2008
9 Drug innovation and development	MOST	MOH and HD- GLD-PLA	6.50	2008
10 Control and treatment of AIDS, hepatitis, and other major diseases	MOH	MOH and HD-GLD-PLA	3.40	2011
11 Large aircraft	State Council	Comac	–	2007
12 High-definition earth observation systems	SASTIND		–	2010
13 Manned aerospace and moon exploration	SASTIND		–	2007

Sources: MOST, 2010: 72–85.

Notes: (a) An organization unit (*qianton zuzhi danwei*) for an MEP is an unit organizing the MEP, whose functions include managing funds of MEPs projects, and organizing the task undertaking unit to draw up the total budget and annual budget. A leading unit (*lingdao xiaozu zuzhang danwei*) is a unit leading the MEP. The leading group (*lingdao xiaozu*), along with the organization unit, is responsible for drawing up the total budget and annual budget and implementing the other funds besides the central funds and the related supporting conditions. (b) CNPC – China National Petroleum Corporation; CBM – China United Coalbed Methane Corporation, Ltd; Comac – Commercial Aircraft Corporation of China Ltd; HD-GLD-PLA: Health Department, General Logistics Department, People's Liberation Army; SNPTC – State Nuclear Power Technology Corporation; MOHURD – Ministry of Housing and Urban-Rural Development; MOEP – Ministry of Environmental Protection. (c)* estimated results and – data of funding not disclosed.

missions of the MEP-DID in the 12th FYP period were the same as those in the 11th FYP period (2006–2010) and a small number of new projects may still be initiated, most of the R&D funds would be used to support the projects that started in the 11th FYP period and the selection would be based on previous research achievements. This means that scientific research units that received government appropriation in the 11th FYP period were likely to continue to do so in the future. In other words, spending of the huge amount of money for the MEP-DID program was decided in the months of August and September 2008. This funding allocation pattern also might have appeared in other MEPs.

After the reform of the NSTPs in 2014, the allocation of funds for the MEPs has been shifted from mission-oriented agencies to the MOST, although the MOIIT, the NHC, the MOA, and the NEA still were managing a part of the funds. Meanwhile, the MEPs accounted for 34.73% of the 102 central government agencies' funds in 2020, up from 9.73% in 2011 (see Table 4.3).

The Progress of the MEPs

Of the 13 civilian MEPs under the MLP, the CHB Program was initiated first, which had three projects – core electronic components, high-end generic chips (HGCs), and basic software of the electronic and information industry – with each project also including several product lines. It is not easy to assess the results due to the program's large number of missions. For example, the program aimed to come up with products oriented partly toward consumers such as operating systems and office software packages, and partly toward POEs and SOEs such as highly efficient embedded CPUs. To be specific, the HGCs project of the program had characteristics similar to those of the Japanese VLSI Program. Unfortunately, in adopting the MMRD model to develop HGCs, the Chinese government implemented the project differently with the VLSI Program. Firstly, the VLSI Program defined a clear mission, but the HGCs project was part of the big program whose focuses were not explicit. Secondly, the MITI organized the VLSI Program through integrating and coordinating major private enterprises in this sector, but government agencies, SOEs, research institutions, and universities, all from public sectors, had dominated the HGCs project and private enterprises seldom participated in it.

These could explain the extent to which different results had come out of Japan's VLSI Program and China's CHB Program.

The AHT Program in health care, on the other hand, was very complex in terms of its R&D network and end users. China's pharmaceutical industry has gone through the marketization reform for a long time, although SOEs, as the supplier, still play an important role. The demander of the industry is mainly public hospitals where doctors prescribe drugs for patients. Meanwhile, prices of most medicines are government sanctioned. But both the market and government mechanism failed to work out. On the one hand, government dominates the pharmaceutical product market through SOEs and public hospitals but does not administer them directly; on the other hand, government intends to regulate the market through the price mechanism, but the price is not determined by the market supply and demand.

Furthermore, the program involved exploratory research. For example, the control and treatment of communicable disease such as AIDS, hepatitis, and tuberculosis remain big challenges in China as well as globally. There is currently no effective cure or vaccine for AIDS while the control and treatment of hepatitis and tuberculosis had only partially succeeded. Considering that the healthcare sector was related to public interests, it was more appropriate and effective for government to fund basic research and small-scale exploratory projects. Generally, given the similarity between the AHT Program and the War on Cancer in terms of the technical goal of the R&D activities, similar to the failure of the War on Cancer in achieving its goal, the MMRD also might be less likely to be the most effective model.

As a developmental state, China prefers to use MMRDs for intervention on R&D and innovation. However, according to our TOM framework, some of selected Chinese MEP cases may not be able to tackle their technical goals as outlined. Thus, it also is necessary to consider whether the way through which the state makes decision is science-based or ideologically driven (Appelbaum *et al.*, 2012). China's state-led innovation model may be better than America's and Europe's for making long-term decisions on MMRDs for the future; however, it does not mean that decision-making for the long term is ultimately correct. Not following a right direction, the state-led innovation model also is facing daunting challenges, many of which may not be easily met. Judged by the evolutionary governance theory, the Chinese decision-making system is characterized by strong path dependence and goal dependence, but more path creation is necessary. Accordingly, flexibility is helpful in overcoming the limitations caused by dependencies as well as steering and planning the creation of new path (Beunen *et al.*, 2015).

Summary and Discussions

The chapter proposes a theoretical TOM framework for adopting a mission-oriented mega-R&D program. It then empirically tests the framework through the analysis of cross-country and cross-sector cases. The MMRD is an appropriate model of R&D intervention when government agencies dominate the R&D network and public actors are end users, and most importantly, the programs have a clear and specific goal. We evaluate the framework based on its application of China's practice, particularly ongoing MEPs.

For making long-term decisions, the developmental state such as China is more likely to use the MMRD model for long-term interests relative to market economies such as the USA. MMRDs may not succeed if they do not meet the criteria of our TOM framework. Our case studies (see Figure 6.3) show that various countries have organized similar or same MMRDs such as the War on Cancer and AHT programs in healthcare, the HGCs and VLSI programs in integrated circuits, Yun–10, Airbus A300 and HSR in mass passenger transportation, among others. Some of these programs have succeeded to achieve their goals but others have failed. The transportation and integrated circuit programs share some common features. The three programs – Yun–10, Airbus A300, and the HSR – all had a clear technological goal, Yun–10 and Airbus A300 even shared a particularly identical technological goal for R&D – developing a passenger-aircraft, with government agencies or SOEs dominating the R&D network and providing services to passengers as end users.[21] But the outcomes of these programs differed enormously.

Indeed, our framework only provides a more substantive foundation for exploring the *necessary* conditions of government intervention through MMRDs. However, these conditions are not *sufficient*,

---

[21] Whether private enterprises could participate in the passenger market depends on a country's institutional arrangement. The governments of China and EU countries prefer SOEs' domination of the passenger market.

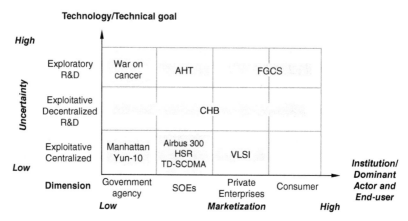

Figure 6.3 Overall summary of the 10 cases
Notes: VLSI – the Very Large-scale Integration Program; HSR – the High Speed Railway Program; FGCS – the Fifth Generation Computer System Program; Yun–10 and A300 are the large passenger-aircraft programs, respectively; AHT – China's MEP of control and treatment of AIDS, hepatitis, and other major diseases; CHB – China's MEP of core electronic components, high-end generic chips, and basic software.

and the success of a program depends on not only the program's context, as discussed in the chapter, but also various uncertainties and risks facing the program. The identified conditions for government intervention are dynamic not static and real-life characteristics of an MMRD could depart from the ideal type, thus rendering the intervention anachronistic and ineffective. An MMRD for the long term also is likely to fail to achieve its goal because of government failure or system failure even if it possesses all the necessary conditions discussed in the chapter.

With the involvement of usually many organizations in an MMRD, governments need to coordinate their activities, which proves to be vital for the outcome of the MMRD. The state as a monolithic whole is just a theoretical assumption; in practice, government agencies compete fiercely for departmental interests and it is not easy to coordinate the interests of these agencies even if the superior authorities intervene in coordination. It also is not easy to coordinate the interests of various participants of MMRDs. For example, the R&D supplier and demander of the Yun–10 Program were all China's government agencies, the HSR Program was organized by China's government agencies but its R&D supplier and demander were SOEs, both of which were similar to the Airbus A300 Program. According to our theoretical framework, the MMRD model was suitable for all three programs and mostly for the Yun–10 Program. However, of the three, the Yun–10 Program was the one that failed its mission due to government failure. Therefore, as the mechanisms of the government's coordination and program organization are central for C919 Program's outcome, it is necessary to avoid government failure and system failure.

In addition, government intervention through MMRDs is economically inefficient, as historical precedents indicate. State's mobilization of resources through MMRDs is to achieve largely a political or public policy goal such as national security or public interests rather than an economic goal. In doing so, government agencies allocate resources under the challenging political or societal pressure rather than out of the pure economic rationale. Under these circumstances, cost usually takes a secondary position. The introduction of the MMRD model during World War II or the Cold War period, national security was the top priority of policymakers and the state had to respond to the potential threats regardless of the cost. As such, government going down to the MMRD path was understandable, although such programs could fail. During the peace period, however, policymakers should pay more attention to economic development, employment, and industrial competitiveness. Therefore, cost or efficiency matters for both government and enterprises.

7 | Toward a Political Economy of Science, Technology, and Innovation in China

In keeping pace with the development of science, technology, and innovation in China, the studies of China's science, technology, and innovation have become an emerging field of scholarly research, corresponding to China's two critical milestones – the formulation of the strategy of "revitalizing the nation through the science and education" in 1995 and the introduction of the *Medium and Long-Term Plan for the Development of Science and Technology (2006–2020)* in 2006. They also have to meet the increased demands from the scholarly and policymaking communities both inside and outside of China to understand what has underpinned China's sharply upward trajectory in science, technology, and innovation (Sun & Cao, 2020). In particular, the studies cover a wide range of research topics and have drawn the interests of scholars from social science disciplines such as political science, sociology (including science, technology, and society), public and business administration, China studies, and others.

Built on and extending this literature, our book represents a systematic and comprehensive effort to put China's state-led innovation model, especially its whole-of-the-nation system (*juguo tizhi*), under the lens of political economy and to examine innovation policymaking involving government ministries, funding for R&D and S&T activities at the central government, effects of the programs attracting high-end talents from overseas, and organization of mission-oriented mega-R&D programs. Focusing on the structure of China's state related to science, technology, and innovation activities, our effort is theoretically driven and evidence-based, from which we have come up with some principles, albeit preliminary, of the political economy of science, technology, and innovation in China.

Our analysis and discussion also reveal the extent to which the state-led innovation model has worked in China and what challenges facing China in its journey to become an innovation-oriented nation and an S&T powerhouse in the world. Of more significance, we explore whether China's innovation model deviates from the developmental state or the state-led innovation model, which the existing literature has touched upon but has not comprehensively investigated. In particular, the Chinese state has played a critical role in the rapid development of science, technology, and innovation, but the question is how government interventions have been institutionalized. What characterizes the China model includes an authoritarian regime that guides science, technology, and innovation development; government agencies' extensive access to and domination of the policymaking process; the difficulty of the formation of interest groups in funding; and efforts to achieve brain gain and brain circulation, and to organize mega R&D programs. However, China has long lacked sufficient policy and institutions tasked with coordinating public–private partnerships (PPP), such as those involved in the mixed-ownership reform of state-owned enterprises (SOEs). Meanwhile, there have been instances of government failure. All these also has implications for the issues discussed in the book.

The Political Economy of Science, Technology, and Innovation in China: The Role of the State

As we have shown in the book, the focal point of our approach toward the political economic study of science, technology, and innovation in China is the role of the state. We care not only about its functions but also about its internal institutions and the relations between state departments. Let us start with a recap of the findings from our research.

Policymaking: Hierarchy, Division of Labor, Collaboration, and Coordination

At the central level, China's state is a hierarchical system, which determines the differences in the efficiency of policies in different agencies. The Communist Party of China's Central Committee (CPC CC) launches the most strategically important initiatives related to science, technology, and innovation, leads and directs policymaking, with inter-organizational units steering the policy network, fostering integration and coordination within and between various participants, and most importantly enabling the state to better attain its objectives. The hierarchy is reflected in organizations issuing science, technology, and innovation policies. A policy that comes from the CPC CC, usually in the format of the decision, is the most authoritative and supposedly most influential, impactful, and effective, followed by a law enacted by the National People's Congress, an administrative statute formulated by the State Council, and a regulation issued by the respective ministries under the State Council. In general, a high-grade policy guides the macro and strategic direction, while a low-grade policy largely is focused on the interpretation of specific issues and the operational mechanisms associated with the macro-level policy. Even though the overall number of CPC CC decisions, laws enacted by the NPC, and State Council statues has been relatively few, in general, their impacts have been the most pronounced.

The respective departments under the CPC CC and ministries under the State Council have a clear division of labor in science, technology, and innovation policymaking. The division of labor is advantageous in that the rights and responsibilities of each department or ministry are clearly defined and allocated, yet no department or ministry wants to relinquish to others their specific prerogatives. During the early years of the reform and opening up, innovation policies tended to be formulated by a single government ministry – the Ministry of Science and Technology for S&T policy, the Ministry of Commerce for industrial policy, and so on. Obviously, this reflects a great deal of parochialism on the part of these ministries. Indeed, the frustrated problems of poor coordination are not simply found in the science, technology, and innovation realm, but are much more generic inside of the Chinese bureaucratic system as a whole.

Chinese inter-agency collaboration has been gradually increasing at the central level. From 1980 to 2005, a total of 36 ministerial level agencies participated in the formation of innovation policies, and 356 distinct agency–efforts were involved in the introduction of 213 pieces of policy, which translates into about 1.67 agencies per policy. From 2006 to 2019, every innovation policy involved 2.8 participating agencies, which shows a marked improvement in inter-agency collaboration. In fact, China's central government has set innovation policymaking agendas through a timetable/summary sheet to routinize and institutionalize cross-agency collaboration and coordination.

Meanwhile, China's policy network for innovation has been sustained through self-organization due to power concentration and heterogeneity dependence. The lead agencies could govern the network through their core positions and act as intermediaries to increase the policy network's operational efficiency. The collaboration between agencies with heterogeneous functions may be a better choice to make a new and more effective policy.

Funding: A Transparent, Restructuring Budgeting Process

As R&D funding is the most important resource for a country to support the development of science, technology, and innovation, it becomes utmost important that the government needs to manage the resource effectively. Opening the "black box" of China's central R&D expenditure allows us to better understand who spends how much money on what at the central government level. Indeed, Chinese government agencies are becoming more transparent in their budget management, with more of them disclosing their S&T budgets. Nevertheless, as more than half of the central S&T appropriation is still not a countable from budgets released by 71 or 102 agencies in 2011 or 2020, respectively, while none of the key agencies with a mission in national defense S&T have made public their budgets, this portion was likely to be spent at these agencies.

The MOST, the Chinese Academy of Sciences (CAS), the National Natural Science Foundation of China (NSFC), and the Ministry of Industry and Information Technology (MOIIT) are key central government agencies in allocating and spending public S&T expenditure. In 2011, the division of labor among these big R&D spenders seems to be clear with the NSFC focusing on basic research, the MOST and the MOIIT on applied research, and the CAS seeing a balance between the two. But the new division of labor and probably a recalibration of power happened in 2020, with the CAS joining the NSFC and focused on basic research and the MOST and the MOIIT turning to Mega-Engineering Programs (MEPs) and seeing their roles increasingly important in organizing such programs. China's R&D landscape has thus been changed significantly.

Chinese budgeting decisions are separated from policy decisions and national plans. The Ministry of Finance (MOF) holds the main responsibility in budgeting but it is not the only agency having the power for the central budget allocation. China's S&T budgeting process involves two rounds of budget requests and guidelines between the MOF and S&T-mission agencies. The role of the MOST in China's national innovation system (NIS) and S&T budgeting process has been decreasing since 2000, due to the reform of the S&T budget system, departmental competition, and especially the initiation of MEPs. The MOST, in addition to making S&T policy, organizes S&T activities and allocates S&T budget while also sharing the policymaking role with the National Development and Reform Commission and the national S&T programs' organizational role with the CAS, the NSFC, and other S&T-mission agencies. Now, the MOST administers the NSFC by macro-management, coordination, supervision, and evaluation, while the NSFC remains to operate relatively independently.

Nevertheless, China lacks an agency like the Office of Management and Budget (OMB) at the US federal government level. Again, inter-agency collaboration and coordination aside, a more focused and coherent agency can mainly assist the top leaders to prepare the budget, to measure the quality of agency programs, policies, and procedures, and to see if the central agencies' budget comply with the national demand and policies. It is in this sense that the institutional reform in 2023 probably will make sense. With a new Central Science and Technology Commission under the CPC CC, with the reorganized MOST running daily operation of the S&T enterprise, inter-agency cooperation and coordination at the macro level are likely to improve. But it is not clear whether the new MOST will work with the MOF to play similar budget functions to OMB in the USA.

Talent: Brain Gain, Shortage, and Controversy

Since the mid-1990s, China's government agencies and institutions of learning have launched a series of talent-attracting programs to get some of the best and the brightest expatriate scientists back to help China's scientific enterprise. While it is rather difficult to figure out the effects of these programs on talents' return, this book devotes one chapter to examine the outcome of one such program, the Young Thousands Talent Program (YTTP).

Since 2009, the Organization Department of the CC CPC has become a headhunter by implementing a new program, the Thousand Talents Program (TTP), targeting the returning of overseas high-level talents. The TTP intended to attract from the world within five to ten years about 2,000 leading scientists and professionals, mostly ethnic Chinese. The program was ambitious, but overseas scholars with high academic ability were less enthusiastic about returning on a fulltime basis than those with low academic ability. The YTTP, the version of the TTP for young scientists, has played its due role in attracting some highly capable overseas young scholars, although it remains unattractive to those with a stable overseas position who were generally reluctant to return and whose willingness to return decreased with age. Nonetheless, the program did successfully allure some scholars whose last employers' academic discipline ranking is among the world's top 100 to give up their overseas positions and return.

Talents recruited into various similar programs have significantly contributed to the development of their affiliated institutions by publishing more and higher impact papers at the international level, extending new research areas, and helping uplift the overall performance of the domestic scientific community (Cao *et al.*, 2020). However, the high-profile TTP with enormous prestige and benefits attached has largely failed to achieve its goal as a significant number of the position holders have not returned to China on a fulltime basis as expected (Zweig & Wang, 2013; Sun *et al.*, 2017; Zweig *et al.*, 2020). Consequently, China is still experiencing a serious shortage of high-end academics and other professionals. Moreover, there has been a new exodus of leading scientists, which may greatly undermine China's efforts to build an innovation-oriented country (Cao *et al.*, 2020).

Moreover, the TTP has become controversial internationally. Amid recent tensions with China, the American government targeted USA-based expatriate Chinese scholars and high-tech professionals, quite a number of whom have not been frank with their involvement in the TTP and similar talent-attracting programs (Zweig *et al.*, 2020). Not only has China halted its talents recruitment efforts in the USA and some other countries, it also has had difficulty sending students and scholars, especially in some high-technology fields and from some specifically targeted universities, abroad. This will undoubtedly have negative impacts on China's technological learning and catch-up (Tang *et al.*, 2021). Overseas talent recruitments may need to pay special attention to the issues of transparency, research integrity and ethics, and intellectual property protection and to especially avoid the part-time "double dipping" phenomenon (JASON, 2019).

Organization: The Whole-of-the-Nation System,
Successes and Failures

China's whole-of-the-nation system toward science, technology, and innovation has its unique merits in organizing R&D activities to tackle major challenges through resource mobilization. In fact, organization of mega-mission-oriented R&D programs originated in the USA, whose early successes such as the Manhattan and Apollo programs have inspired a succession of similar programs globally. The War on Cancer in the USA and the VLSI program in Japan were some of the examples of such programs involving enormous government efforts. International experience suggests that the mission-oriented mega-R&D (MMRD) model is only appropriate for R&D programs dominated by government agencies with public actors being end-users while the programs have a clearly defined and specific goal. That is, the mobilization of resources is neither applicable to all R&D programs, nor does it lead to the solution of a particular mission.

Accordingly, our framework of technology–organization–market (TOM) for adopting MMRDs includes technology goal, effective organization, and market user. We have used the insights from the framework and international experiences to assess China's practice, particularly ongoing MEPs. It is understandable that China, as a developmental state, favors the whole-of-the-nation system in achieving long-term interests or public policy goals relative to market-oriented economies (Appelbaum *et al.*, 2011).

Although MEPs bear a remarkable similarity to some of the alike programs in developed countries, it is worth noting the applicability of the MMRD model in different market regimes. The developed countries emphasize more on the coordination of the public sector, as their private sector is highly efficient. In developing countries, the government is strong in coordination, but the level of commercialization in the private sector is relatively weak. The public and private partnerships might be essential for the viability of the whole-of-the-nation system.

Tensions in China's State-led Science, Technology, and Innovation System

At present, there exist multiple tensions in China's science, technology, and innovation system, which means that the state is not omnipotent. The tensions are not only the main feature of the transition period but also the new challenges brought by the ongoing institutional reform. How to overcome these tensions is the key to the political economy of science, technology, and innovation in China.

The Tension between Research and Development

As the second largest R&D spender in the world, China sees a level of the gross expenditure on R&D (GERD) very close to that of the USA (NSB & NSF, 2022). Although it did not fulfill the R&D intensity target set for 2020, as mentioned, China has retained the momentum to increase its investment in R&D, which is helpful in transforming its economic structure and stimulating the next stage of economic and social development driven by technology and innovation.[1]

It is known that R&D covers three types of activities: basic research, applied research, and experimental development (OECD, 2015). However, in China, the share of GERD spent on basic research had been hovering around 5 percent for a couple of decades until it finally reached 6 percent in 2019, compared with 18.6 percent for the UK and 16.6 percent for the USA in 2018. Moreover, not only has the proportion of the expenditure allocated to applied research been low and declining (11.3 percent in 2019, compared with 19.15 percent for USA in 2018) but the issue of the chronic imbalance in favor of experimental development has been largely ignored in policy. That is, China has overspent its R&D expenditure on development at the expense of scientific research – basic and applied, which may jeopardize the long-term prospect of the country's scientific, economic, and social development.

Less government R&D spending has led to less expenditure on scientific research at research-intensive universities and public research institutes that depend upon the government for funding (Sun & Cao, 2014). Although the *Medium and Long-Term Plan for the Development of Science and Technology (2006–2020)* (MLP) called on the government to maintain its contribution to GERD at 40 percent between 2010 and 2020 (Jia *et al.*, 2006: 49), in reality, between 2000 and 2020, governments – central and local – decreased their share in GERD from 40 percent to 20 percent despite overall rising funding. Governments have mistaken strengthening an enterprise-centered innovation system for their less contributions to GERD.

---

[1] China spent 3.09 trillion RMB, or 2.55% of its GDP, on R&D in 2022 (NBS 2023).

The orientation of the reform of China's S&T system toward commercialization may have hindered the development of basic research, reflected in the preference of the government's R&D expenditure on applied research. Meanwhile, the expenditure on experimental development is mainly funded and performed by enterprises, but their numbers may be dubious. A study finds that more than half of the sample companies reported materially discrepant profit numbers to the local branches of the then State Administration of Industry and Commerce and the MOST so as to take advantage of government's incentives (Stuart & Wang, 2016). This indicates that the decline of government proportion in GERD also is partly attributed to government misincentives and enterprises' fraudulent behavior.

The Tension between the State-Led and Enterprise-Centered Innovation

The tension between research and development is essentially the tension between the state-led and enterprise-centered innovation models. The state-led innovation is the main advantage of China's science, technology, and innovation system. And the state-led innovation is reflected and achieved in the public research-oriented universities, public research institutions, SOEs, NSTPs, national S&T awards, and so on. The MLP clearly stated that China's NIS is state-led. However, the proportion of R&D funds from the government in the GERD has continued to decline, remaining at only 20 percent, thus seriously weakening the function of state-led scientific research (basic research and applied research). China's state-led science, technology, and innovation system should be more inclined to invest in scientific research. But, the scientific research accounts for only about 15 percent of GERD in China, compared with about 30 percent in major developed countries (Sun & Cao, 2014).

The goal of China's reform of its S&T system is to better link S&T and the economy, as well as supporting and encouraging enterprises to become the center of technological innovation. For the latter goal, the state has set up an impressive policy goal, requiring that enterprises spending on R&D account for more than 50 percent of GERD. In reality, in 2020, enterprises spending on R&D reached 76.6 percent of GERD, higher than the average level of OECD countries, which is 63.84 percent in 2019 (OECD, 2022). Enterprises have become the main vehicle of technological innovation resources. However, the establishment of an enterprises-centered NIS remains in form than substance. Within the enterprises-centered NIS, enterprises are not only the main vehicle of innovation resources but also the center of innovation decision-making, research organization, and S&T achievement transformations.

In fact, SOEs are at the intersection of the tension between state-led and enterprises-centered innovation models. According to the State-owned Assets Supervision and Administration Commission (SASAC), the central SOEs invested 904.59 billion RMB in R&D in 2021, or 32.4 percent of GERD and more than 40 percent of R&D spending at enterprises (SASAC, 2021). SOEs feature the characteristics of both the state and enterprises. On the one hand, SOEs are guided by the state's administrative and institutional arrangement; on the other hand, they need to allocate resources to meet market's demands. In this sense, SOEs are not genuine enterprises in the Chinese context and much of the R&D spending at these enterprises comes from public finance. Thus, the key to establishing an enterprises-centered system is to allow SOEs make their own decisions, rather than press by government, on innovation to meet the market's demands, especially in terms of investment in R&D, organization of innovation activities, and transform S&T achievements from and collaborating with institutions of learning.

Indeed, China's NIS has been state-led in nature under the centrally planned economy system as well as the socialist market-oriented economy system. The key to solving the tension between state-led and the enterprises-centered innovation models is also to clarify the roles and functions of the state and the market and further handle the relations between government and the market, so that the market can play a decisive role in the allocation of resources. The government needs to do a better job in the supply of public goods in science and generic technologies, especially in areas where enterprises lack incentives to venture their endeavors. The government needs to establish a good PPP model to give full play to the enthusiasm of the private sector to participate in public affairs. Most importantly, the government needs to level the playing field on which different types of enterprises are encouraged to compete and prevail.

The Tension between Investigator-Initiated Research and Mission-Oriented Research

An important advantage of China's state-led innovation is its mission-oriented governance mode or the whole-of-the-nation system. That is, government leads resource allocation to meet national strategic needs. NSTPs are an important way for the government to support science, technology, and innovation activities through state funds. In 2006, when the MLP started, there were two types of NSTPs in China: basic programs and MEPs. The basic programs provide public S&T goods, covering a wide range of S&T areas and requiring long-term and stable funding. Mission-oriented MEPs had been set up around national strategic goals. The reform thereafter highlighted the role of MEPs in the NSTPs. For a period, China had decentralized these programs.

However, mission orientation could be at the expense of investigator-initiated research, which is derived from scientists' own interests and curiosity, emphasizing autonomy and creativity. Funding for investigator-initiated research is distributed through a peer-review process focused on identifying and funding the best science and choosing a project on its scientific merits. After the reform of NSTPs in 2014, the NSFC has become the main funding agency for investigator-initiated basic research. According to the 2020 Annual Performance Evaluation Report of the NSFC (CNCSTE, 2021), done by China's National Center for Science and Technology Evaluation at the NSFC's request, the proportion of NSFC's funding for the investigator-initiated programs such as the general program and the program for young scientists is relatively low, and the investigator-initiated programs accounted for 58.62 percent of the total funding of the NSFC in 2020. If this situation allows to last for a prolonged period of time, the NSFC would deviate from its mission for funding scientific research.

The tension between investigator-initiated and mission-oriented research may pose some challenges. The reform in 2014 has turned out to complicate rather than simplify the funding for the NSTPs. For example, the National Key R&D Programs aim to link basic research, applied research, and technological development, as well as accelerating the transformation and commercialization of achievements. Yet, it is impossible for a mission-oriented project to engage purely investigator-initiated basic research. Such arrangements may end up weakening basic research and directing most projects toward application and short-termness. The continuous expansion of mission-oriented programs at funding agencies including the NSFC may cause a large number of scientists doing basic research to lose their enthusiasm for free inquiry and instead pursue more projects with reachable goals, as it is difficult for them to get funding for their engagement in explorative but risky research approaches.

Therefore, it is necessary to clarify the functions of and division of labor between funding agencies. The NSFC should maintain its responsibility for distributing investigator-initiated grants through the peer-review process, the mission-oriented agencies should be in charge of allocating grants to mission-oriented projects through contracts and the operation of research centers and distributing funding via requests for applications (Sampat, 2012), and it is meaningful that the new MOST works with the MOF to play similar budget functions to OMB in the USA.

The Tension between Indigenous Innovation and Open Innovation

The international community has been generally concerned about whether China's state-led science, technology, and innovation model and the indigenous innovation strategy would lead to the country's embrace of techno-nationalism and protectionism. China has been following a long-term strategy of reducing its dependence on foreign technology and capabilities, which has been seen as a strategic challenge to decoupling (Black & Morrison, 2021).

Since 1999, the Chinese central government has been the leading force in reforming its innovation system with "Chinese characteristics" (Sun & Liu, 2010). After 2003, the government has directly intervened in specific industrial sectors, thus showing a dramatic return to "techno-industrial policy" and changing China's trajectory of economic reform and marketization (Chen & Naughton 2016). Furthermore, the MLP prioritized significant domestic S&T resources and tried to reduce China's over-dependence on foreign technologies (Liu *et al.*, 2011). However, the strategy of indigenous innovation anchored in the MLP may have endangered international technology transfer (Cao *et al.*, 2006; Serger & Breidne, 2007; Appelbaum *et al.*, 2016). The Made in China 2025 has raised further concerns regarding China's aim to control over the most profitable segments of the global supply chain and production networks through systematically acquiring cutting-edge technology and generating large-scale technology transfer (Wübbeke *et al.*, 2016).

Amid such developments and interruptions caused by the COVID-19 pandemic, "de-globalization" and "re-globalization" have begun its co-existence with techno-nationalism. As a type of mercantilist thinking, the techno-nationalism links technological innovation and capabilities directly to a nation's economic prosperity, national security, and social stability (Ostry & Nelson, 1995). In 2018, when a trade war broke between the USA and China, the cut-off of Chinese companies such as ZTE and Huawei from the supply of key basic components, key basic materials, and advanced basic technologies has fully exposed China's bottlenecks in high-tech development. In 2021, the Chinese state proposed to become S&T self-relied and self-improved at the high-level, which is a demand not only for national development but also for opening up and innovation. Only by strengthening its own capacity for innovation and achieving self-reliance in advanced S&T can China gain an advantageous position in the global value chain and technological competition.

Indeed, China has been making efforts to reduce its dependence on foreign technology and capabilities (Grimes & Sun, 2014). China's indigenous innovation policy has prioritized domestic companies in government procurement (Dedrick *et al.*, 2012). In the post-MLP era, China has sought to develop its own intellectual properties (IPs), core technologies, and technical standards. But China does not want to be decoupled from the international frontier of science, technology, and innovation in terms of acquiring advanced foreign technology, pursuing international collaboration, harvesting the benefits from a globally mobile talent pool, and embedding its companies in the global value chain and innovation network. The indigenous innovation strategy would only succeed under globalization. Indigenous innovation cannot be equated to autarky or an unwillingness to open up. It is very unlikely that China will ever close its door to the outside world and indigenously innovate on its own while ignoring the ultimate purpose of innovation, which is the creation of new technologies and products with international competitiveness. Therefore, foreign companies have taken a realistic view of the market potential against the risks of exposing IPs to China's complex and uncertain environment (Sun & Grimes, 2018). In fact, in recent years, foreign-invested enterprises contribute 12–16 percent of China's R&D expenditure (MOST & NBS, various years).

A new round of S&T revolution and industrial transformation is in the making. The COVID-19 pandemic is not over yet. Economic globalization is facing undercurrents. Nationalism and protectionism are on the rise. Thus, the dialectical unity between indigenous innovation and open innovation has been another tension for S&T governance, in China as well as in the world. Indigenous innovation and internationalization are mutually reinforcing. China has fully utilized the convenience of resource sharing induced by globalization. It also will be more conducive for China to implement an indigenous innovation strategy oriented toward globalization. Moreover, as it has achieved a certain level of S&T development and become a more prominent power, China needs to promote the process of internationalization by following market rules, such as fair competition, equal and reciprocal treatment of domestic and foreign-invested enterprises, and protecting property rights.

Government and Governance

China has delivered an unnerving and rousing performance in science, technology, and innovation for some four decades. It has learned from international, and especially Western sources, the experience of developing and governing scientific research. In turn, its governance experience has caused the attention of the world scientific community and S&T policymakers.

The State as a Double-Edged Effort in Governance

The state-led development could be a double-edged effort. Such a model is advantageous in its ability of mobilizing substantial resources to meet specific national goals; or the state could mobilize the country's entire resources on the strategic undertaking. However, as noted, this model is not a cure for all science, technology, and innovation challenges. Therefore, there is the need to delicately balance the role of the state and the market in innovation.

Utilizing the whole-of-the-nation system to mobilize and concentrate resources, China has taken full advantage of the benefits as a latecomer and achieved the catching-up with developed countries in certain technological areas. The system is most suitable for sectors with clear goals, such as high-speed rail and large passenger-aircrafts. However, such a system does not always work as it often fails in consumer-centered sectors (e.g., the automobile industry) and in areas where there is no leader to follow. It is less effective and efficient in market-oriented or exploratory fields in which goals are a moving target.

In market-oriented economies, government intervenes as an autonomous self-regulating order through investing in R&D, especially basic research, out of the market failure concern (Mowery, 2009) and through nurturing a fair, open, and competitive environment. The state also could be "entrepreneurial" by making visionary and strategic public investments, distributing resources across the innovation chain, and providing private businesses with growth opportunities (Mazzucato, 2013).

As China still is in its transition from a centrally planned economy to a socialist market economy, the state's main focus remains science-, technology-, and innovation-driven economic development. On the one hand, as the government's "unlimited power" features an innovation system with "Chinese characteristics," the state subjects the market to the state-centered or state-led order (Fang, 2010). The state operates the S&T system and allocates resources for science, technology, and innovation activities. But this approach has its limits.

During the global financial crisis, for example, China dramatically increased direct government intervention on industrial development, as part of a massive stimulus program, to mitigate its negative effects on both emerging sectors and hard-hit traditional industries. But in doing so, the state largely ignored the more fundamental issues of the reform of the S&T system and even missed the best window of opportunity to proceed with the reform. Afterward, most developed economies dialed back their stimulus efforts, but China still was stuck in its industrial policy initiatives (Naughton, 2021: 67). The direct government intervention also distorted the market-oriented mechanism which otherwise could expand the potential contribution to science, technology, and innovation progress. As a result, China's total factor productivity, a global benchmark for economic efficiency and innovation, has experienced a significant slowdown in growth, from 3.51 percent in the ten years before the global financial crisis to 1.55 percent in 2008–2017 (World Bank Group & Development Research Centre of China's State Council, 2019).

On the other hand, the state needs to allow for the autonomous operation of the scientific community and the true market orientation for enterprises in innovation. For one thing, He Jiankui's gene-edited baby scandal, exposed in 2018, relates to one of the most critical issues in research ethics, procreative ethics, and medical practice. The research did not go through the mandatory ethical review process and He applied the gene-editing technology to human-assisted procreative medicine in a hospital. It was claimed that none of these had been known to government departments or the scientific community before He made them public. In 2019, He was prosecuted and sentenced for a three-year jail term for illegal medical practices, as there were no other terms applicable to his crime (Lei & Qiu, 2020). It is until 2020 that a provision on illegal gene-editing was written into Chinese *Criminal Law* and in 2023 relevant government agencies came up with a new regulation on ethical reviews of life sciences and medical research involving humans. Indeed, while laws and regulations constrain the behaviors of scientists, research ethics and integrity should be within the purview of the scientific community.

Similarly, government intervention should not substitute the market's proper function as the intervention may distort incentives. For example, Chinese firms filed more patent applications to take advantage of the subsidies offered by local governments (Eberhardt *et al.*, 2017); academics published more papers that carried significant weight in performance evaluation. Now, aware of such distortions, the central government has taken action to correct overemphasis on publications, professional titles, credentials, and awards in the performance evaluation of scientists and institutions, and is likely to abolish patent subsidies soon.

The Asymmetric Structure of Actors in Governance

As the world's second-largest economy, after the USA, China is growing its economy at a slower pace now than in the earlier decades of the reform and opening up. Along with structural issues, such as export-oriented growth and insufficient domestic consumption, the economy has been further perturbed by a disruptive, prolonged trade dispute with the USA since 2018. The trade dispute has spilled over into issues such as technology and talent with sources of the tensions including high-tech competition, technology transfer, IP protection, and the TTP. There is real risk of decoupling in technology and talent between

China and the USA as the USA has taken more aggressive actions targeting China's efforts in science, technology, and innovation. In fact, the decoupling rhetoric has originated from mutual suspicions between the two countries when a rapidly rising nation is perceived to challenge the incumbent power that wants to maintain its supremacy in economic, technological, and geopolitical terms. And the tension has started to involve other developed countries, which is likely to undermine China's efforts to become an innovation-driven nation and a world's leading S&T power.

In order to achieve its ambition to become an innovation-oriented country, China has to overcome its asymmetric governance system between the perceived omnipresent state and other actors including universities, research institutions, and enterprises that are significantly less powerful. Or, there needs a balance between government, market, and the research community. The state-led innovation system may allocate resources through a less market-based mechanism and may lead to a less autonomous research community. To correct the distorted performance of the market and the research community, China needs to modernize its governance system by diversifying participants, rather than depending solely on the state, appropriately balancing power structure of the participants, and making the research community self-organized and autonomous.

The state-led innovation system also is less effective in making macro-level coordination. The state is not one entity within itself but is made up of many agencies and departments with their own interests that might be in conflict with each other. China's National Leading Group on Science & Technology (NLGST), for example, has not fully functioned coordinating agencies at the macro level. The MOST oversees S&T affairs, but it is only one ministry among many within the State Council and probably a weak one in terms of clout (Cao *et al.*, 2013). In addition, it is the MOF that directly appropriates S&T budget.

Less effective macro-level coordination remains a major challenge, although the problem has been improved through the reform of funding system in 2014 and the reform of state institutions in 2018. Starting from 2014, the MOST convened a new inter-ministerial joint conference, with participation from the MOF and other agencies whose administrative ranks seemingly are the same (Cao & Suttmeier, 2017). After the 2018 reform, the MOST absorbed the State Administration of Foreign Experts Affairs (SAFEA), which was previously under the Ministry of Human Resources and Social Security (MOHRSS), and the independent NSFC. The merger seemed to consolidate the role of the ministry in administering China's NSTPs, but not necessarily in managing the S&T budget and other administrative tasks. After the 2023 reform, the SAFEA comes back to the MOHRSS. There exist a the functional equivalent in China of a national science advisory system to coordinate S&T affairs between agencies (Cao & Suttmeier, 2017). Even with such an advisory apparatus, as there is an apparent redundancy, the question lies in how to coordinate several organizations with similar, albeit not necessarily the same, functions, or whether to consolidate one organization while abolishing others. In fact, the 2023 reorganization of the S&T system, among others, will abolish the NLGST but retain the National Science and Technology Advisory Committee. The State Committee for Science and Technology Ethics will be retained, reporting directly to the Central Science and Technology Commission under the CPC CC.

Planning as an Approach of S&T Governance

To a certain extent, China's rising capability in science, technology, and innovation has to do with "a grand experiment" that started in 2006 (Cao *et al.*, 2006). In early that year, China's State Council released the MLP, thus launching the indigenous innovation strategy and setting up goals to turn China into an innovation-oriented country and a scientific power in the world. The junction at which the old MLP phased out and a new MLP (2021–2035) may be introduced holds greater historical and practical significance for the Chinese and international scientific communities to make sense of planning for science, as a dominant model of S&T governance in China, if not globally.

China has a long history of formulating five-year plans (FYPs) for national economic and social development (since 1953) and FYPs usually include an S&T component. The MLP to 2020 was particularly inspired by the *Long-term Plan for the Development of Science and Technology (1956–1967)*, or the 12-year plan, the most celebrated of China's past S&T plans, which not only laid the foundation for modern science in China but also has been recognized as an important milestone in S&T planning (Cao *et al.*, 2006). Corresponding to China's FYPs for economic and social development, the MOST leads the formulation of FYPs for S&T development, which are important vehicles for the implementation of the MLP, FYPs, and annual plans.

In fact, several developed countries also have adopted the practice of planning S&T development, albeit not necessarily in the Chinese approach. For example, as mentioned, since 1996, Japan has drawn up S&T basic plans every five years, according to its *Science and Technology Basic Law* enacted in 1995. Now, the country is working on its sixth *Science and Technology Basic Plan*. The *S&T Basic Plans* of South Korea and the *Framework Programmes* of the European Union have some planning characteristics. In addition, the American Academy of Arts and Sciences (2014) proposed the introduction of a more strategic, long-term approach toward S&T policymaking at the US federal level as a way of restoring the vital role of research.

Applying Goodhart's Law that "when a measure becomes a target, it ceases to be a good measure" (Varela *et al.*, 2014), measuring China's S&T capability by its plan's targets might be problematic. For example, China has increased its payments for the use of foreign intellectual property significantly from $6.63 billion to $37.78 billion between 2006 and 2020, while its receipts increased from $0.2 billion to $8.5 billion during the same period. That is, China ran a larger IP deficit in 2020, although its average annual growth rate of IP receipts is faster than that of IP payments, and more importantly, its degree of dependence upon foreign technology, an indicator that was set in the MLP but the Chinese government no longer uses, declined to 31.2 percent in 2016, attributing to rapid growth of domestic investment in R&D and shrinking foreign technology imports (Sun & Cao, 2021).[2] As a latecomer, China needs to acquire an increasing amount of foreign technology including IPs in developing its industry, moving toward the international frontier of technology, and moving up its value chain. China has become the world's second largest R&D spender but its large amount of R&D activities have not generated enough technologies and IPs for usage in its industrial development.

---

[2] Similar problems exist in other countries, where government's planning targets are not being met on time. For example, the Lisbon strategy stipulated the EU investing 3 percent of its GDP on R&D by 2010, but the majority of its member states remained far from the target by 2020.

Consequently, the country still has to spend a significant amount of its money acquiring foreign IPs, which is not included in R&D expenditure.[3]

Going forward, China should strive to build an enterprises-centered, market-oriented, and open and indigenous NIS by deeply integrating a variety of actors, from governments, enterprises, universities, research institutions, and users. As well as playing the role in making science, technology, and innovation policies, distributing funds, attracting and retaining talents, and organizing projects crucial to the nation's strategic missions, the state needs to nurture an environment conducive to the advancement of science, technology, and innovation. Such an environment includes elements such as upholding norms and values, or the cultural aspects for the carrying out of scientific research and technological innovation, creating a market of ideas where different views are allowed to collide and contend, encouraging independent and thinking, among others (Cao, 2014).

---

[3] In 2019, China's GERD is RMB 2.2 trillion (about $320.98 billion) and its IP payment is $34.37 billion, or some 10 percent of the R&D expenditure.

References

Abbasi, A., Hossain, L., & Leydesdorff, L. (2012). Betweenness centrality as a driver of preferential attachment in the evolution of research collaboration networks. *Journal of Informetrics*, 6(3), 403–412.

Abelson, P. (1979). Education, science, and technology in China. *Science*, 203(4380), 505–509.

Abernathy, W.J. & Chakravarthy, B.S. (1979). Government intervention and innovation in industry: A policy framework. *Sloan Management Review*, 20(3), 13–18.

Acemoglu, D., Johnson, S. & Robinson, J.A. (2005). Institutions as a fundamental cause of long-run growth. In P. Aghion & S. Durlauf, eds. *Handbook of Economic Growth*. Amsterdam: North-Holland Publishing Company, vol. 1A, pp. 385–472.

Ackers, L. (2005). Moving people and knowledge: Scientific mobility in the European Union. *International Migration*, 43(5), 99–131.

Adner, R. (2006). Match your innovation strategy to your innovation ecosystem. *Harvard Business Review*, 84(4), 98–107.

Aghion, P., David, P.A. & Foray, D. (2008). Science, technology and innovation for economic growth: Linking policy research and practice in "STIC systems." *Research Policy*, 38(4), 681–693.

Ahuja, G., Soda, G. & Zaheer, A. (2012). The genesis and dynamics of organizational networks. *Organization Science*, 23(2), 434–448.

Aldrich, H.E. & Fiol, C.M. (1994). Fools rush in? The institutional context of industry creation. *Academy of Management Review*, 19(4), 645–670.

Allen, R. & Tommasi, D. (2001). *Managing Public Expenditure: A Reference Book for Transition Countries*. Paris: OECD Press.

American Academy of Arts and Sciences. (2014). Restoring the Foundation: The Vital Role of Research in Preserving the American Dream. Available at www.amacad.org/sites/default/files/publication/downloads/American Acad_RestoringtheFoundation.pdf (accessed December 3, 2021).

Amin, A. & Cohendet, P. (2004). *Architectures of Knowledge: Firms, Capabilities, and Communities*. Oxford: Oxford University Press.

Amos, P. & Bullock, R.G. (2011). Governance and structure of the railway industry: Three pillars. *China Transport Topics*, 2(12), 53–60.

Amsden, A.H. (1998). Bringing production back in: Understanding government's economic role in late industrialization. *World Development*, 25(4), 469–480.

Anadón, L.D. (2012). Missions-oriented R&D institutions in energy between 2000 and 2010: A comparative analysis of China, the United Kingdom, and the United States. *Research Policy*, 41(10), 1742–1756.

Appelbaum, R.P., Cao, C., Han, X., Parker, R. & Simon, D. (2018). *Innovation in China: Challenging the Global Science and Technology System*. Cambridge, UK: Polity.

Appelbaum, R.P., Cao, C., Parker, R. & Motoyama, Y. (2012). Nanotechnology as industrial policy: China and the United States. In B.H. Harthorn & J.W. Mohr, eds. *The Social Life of Nanotechnology*. New York: Routledge, pp. 111–133.

Appelbaum, R.P., Gebbie, M.A., Han, X., Stocking, G. & Kay, L. (2016). Will China's quest for indigenous innovation succeed? Some lessons from nanotechnology. *Technology in Society*, 46, 149–163.

Appelbaum, R.P., Parker, R. & Cao, C. (2011). Developmental state and innovation: Nanotechnology in China. *Global Networks*, 11(3), 298–314.

Argyres, N.S. & Silverman, B.S. (2004). R&D, organization structure, and the development of corporate technological knowledge. *Strategic Management Journal*, 25(8–9), 929–958.

Baldwin, R. & Krugman, P. (1988). Industrial policy and international competition in wide-bodied jet aircraft. In R. Baldwin, ed. *Trade Policy Issues and Empirical Analysis*. Chicago, IL: University of Chicago Press, pp. 45–78.

Barabási, A. & Albert, R. (1999). Emergence of scaling in random networks. *Science*, 286(5439), 509–512.

Baruffaldi, S.H. & Landoni, P. (2012). Return mobility and scientific productivity of researchers working abroad: The role of home country linkages. *Research Policy*, 41(9), 1655–1665.

Baudassé, T. & Bazillier, R. (2014). Gender inequality and emigration: Push factor or selection process? *International Economics*, 139, 19–47.

Bazhal, I. (2017). *The Political Economy of Innovation Development: Breaking the Vicious Cycle of Economic Theory*. Berlin: Palgrave Macmillan.

Becker, G.S. (1964). *Human Capital*. Chicago, IL: The University of Chicago Press.

Berardo, R. & Scholz, J.T. (2010). Self-organizing policy networks: Risk, partner selection, and cooperation in estuaries. *American Journal of Political Science*, 54(3), 632–649.

Besussi, E. (2006). *Policy Networks: Conceptual Developments and Their European Applications (CASA Working Papers)*. London: Centre for Advanced Spatial Analysis, University College London. Available at http://discovery.ucl.ac.uk/3280/1/3280.pdf (accessed December 3, 2021).

Beunen, R., Van Assche, K. & Duineveld, M. (2015). *Evolutionary Governance Theory: An Introduction*. Heidelberg: Springer.

Black, J.S. & Morrison, A.J. (2021). The strategic challenges of decoupling. *Harvard Business Review*, July–August 2–7.

Blom-Hansen, J. (1997). A "new institutional" perspective on policy networks. *Public Administration*, 75(4), 669–693.

Borgatti, S.P., Brass, J.D. & Halgin, S.D. (2014). Social network research: Confusions, criticisms, and controversies. *Research in the Sociology of Organizations*, 40, 1–29.

Borjas, G.J. (1994). The economics of immigration. *Journal of Economic Literature*, 32(4), 1667–1717.

Borrás, S. & Edquist, C. (2013). The choice of innovation policy instruments. *Technological Forecasting and Social Change*, 80(8), 1513–1522.

Boston, J. & Lempp, F. (2011). Climate change: Explaining and solving the mismatch between scientific urgency and political inertia. *Accounting, Auditing and Accountability Journal*, 24(8), 1000–1021.

Boston, J. & Prebble, R. (2013). The role and importance of long-term fiscal planning. *Policy Quarterly*, 9(4), 3–8.

Braun, D. (2008). Lessons on the political coordination of knowledge and innovation policies. *Science and Public Policy*, 35(4), 289–298.

Breznitz, D. (2007). Industrial R&D as a national policy: Horizontal technology policies and industry-state co-evolution in the growth of the Israeli software industry. *Research Policy*, 36(9), 1465–1482.

Breznitz, D. & Murphree, M. (2011). *Run of the Red Queen: Government, Innovation, Globalization, and Economic Growth in China*. New Haven, CT: Yale University Press.

Buesa, M., Heijs, J., Martínez Pellitero, M. & Baumert, T. (2006). Regional systems of innovation and the knowledge production function: The Spanish case. *Technovation*, 26(4), 463–472.

Bullock, R.H., Salzberg, A. & Jin, Y. (2012). *High-Speed Rail-The First Three Years: Taking the Pulse of China's Emerging Program*. China Transport Topics No. 2. World Bank.

Burt, R.S. (2005). *Brokerage and Closure: An Introduction to Social Capital*. New York: Oxford University Press.

Busse, T.V. & Mansfield, R.S. (1984). Selected personality traits and achievement in male scientists. *Journal of Psychology: Interdisciplinary & Applied*, 116(1), 117–131.

Cadien, N. (1980). Budgeting in poor countries: Ten common assumptions re-examined. *Public Administration Review*, 40(1), 40–46.

Caixin. (2012). A professor at Beijing University of Chemical Technology has been fired for embezzling other people's papers (in Chinese). Available at https://china.caixin.com/2012-07-29/100416446.html (assessed February 23, 2022).

Cao, C. (2008). China's brain drain at the high end: Why government policies have failed to attract first-rate academics to return. *Asian Population Studies*, 4(3), 331–345.

Cao, C. (2014). The universal values of science and China's Nobel Prize pursuit. *Minerva*, 52(2), 141–160.

Cao, C., Baas, J., Wagner, C.S. & Jonkers, K. (2020). Returning scientists and the emergence of Chinese science system. *Science and Public Policy*, 47(2), 172–183.

Cao, C., Li, N., Li, X. & Liu, L. (2013). Reforming China's S&T system. *Science*, 341(6145), 460–462.

Cao, C. & Simon, D.F. (2021). China's talent challenges revisited. In E. Baark, B. Hofman, & J. Qian, eds. *Innovation and China's Global Emergence*. Singapore: National University of Singapore Press, pp. 90–112.

Cao, C., Simon, D.F. & Suttmeier, R.P. (2009). China's innovation challenge. *Innovation: Management, Policy & Practice*, 11(2), 253–259.

Cao, C. & Suttmeier, R.P. (2001). China's new scientific elite: Distinguished young scientists, the research environment, and hopes for Chinese science. *The China Quarterly*, 168, 960–984.

Cao, C. & Suttmeier, R.P. (2017). Challenges of S&T system reform in China. *Science*, 355(6329), 1019–1021.

Cao, C., Suttmeier, R.P. & Simon, D.F. (2006). China's 15-year science and technology plan. *Physics Today*, 59(12), 38–43.

Cervantes, M. & Guellec, D. (2002). The brain drain: Old myths, new realities. *OECD Observer*, 4(230), 40–42.

Chang, P.L. & Shih, H.Y. (2004). The innovation systems of Taiwan and China: A comparative analysis. *Technovation*, 24(7), 529–539.

Chen, Z. (2009). A brief history of China's Y-10: Imitation versus innovation. *Technology in Society*, 31(4), 414–418.

Chen, L., & Naughton, B. (2016). An institutionalized policy-making mechanism: China's return to techno-industrial policy, *Research Policy*, 45(10), 2138–2152.

Cheung, T.M. (2013). The Chinese Defense Economy Takes Off: Sector-By-Sector Assessments and the Role of Military End-Users. The University of California Institute on Global Conflict and Cooperation. Available at http://igcc.ucsd.edu/assets/001/504355.pdf (accessed December 3, 2021).

Chiang, J.T. (1991). From 'mission-oriented' to 'diffusion-oriented' paradigm: The new trend of US industrial technology policy. *Technovation*, 11(6), 356–339.

China's National Center for Science and Technology Evaluation (CNCSTE). (2021). *The Annual Performance Evaluation Report of NSFC in 2020* (in Chinese). Available at www.nsfc.gov.cn/Portals/0/fj/fj20210525_01 .pdf (accessed May 3, 2022).

Chinese Academy of Science, ed. (2012). *The Successful Practice of the National Innovation System Construction with Chinese Characteristics: An Assessment Report of Knowledge Innovation Program (in Chinese)*. Beijing: Science Press.

Chinese Central Government's DAR. (2012). Available at www.gov.cn/ gzdt/201207/11/content_2181165.htm (assessed on February 23, 2013).

Clark, N. (1985). *The Political Economy of Science and Technology*. Oxford: Blackwell.

Coase, R. & Wang, N. (2012). *How China Became Capitalist*. New York: Palgrave Macmillan.

Coe, N.M. & Bunnell, T.G. (2003). Spatializing knowledge communities: Towards a conceptualization of transnational innovation networks. *Global Networks*, 3(4), 437–456.

Commander, S., Kangasniemi, M. & Winters, L.A. (2004). The brain drain: Curse or boon? A survey of the literature. In R.E. Baldwin & R.E. Winters, eds. *Challenges to Globalization: Analyzing the Economics*. Chicago, IL: University of Chicago Press, pp. 235–278.

Communist Party of China's Central Committee and the State Council. (2016). *Outline of the Innovation-Driven Development Strategy* (in Chinese). Available at www.gov.cn/zhengce/2016-05/19/content_5074812 .htm(accessed August 30, 2022).

Compston, H. (2009). *Policy Networks and Policy Change: Putting Policy Network Theory to the Test*. Basingstoke: Palgrave Macmillan.

Congleton, R.D. (1992). Political institutions and pollution control. *Review of Economics and Statistic*, 74(3), 412–421.

Cross, M. (1989). Japan's fifth generation computer project successes and failures. *Futures*, 21(4), 401–403.

Dai, S. & Taube, M., eds. (2019). *China's Quest for Innovation: Institutions and Ecosystems*. London and New York: Routledge.

Datta-Chaudhuri, M. (1990). Market failure and government failure. *Journal of Economic Perspectives*, 4(3), 25–39.

David, P.A., Hall, B.H. & Toole, A.A. (2000). Is public R&D a complement or substitute for private R&D? A review of the econometric evidence. *Research policy*, 29(4–5), 497–529.

De Schutter, O. (2019). The political economy approach to food systems reform. In J. Harris, M. Anderson, C. Clément, & N. Nisbett, eds. *The Political Economy of Food*. IDS Bulletin 50.2. Brighton: Institute of Development Studies, pp. 13–26.

Dedrick, J., Tang, J. & Kraemer, K.L. (2012) China's indigenous innovation policy: Impact on multi-national R&D, *Computer*, 45, 70–78.

Dobrev, S.D. & Barnett, W.P. (2005). Organizational roles and transition to entrepreneurship. *Academy of Management Journal*, 48(3), 433–449.

Docquier, F., Marfouk, A., Salomone, S. & Sekkat, K. (2012). Are skilled women more migratory than skilled men? *World Development*, 40(2), 251–265.

Dolfsma, W. & Seo, D.B. (2013). Government policy and technological innovation-a suggested typology. *Technovation*, 33(6–7), 173–179.

Dolla, V.S. (2015). *Science and Technology in Contemporary China: Interrogating Policies and Progress*. Cambridge and New Delhi: Cambridge University Press.

Dowding, K. (1995). Model or metaphor? A critical review of the policy network approach. *Political Studies*, 43(1), 136–158.

Dustmann, C. (1996). Return migration: The European experience. *Economic Policy*, 11(22), 213–250.

Dustmann, C., Fadlon, I. & Weiss, Y. (2011). Return migration, human capital accumulation and the brain drain. *Journal of Development Economics*, 95(1), 58–67.

Eberhardt, M., Helmers, C., Yu, Z.H. (2017). What can explain the Chinese patent explosion? *Oxford Economic Papers*, 69(1), 239–262.

Eisenhardt, K.M. (1989). Building theories from case study research. *Academy of Management Review*, 14(4), 532–550.

Ergas, H. (1987). *Does Technology Policy Matter? Technology and Global industry: Companies and Nations in the World Economy*. Washington, DC: The National Academies Press.

European Commission. (2000). *Innovation Policy in a Knowledge-Based Economy*. Luxembourg: European Commission. Available at http://ftp .cordis.lu/pub/innovation-policy/studies/studies_knowledge_based_ economy.pdf (accessed December 3, 2021).

Fang, X. (2010). Re-examining the reform of China's science and technology system: A historical perspective. *Journal of Science and Technology Policy in China*, 1(1), 7–17.

Fang, J.Q. (2015). Survival analysis. In M. Gail & J.M. Samet, eds. *Statistics for Biology & Health*. New York: Springer, pp. 211–220.

Flanagan, K., Uyarra, E. & Laranja, M. (2011). Reconceptualising the "policy mix" for innovation. *Research Policy*, 40(5), 702–713.

Foray, D., Mowery, D.C. & Nelson, R.R. (2012). Public R&D and social challenges: What lessons from mission R&D programs? *Research Policy*, 41(10), 1697–1702.

Foreman-Peck, J. & Federico, G. (1999). *European Industrial Policy: The Twentieth-Century Experience*. New York: Oxford University Press.

Freeman, C. (1987). *Technology Policy and Economic Performance: Lessons from Japan*. London: Pinter.

Freeman, L.C. (1979). Centrality in social networks conceptual clarification, *Social Networks*, 1(3), 215–239.

Freeman, C. & C. Perez. (1988). Structural crisis of adjustment, business cycles and investment behavior. In G. Dosi, C. Freeman, R. Nelson, G. Silverberg, & L. Soete, eds. *Technical Change and Economic Theory*. London: Pinter, pp. 38–66.

Freeman, L.C., White, D.R. & Romney, A.K., eds. (1989). *Research Methods in Social Network Analysis*. Fairfax, VA: George Mason University Press.

Freeman, C. (1995). The "National System of Innovation" in historical perspective. *Cambridge Journal of Economics*, 19(1), 5–24.

Fu, X., Pietrobelli, C. & Soete, L. (2011). The role of foreign technology and indigenous innovation in the emerging economies: technological change and catching-up. *World Development*, 39(7), 1204–1212.

Fu, X., McKern, B. and Chen, J. eds. (2021). *Oxford Handbook of China Innovation*, Oxford: Oxford University Press.

Fuchs, E.R. (2010). Rethinking the role of the state in technology development: DARPA and the case for embedded network governance. *Research Policy*, 39(9), 1133–1147.

Fuller, D.B. (2016). *Paper Tigers, Hidden Dragons: Firms and the Political Economy of China's Technological Development*. Oxford: Oxford University Press.

Gaillard, J. & Gaillard, A.M. (1997). Introduction: The international mobility of brains: exodus or circulation? *Science Technology and Society*, 2(2), 195–228.

Gao, X. (2014). A latecomer's strategy to promote a technology standard: The case of Datang and TD-SCDMA. *Research Policy*, 43(3), 597–607.

Gaughan, M. (2009). Using the curriculum vitae for policy research: An evaluation of National Institutes of Health center and training support on career trajectories. *Research Evaluation*, 18(2), 117–124.

Gaughan, M. & Robin, S. (2004). National science training policy and early scientific careers in France and the United States. *Research Policy*, 33(4), 56–581.

Giesecke, S. (2000). The contrasting roles of government in the development of biotechnology industry in the US and Germany. *Research policy*, 29(2), 205–223.

Gosling F.G. (2005). *The Manhattan Project: Making the Atomic Bomb*. Stockton, CA: University Press of the Pacific.

Griliches, Z. (1990). Patent statistics as economic indicators: A survey. *Journal of Economic Literature*, 28(4), 1661–1707.

Grimes, S. & Sun, Y. (2014). Implications of China's on-going dependence on foreign technology. *Geoforum*, 54(7), 59–69.

Guan, J. & Yan, Y. (2016). Technological proximity and recombinative innovation in the alternative energy field. *Research Policy*, 45(7), 1460–1473.

Gulati, R. & Gargiulo, M. (1999). Where do interorganizational networks come from? *American Journal of Sociology*, 104(5), 1439–1493.

Haapanen, M., Lenihan, H. & Mariani, M. (2014). Government policy failure in public support for research and development. *Policy Studies*, 35(6), 557–575.

Hall, A. & Clack, N. (2010). What do complex adoptive systems look like and what are the implications for innovation policy. *Journal of International Development*, 22(3), 308–324.

Hall, P. & Taylor, R. (1996). Political science and the three new institutionalisms. *Political Studies*, 44(5), 936–957.

Hao, X. (2009). Help wanted: 2000 leading lights to inject a spirit of innovation. *Science*, 325(5940), 534–535.

Hao, X. (2011). High-priced recruiting of talent abroad raises hackles. *Science*, 331(6019), 834–835.

Hays, S.P. & Glick, H.R. (1997). The role of agenda setting in policy innovation: An event history analysis of living-will laws. *American Politics Quarterly*, 25(4), 497–516.

Hekkert, M.P., Suurs, R.A.A., Negro, S.O., Kuhlmann, S. & Smits, R.E.H.M. (2007). Functions of innovation systems: A new approach for analysing technological change. *Technological Forecasting and Social Change*, 74(4), 413–432.

Helpman, E. (1998). *General Purpose Technologies and Economic Growth*. Cambridge, MA: MIT Press.

Henderson, J. & Appelbaum, R.P. (1992). Situating the state in the East Asian development process. In R.P. Appelbaum & J. Henderson, eds. *States and Development in the Asian Pacific Rim*. London: Sage Publications, pp. 1–26.

Hewlett, R.G & Anderson, O.E. (1962). *A History of the United States Atomic Energy Commission: The New World, 1939–1946*. University Park, PA: The Pennsylvania State University Press.

Hitch, C.J. & McKean, R.N. (1960). *The Economics of Defense in the Nuclear Age*. Santa Monica, CA: RAND Corporation.

Hobday, M. (1994). Export-led technology development in the four dragons: The case of electronics. *Development and Change*, 25(2), 333–361.

Hsu, D.H., Roberts, E.B. & Eesley, C.E. (2007). Entrepreneurs from technology-based universities: Evidence from MIT. *Research Policy*, 36(5), 768–788.

Hu, A.G. (2001). Ownership, government R&D, private R&D, and productivity in Chinese industry. *Journal of Comparative Economics*, 29(1), 136–157.

Hu, M.C. & Mathews, J.A. (2005). National innovative capacity in East Asia. *Research Policy*, 34(9), 1322–1349.

Huang, C., Amorim, C., Spinoglio, M., Gouveia, B. & Medina, A. (2004). Organization, programme and structure: An analysis of the Chinese innovation policy framework. *R&D Management*, 34(4), 367–387.

Huang, C. & Sharif, N. (2016). Global technology leadership: The case of China. *Science and Public Policy*, 43(1), 62–73.

Ibata-Arens, K. (2003). The comparative political economy of innovation. *Review of International Political Economy*, 10(1), 147–165.

Ja, H. (2012). The special funding policy for the MEPs of new drugs will be changed. Available at news.sciencenet.cn/htmlnews//2009/8/222552 .shtm (accessed on December 12, 2012).

Jacobs, A. (2011). *Governing for the Long-Term: Democracy and the Politics of Investment*. Cambridge: Cambridge University Press.

Jakobson, L. (2007). *Innovation with Chinese Characteristics: High-Tech Research in China*, Hampshire: Palgrave Macmillan.

James, H. (2008). Avoiding another AI winter. *IEEE Intelligent Systems*, 23(2), 2–4.

Jansen, J.J.P., Van Den Bosch, F.A.J. & Volberda, H.W. (2006). Exploratory innovation, exploitative innovation, and performance: Effects of organizational antecedents and environmental moderators. *Management science*, 52(11), 1661–1674.

JASON (2019). *Fundamental Research Security*. McLean, VA: The MITRE Corporation.

Jia, K., *et al.* (2006). *Research on Science & Technology Expenditure and Its Management Model (in Chinese)*, Beijing: China Financial & Economic Publishing House.

Jia, N (2012). A new chapter on the spectrum of indigenous innovation (in Chinese). Available at www.stats.gov.cn/tjfx/grgd/t20121025_402845413 .htm (accessed November 12, 2012).

Johnson, C. (1982). *MITI and the Japanese Miracle: The Growth of Industrial Policy, 1925–1975*. Stanford, CA: Stanford University Press.

Jones, V.C. (1985). *Manhattan: The Army and the Atomic Bomb*. Washington, DC: United States Army Center of Military History.

Kayser, V., Blind, K. (2017). Extending the knowledge base of foresight: The contribution of text mining. *Technological Forecasting and Social Change*. 116(3), 208–215.

Kapur, D. (2010). *Diaspora, Development, and Democracy: The Domestic Impact of International Migration from India*, Princeton, NJ: Princeton University Press.

Kenis, P. & Schneider, V. (1991). Policy networks and policy analysis: Scrutinizing a new analytical toolbox. In B. Marin & R. Mayntz, eds. *Policy*

Networks: Empirical Evidence and Theoretical Considerations. Frankfurt am Main, Germany: Campus Verlag, pp. 25–59.

Kennedy, S. (2005). *The Business of Lobbying in China*, Cambridge, MA: Harvard University Press.

Kennedy, S., Suttmeier, R.P. & Su, J. (2008). *Standards, Stakeholders, and Innovation: China's Evolving Role in the Global Knowledge Economy.* Seattle, WA: National Bureau of Asian Research.

Keynes, J.M. (1936). *The General Theory of Employment, Interest and Money.* London: Macmillan.

Kim, H. & Song, J. (2013). Social network analysis of patent infringement lawsuits. *Technological Forecasting and Social Change*, 80(5), 944–955.

Klijn, E. (1996). Analyzing and managing policy processes in complex networks: A theoretical examination of the concepts policy networks and its problems. *Administration & Society*, 28(1), 90–119.

Klijn, E., Koppenjan, J. (2012). Governance network theory: past, present and future. *Policy & Politics*, 40(4), 587–606.

Knell, M. (2018). *Friedrich List and the American system of innovation.* In *The Economic Thought of Friedrich List.* New York & London: Routledge, pp. 179–197.

Kolata, G. (2009). Playing it safe in cancer research. *The New York Times*, June 28, pp. A1 & A18.

Krueger, A.O. (1990). Government failures in development. *Journal of Economic perspectives*, 4(3), 9–23.

Kuhlmann, S. (2001). Future governance of innovation policy in Europe: Three scenarios. *Research Policy*, 30(6), 953–976.

Kvint, V. (2009). *The Global Emerging Market: Strategic Management and Economics.* New York and London: Routledge.

Lanahana, L. & Feldman, M.P. (2015). Multilevel innovation policy mix: A closer look at state policies that augment the federal SBIR program. *Research Policy*, 44(7), 1387–1402.

Lee, Y., Lee, I.W. & Feiock, R.C. (2012). Interorganizational collaboration networks in economic development policy: An exponential random graph model analysis. *Policy Studies Journal*, 40(3), 547–573.

Lei R. & Qiu R. (2020). Chinese Bioethicists: He Jiankui's crime is more than illegal medical practice. Available at www.thehastingscenter.org/chinese-bioethicists-he-jiankuis-crime-is-more-than-illegal-medical-practice/ (accessed December 3, 2021).

Lempert, R.J, Popper, S.W., Min, E.Y., Dewar, J.A., Light, P.C., Pritchett, L. & Treverton, G.F. (2009). *Shaping Tomorrow Today: Near-Term Steps Towards Long-Term Goals*, Santa Monica, CA: RAND Corporation. Available at https://eric.ed.gov/?id=ED506396 (accessed December 3, 2021).

Levi-Faur, D. (1997). Friedrich List and the Political Economy of the Nation-State. *Review of International Political Economy*, 4(1), 154–178.

Lewis, J.M. (2011). The future of network governance research: Strength in diversity and synthesis. *Public Administration*, 89(4), 1221–1234.

Lieberthal, K. & Oksenberg, M. (1988). *Policy Making in China: Leaders, Structures, and Processes*. Princeton, NJ: Princeton University Press.

Lindtner, S.M. (2020). *Prototype Nation: China and the Contested Promise of Innovation*. Princeton, NJ: Princeton University Press.

List, F. (1841 [2005]). *National System of Political Economy*, New York: Cosimo.

Liu, S. & Li, l. (2002). Current practice of statistics on China's government R&D investment and suggestion for improvement (in Chinese). *Forum on Science and Technology in China*, 5, 56–61.

Liu, F., Simon, D., Sun, Y. & Cao, C. (2011). China's innovation policies: Evolution, institutional structure, and trajectory. *Research Policy*, 40(7), 917–931.

Liu, X. & White, S. (2001). Comparing innovation systems: A framework and application to China's transitional context. *Research Policy*, 30(7), 1091–1114.

Lundvall, B.-Å. ed. (1992). *National Systems of Innovation: Towards a Theory of Innovation and Interactive Learning*, London: Pinter.

Lundvall, B.-Å. & Borrás, S. (2005). Science, technology, and innovation policy. In J. Fagerberg, D.C. Mowery & R.R. Nelson, eds. *The Oxford Handbook of Innovation*. Oxford: Oxford University Press, pp. 599–631.

Ma, J. & Yu, L. (2007). A study on the core budget office in China: A case study of a metropolitan government in central China (in Chinese). *Journal of Huazhong Normal University (Humanities and Social Sciences)*, 46(2), 17–25.

Mahdjoubi, D. (1997). Non-linear models of technological innovation: Background and taxonomy. Available at www.ischool.utexas.edu/~darius/04-Linear%20Model.pdf.

Mahroum, S. (2000). Highly skilled globetrotters: Mapping the international migration of human capital. *R&D Management*, 30(1), 23–32.

Martin, B.R. & Nightingale, P. eds. (2000). *The Political Economy of Science, Technology and Innovation*. Cheltenham: Edward Elgar Publishing.

Masiello, B., Izzo, F. & Canoro, C. (2015). The structural, relational and cognitive configuration of innovation networks between SMEs and public research organisations. *International Small Business Journal*, 33(2), 169–193.

Massey, D.S., Arango, J., Hugo, G., Kouaouci, A., Pellegrino, A. & Taylor, J.E. (1993). Theories of international migration: A review and appraisal. *Population and Development Review*, 19(3), 431–466.

Mathews, J.A. (2002). The origins and dynamics of Taiwan's R&D consortia. *Research Policy*, 31(4), 633–651.

Mazzucato, M. (2013). *The Entrepreneurial State: Debunking the Public vs. Private Myth in Risk and Innovation*, London: Anthem Press.

Mazzucato, M. (2018). Mission-oriented innovation policies: Challenges and opportunities. *Industrial and Corporate Change*, 27(5), 803–815.

McGregor, J. (2010). *China's Drive for "Indigenous Innovation": A Web of Industrial Policies*. Washington, DC: US Chamber of Commerce.

Medeiros, E.S., Cliff, R., Crane, K. & Mulvenon, J.C. (2005). *A New Direction for China's Defense Industry*. Santa Monica, CA: RAND Corporation. Available at www.dtic.mil/dtic/tr/fulltext/u2/a449324.pdf (accessed December 3, 2021).

Meng, W., Hu, Z. & Liu, W. (2006). Efficiency evaluation of basic research in China. *Scientometrics*, 69(1), 85–101.

Meyer, J.B., Kaplan, D. & Charum, J. (2001). Scientific nomadism and the new geopolitics of knowledge. *International Social Science Journal*, 53(168), 309–321.

Min, Q. (2014). China mobile's dead end on the 3G Highway. Available at http://english.caixin.com/2014-12-15/100762382.html (accessed December 3, 2021).

Ministry of Finance (MOF). (2007). Administrative measures on the project expenditure budget at the central level (in Chinese). Available at http://yss.mof.gov.cn/zhengwuxinxi/zhengceguizhang/200805/t20080522_33871.html (accessed December 3, 2021).

Ministry of Education (MOE). (2021). Number of students in higher education institutions (in Chinese). Available at (accessed August 30, 2022).

Ministry of Science and Technology (MOST). (2009). A compilation of policy implementation details accompanying the medium- and long-term plan for the development of science and technology (2006–2020) (in Chinese). Available at www.most.gov.cn/ztzl/gjzctx/index.htm (accessed December 3, 2021).

Ministry of Science and Technology (MOST). (2009). *China Science and Technology Indicators 2008 (in Chinese)*. Beijing: Scientific and Technical Documentation Press.

Ministry of Science and Technology (MOST). (2010). *China Science and Technology Development Report 2010* (in Chinese). Available at www.most.gov.cn/kjfz/kjxz/ (accessed December 3, 2021).

Ministry of Science and Technology (MOST). (2011). *Annual Report of the National Programs of Science and Technology Development 2011* (in Chinese). Available at www.most.gov.cn/ndbg/ (accessed December 3, 2021).

Ministry of Science and Technology (MOST). (2011). *China Science and Technology Indicators 2010 (in Chinese)*. Beijing: Scientific and Technical Documentation Press.

Ministry of Science and Technology (MOST). (2012). *Annual Report of the National Programs of Science and Technology Development 2012* (in Chinese). Available at www.most.gov.cn/ndbg/ (accessed December 3, 2021).

Ministry of Science and Technology (MOST) and National Bureau of Statistics of China (NBS). (Various years). *China Statistical Yearbook on Science and Technology*. Beijing: National Statistics Press.

Mintzberg, H. & Waters, J.A. (1985). Of strategies, deliberate and emergent. *Strategic Management Journal*, 6(3), 257–272.

Morano-Foadi, S. (2005). Scientific mobility, career progression, and excellence in the European research area. *International Migration*, 43(5), 133–162.

Morlacchi, P. & Martin, B.R. (2009). Emerging challenges for science, technology and innovation policy research: A reflexive overview. *Research Policy*, 38(4), 571–582.

Mowery, D.C. (2009). Plus ca change: Industrial R&D in the "Third Industrial Revolution." *Industrial and Corporate Change*, 18(1), 1–50.

Mowery, D.C. (2012). Defense-related R&D as a model for "Grand Challenges" technology policies. *Research Policy*, 41(10), 1703–1715.

Mowery, D.C. & Nelson, R.R., eds. (1999). *Sources of Industrial Leadership: Studies of Seven Industries*, Cambridge and New York: Cambridge University Press.

Mowery, D.C., Nelson, R.R. & Martin, B.R. (2010). Technology policy and global warming: Why new policy models are needed (or why putting new wine in old bottles won't work). *Research Policy*, 39(8), 1011–1023.

National Bureau of Statistics (NBS) & Ministry of Science and Technology (MOST). (2009). *2008 China Statistical Yearbook on Science and Technology*. Beijing: China Statistics Press.

National Bureau of Statistics (NBS), Ministry of Science and Technology (MOST) & Ministry of Finance (MOF). (2012). Statistical bulletin of national S&T expenditures in 2011 (in Chinese). Available at www.stats.gov.cn/tjgb/rdpcgb/qgrdpcgb/t20121025_402845404.html (accessed December 3, 2021).

National Bureau of Statistics of China (NBS) (comp.). (2021). *2021 China Statistical Yearbook*. Beijing: China Statistics Press.

National Bureau of Statistics of China (NBS). (2022). Statistical communiqué of the People's Republic of China on national economic and social development in 2021 (in Chinese). Available at www.gov.cn/xinwen/2022-02/28/content_5676015.htm (accessed July 15, 2022).

National Natural Science Foundation of China (NSFC). (2012). *International Evaluation of Funding and Management of the National Natural Science Foundation of China*. Available at www.nsfc.gov.cn/english/03re/ index.html (accessed December 3, 2021).

National Science Board (NSB). (2020). *Science & Engineering Indicators 2020*. Available at https://ncses.nsf.gov/pubs/nsb20201 (accessed December 3, 2021).

National Science Board (NSB). (2023). Chief Statistician Li Ying of the Department of Society, Science and Technology, and Cultural Industries, National Bureau of Statistics, Interprets Data on R&D Expenditure (in Chinese). Available at: www.stats.gov.cn/tjsj/sjjd/202301/ t20230119_1892374.html (accessed February 19, 2023).

National Science Board (NSB) & National Science Foundation (NSF). (2022). Research and Development: U.S. Trends and International Comparisons. *Science and Engineering Indicators 2022*. NSB-2022-5. Alexandria, VA. Available at https://ncses.nsf.gov/pubs/nsb20225/ (accessed August 30, 2022).

Naughton, B. (2009). China's emergence from economic crisis. *China Leadership Monitor*, 29. Available at http://media.hoover.org/documents/ CLM29BN.pdf (accessed December 3, 2021).

Naughton, B. (2021). *The Rise of China's Industrial Policy, 1978 To 2020*. Available at https://dusselpeters.com/CECHIMEX/Naughton2021_Industrial_ Policy_in_China_CECHIMEX.pdf (accessed December 3, 2021).

Neal, H.A., Smith, T.L. & McCormick, J.B. (2008). *Beyond Sputnik: U.S. Science Policy in the 21st Century*. Ann Arbor, MI: University of Michigan Press.

Nelson, R.R. (1959). The simple economics of basic scientific research. *Journal of Political Economy*, 67(3), 297–306.

Nelson, R.R., ed. (1993). *National Innovation Systems: A Comparative Analysis*. Oxford: Oxford University Press.

Neven, D. & Seabright, P. (1995). European industrial policy: The Airbus case. *Economic policy*, 10(21), 313–358.

Nielsen, J. (1988). *Fifth Generation 1988 Trip Report*. Oxford: Nielsen Norman Group. Available at www.nngroup.com/articles/trip-report-fifth-generation/ (accessed December 3, 2021).

Nolan, C.J. (2002). *The Greenwood Encyclopaedia of International Relations*. Westport, CT: The Greenwood Press.

Obama, B. (2016). *State of the Union 2016*. Available at http://edition.cnn .com/2016/01/12/politics/state-of-the-union-2016-transcript-full-text/ index.html (accessed December 3, 2021).

Office of Scientific Research and Development (OSRD) US. (1945). *Science, the Endless Frontier: A Report to the President*. Ann Arbor, MI: University of Michigan Library.

Office of the Under Secretary of Defense (OUSD). (1990). *VHSIC Final Program Report (1980–1990)*. Available at http://oai.dtic.mil/oai/oai?ve rb=getRecord&metadataPrefix=html&identifier=ADA230012. (accessed December 3, 2021).

Okimoto, D.I. (1989). *Between MITI and the Market: Japanese Industrial Policy for High Technology*. Stanford, CA: Stanford University Press.

Organization for Economic Cooperation and Development (OECD). (1997). *National Innovation Systems*. Paris: OECD Publishing.

Organization for Economic Cooperation and Development (OECD). (2002). *Frascati Manual*. Paris: OECD Press.

Organization for Economic Cooperation and Development (OECD). (2005). *China in Global Economy: Governance in China*. Paris: OECD.

Organization for Economic Cooperation and Development (OECD). (2008). *OECD Reviews of Innovation Policy: China*. Paris: OECD.

Organization for Economic Cooperation and Development (OECD). (2013). *OECD Science, Technology and Industry Scoreboard 2013: Innovation for Growth*, Paris: OECD.

Organization for Economic Cooperation and Development (OECD). (2015). *Frascati Manual 2015 – Guidelines for Collecting and Reporting Data on Research and Experimental Development*. Paris: OECD. Available at www.oecd.org/sti/inno/Frascati-Manual.htm (accessed December 3, 2021).

Organization for Economic Cooperation and Development (OECD). (2022). *Main Science and Technology Indicators*. www.oecd.org/sti/msti .htm (accessed August 30, 2022).

Ostry, S. & Nelson, R.R. (1995). *Techno-Nationalism and Techno-Globalism: Conflict and Cooperation*. Washington, DC: Brookings Institution Press.

Pan, S.Y. (2010). Changes and challenges in the flow of international human capital: China's experience. *Journal of Studies in International Education*, 14(3), 259–288.

Party Literature Research Office (PLRO) & the Central Committee of the Communist Party of China (CC CPC). (2004). *A Chronicle of Deng Xiaopeng's Life (1975–1997) (in Chinese)*. Beijing: The Central Literature Press.

Pavitt, K. & Walker, W. (1976). Government policies towards industrial innovation: A review. *Research policy*, 5(1), 11–97.

Perelman, M. (1978). Karl Marx's theory of science. *Journal of Economic Issues*, 12(4), 859–870.

Pierson, P. (2000). Increasing returns, path dependence, and the study of politics. *American Political Science Review*, 94(2), 251–267.

Popper, K. (2002). *The Logic of Scientific Discovery*, New York: Routledge.

Powell, W.W., Koput, K.W. & Smith-Doerr, L. (1996). Interorganizational collaboration and the locus of innovation: Networks of learning in biotechnology. *Administrative Science Quarterly*, 41(1), 116–145.

Qiu, J. (2009). China targets top talent from overseas. *Nature*, 457(7229), 522.

Research Department of the Ministry of Science and Technology (MOST) & General Office and the Chinese Academy of Science and Technology for Development (CASTED). (2006). *Analysis and Study of National Policies Promoting Indigenous Innovation (1980–2005)* (in Chinese).

Rockett, K. (2010). Property rights and invention. In B.H. Hall & N. Rosenberg, eds. *Handbook of the Economics of Innovation*. Amsterdam, The Netherland: North-Holland, vol. 1, pp. 315–380.

Rhodes, R.A.W. (2006). Policy network analysis. In M. Moran, M. Rein, R.E. Goodin, eds. *The Oxford Handbook of Public Policy*. Oxford: Oxford University Press, pp. 423–445.

Rhodes, R.A.W. (2013). How to manage your policy network. *Discussion Paper Prepared for the Commonwealth Secretariat*. Available online at www.raw-rhodes.co.uk/wp-content/uploads/2013/07/Com-Sec-2013-v2 .pdf (accessed December 3, 2021).

Robins, G., Lewis, M.J. & Wang, P. (2012). Statistical network analysis for analyzing policy networks. *The Policy Studies Journal*, 40 (3), 375–400.

Romer, P.M. (1990). Endogenous technological change. *Journal of Political Economy*, 98(5), 71–102.

Romer, P.M. (2000). Should the government subsidize supply or the demand in the market for scientists and engineers? *Innovation Policy and the Economy*, 1, 221–252.

SASAC. (2021). Text record of the press conference on the economic operation of central enterprises in 2021 (in Chinese). Available at www .sasac.gov.cn/n2588020/n2877938/n2879597/n2879599/c22813392/ content.html (accessed May 5, 2022).

Sagasti, F. (1989). Science and technology policy research for development: An overview and some priorities from a Latin American perspective. *Bulletin of Science, Technology & Society*, 9(1), 50–60.

Sakakibara, K. (1983). *From Imitation to Innovation: The Very Large Scale Integrated (VLSI) Semiconductor Project in Japan*. Cambridge, MA: Massachusetts Institute of Technology.

Sampat, B.N. (2012). Mission-oriented biomedical research at the NIH. *Research Policy*, 41(10), 1729–1741.

Sandström, A. & Carlsson, L. (2008). The performance of policy networks: The relation between network structure and network performance. *The Policy Studies Journal*, 36(4), 497–520.

Sarewitz, D. (2016). Saving science. *The New Atlantis*, 49(1), 4–40.

Saxenian, A.L. (2005). From Brain Drain to Brain Circulation: Transnational Communities and Regional Upgrading in India and China. *Studies in Comparative International Development*, 40(2), 35–61.

Scharpf, F.W. (1997). *Games Real Actors Play, Actor-Centered Institutionalism in Policy Research*. Boulder, CO: Westview Press.

Schumpeter, J.A. (1939). *Business Cycles: A Theoretical, Historical, and Statistical Analysis of the Capitalist Process*. New York: McGraw-Hill.

Serger, S.S. & Breidne, M. (2007). China's fifteen-year plan for science and technology: An assessment. *Asia Policy*, 4(1), 135–164.

Shi, D., Liu, W., & Wang, Y. (2023). Has China's Young Thousand Talents program been successful in recruiting and nurturing top-caliber scientists? *Science*, 379(6627), 62–65.

Shi, Y. & Rao, Y. (2010). China's research culture. *Science*, 329(5996), 1128.

Simon, D.F. & Cao, C. (2009). *China's Emerging Technological Edge Assessing the Role of High-End Talent*. New York: Cambridge University Press.

Simon, D.F. & Cao, C. (2012). Examining China's science and technology statistics: A systematic perspective. *Journal of Science and Technology Policy in China*, 3(1), 26–48.

Smith, A. (1776 [1999]). *The Wealth of Nations*, New York: Penguin Books.

Snijders, T.A.B., van de Bunt, G.G. & Steglich, C. (2010). Introduction to actor-based models for network dynamics. *Social Networks*, 32(1), 44–60.

Soete, L., B. Verspagen, & B.R. Weel. (2010). Systems of innovation. In B.H. Hall and N. Rosenberg, eds. *Handbook of the Economics of Innovation*, Amsterdam: North-Holland, vol. 2, pp. 1159–1180.

Solow, R. (1956). A contribution to the theory of economic growth. *Quarterly Journal of Economics*, 70, 65–94.

Sørensen, E. & Torfing, J., eds. (2007). *Theories of Democratic Network Governance*. Basingstoke: Palgrave Macmillan.

Spector, R. (2010). The War on Cancer: A progress report for skeptics. *Skeptical Inquirer*, 34(1), 25–31. Available at www.csicop.org/si/show/war_on_cancer_a_progress_report_for_skeptics (accessed December 3, 2021).

Stark, O. (2004). Rethinking the brain drain. *World Development*, 32(1), 15–22.

Stark, O., Helmenstein, C. & Prskawetz, A. (1997). A brain gain with a brain drain. *Economics Letters*, 55(2), 227–234.

Stark, O., Helmenstein, C. & Prskawetz, A. (1998). Human capital depletion, human capital formation, and migration: A blessing or a "curse"? *Economics Letters*, 60(3), 363–367.

Stephan, P.E. (2012). *How Economics Shapes Science*. Cambridge, MA: Harvard University Press.

Stuart, T. & Wang, Y. (2016). Who cooks the books in China, and does it pay? Evidence from private, high-technology firms. *Strategic Management Journal*, 37(13), 2658–2676.

Sun, Z. (2012). More than five billion RMB has been spent on the MEPs of developing new drugs. Available at news.sciencenet.cn/html-news//2009/5/218970.html (accessed on December 12, 2012).

Sun, Y. & Cao, C. (2014). Demystifying central government R&D spending in China: Should funding focus on scientific research? *Science*, 345(6200), 1006–1008.

Sun, Y. & Cao, C. (2015). Intra-and inter-regional research collaboration across organizational boundaries: Evolving patterns in China. *Technological Forecasting and Social Change*, 96, 215–231.

Sun, Y. & Cao, C. (2016). China: Standardize R&D costing. *Nature*, 536(7614), 30.

Sun, Y. & Cao, C. (2020). The dynamics of the studies of China's science, technology and innovation (STI): A bibliometric analysis of an emerging field. *Scientometrics*, 124(2), 1335–1365.

Sun, Y. & Cao, C. (2021). Planning for science: China's "grand experiment" and global implications. *Humanities and Social Sciences Communications*, 8(1), 215.

Sun, Y. & Grimes, S. (2016). The emerging dynamic structure of national innovation studies: A bibliometric analysis. *Scientometrics*, 106(1), 17–40.

Sun, Y. & Grimes, S. (2018). *China and Global Value Chains: Globalization and the Information and Communications Technology Sector*. London and New York: Routledge.

Sun, Y., Guo, R. & Zhang, S. (2017). China's brain gain at the high end: An assessment of Thousand Youth Talents Program. *Asian Journal of Innovation and Policy*, 6(3), 274–294.

Sun, Y. & Liu, F. (2010). A regional perspective on the structural transformation of China's national innovation system since 1999. *Technological Forecasting and Social Change*, 77(8), 1311–1321.

Sun, Y. & Liu, F. (2014). New trends in Chinese innovation policies since 2009: A system framework of policy analysis. *International Journal of Technology Management*, 65(1–4), 6–23.

Sun, Y. & Liu, K. (2016). Proximity effect, preferential attachment and path dependence in inter-regional network: A case of China's technology transaction. *Scientometrics*, 108(1), 201–220.

Suttmeier, R.P. (1981). *Science, Technology and China's Drive for Modernization*. Stanford, CA: Hoover Institution.

Suttmeier, R.P., Cao, C. & Simon, D.F. (2006). China's innovation challenge and the remaking of the Chinese Academy of Sciences. *Innovations: Technology, Governance, & Globalization*, 1(3), 78–97.

Suttmeier, R.P. & Shi, B. (2008). Success in "Pasteur's quadrant"? The Chinese Academy of Sciences and its role in the national innovation system. In H.S. Rowen, M.G. Hancock & W.F. Miller, eds. *Great China's Question for Innovation*, Washington, DC: Brookings Institute Press, pp. 35–56.

Suttmeier, P.R. & Yao, X. (2011). *China's IP Transition. NBR Special Report #29*. Seattle, WA: The National Bureau of Asian Research. Available at https://china-us.uoregon.edu/pdf/IP_report.pdf (accessed December 3, 2021).

Tai, Q. & Rory, T. (2015). Public opinion towards return migration: A survey experiment of Chinese netizens. *The China Quarterly*, 223, 770–786.

Tang, L., Cao, C., Wang, Z. & Zhou, Z. (2021). Decoupling in science and education: A collateral damage beyond deteriorating US–China relations. *Science and Public Policy*, 48(5), 630–634.

Taylor, M.Z. (2016). *The Politics of Innovation: Why Some Countries Are Better than Others at Science and Technology*. New York: Oxford University Press.

The Center for Knowledge Societies. (2008). Emerging economy report: Societal intelligence for business innovation. Available at http://cks.in/wp-content/uploads/2012/10/01_Report-Introduction.pdf (accessed December 3, 2021).

Tian, F. (2013). Skilled flows and selectivity of Chinese scientists at global leading universities between 1998 and 2006. *Journal of Science & Technology Policy in China*, 4(2), 99–118.

Trippl, M. & Maier, G. (2010). Knowledge spillover agents and regional development. *Papers in Regional Science*, 89(2), 229–233.

Utterback, J.M. & Abernathy, W.J. (1975). A dynamic model of process and product innovation. *Omega*, 3(6), 639–656.

Uzzi, B., Amaral, L. & Reed-Tsochas, F. (2007). Small world networks and management science research: A review. *European Management Review*, 4(2), 77–91.

Van Noorden, R. (2012). Global mobility: Science on the move. *Nature*, 490(7420), 326–329.

Van Waarden, F. (2001). Institutions and innovation: The legal environment of innovating firms. *Organization Studies*, 22(5), 765–795.

Varela, D., Benedetto, G. & Sanchez-Santos J.M. (2014). Editorial statement: Lessons from Goodhart's law for the management of the journal. *European Journal of Government and Economics*, 3(2), 100–103.

Vasudeva, G. (2009). How national institutions influence technology policies and firms' knowledge-building strategies: A study of fuel cell innovation across industrialized countries. *Research Policy*, 38(8), 1248–1259.

Verschraegen, G. & Vandermoere, F. (2017). Introduction: Shaping the future through imaginaries of science, technology and society. In G. Verschraegen, F. Vandermoere, L. Braeckmans, & B. Segaert, eds. *Imagined Futures in Science, Technology and Society*. London: Routledge, pp. 1–17.

Vink, M., van der Steen, M.A. & Dewulf, A. (2016). Dealing with long-term policy problems: Making sense of the interplay between meaning and power. *Futures*, 76, 1–6.

Wang, S. (2008). Changing models of China's policy agenda setting. *Modern China*, 34(1), 56–87.

Wang, H. & Guo, J. (2012). *Annual Report on the Development of China's Study Abroad (No. 1) (in Chinese)*. Beijing: Social Sciences Academic Press.

Wang, C.C. & Lin, G.C.S. (2008). The growth and spatial distribution of China's ICT industry: New geography of clustering and innovation. *Issues & Studies*, 44(2), 145–192.

Wang, Z.Z. & Zhu, J.J. (2014). Homophily versus preferential attachment: Evolutionary mechanisms of scientific collaboration networks. *International Journal of Modern Physics C*, 25(5), 1440014.

Watts, D.J. & Strogatz, S.H. (1998). Collective dynamics of "small-world" networks. *Nature*, 393(6684), 440–442.

Wen, J. (2013). The Regulations on the Disclosure of Government Information of the People's Republic of China. Available at www.gov.cn/zwgk/2007-04/24/content_592937.htm (assessed March 13, 2013).

Wong, J. (2011). *Betting on Biotech: Innovation and the Limits of Asia's Developmental State*. Ithaca, NY: Cornell University Press.

Woolthuis, R.K., Lankhuizen, M. & Gilsing, V. (2005). A system failure framework for innovation policy design. *Technovation*, 25(6), 609–619.

World Bank Group, Development Research Centre of the State Council & The People's Republic of China. (2019). *Innovative China: New Drivers for Growth*. Washington, DC: World Bank.

World Intellectual Property Organization (WIPO). (2021). *Global Innovation Index 2021: Tracking Innovation through the COVID-19 Crisis*. Geneva: WIPO.

World Intellectual Property Organization (WIPO). (2022). *Innovative Activity Overcomes Pandemic Disruption – WIPO's Global Intellectual Property Filing Services Reach Record Levels*. Geneva: WIPO. Available at www.wipo.int/pressroom/en/articles/2022/article_0002.html (accessed July 15, 2022).

White, G. & Wade, R. (1988). Developmental states and markets in East Asia: An introduction. In G. White, ed., *Developmental States in East Asia*. London: Macmillan, pp. 1–29.

Wübbeke, J., Meissner, M., Ives, M.J.Z.J., and Conrad, B. (2016). *Made in China 2025 – The Making of a High-Tech Superpower and Consequences for Industrial countries*. Berlin: Mercator Institute for China Studies (MERICS).

Xue, L. (1997). A historical perspective of China's innovation system reform: A case study. *Journal of Engineering and Technology Management*, 14(1), 67–81.

Yang, W. (2016). Policy: Boost basic research in China. *Nature*, 534(76080), 467–469.

Yin, R.K. (2014). *Case Study Research: Design and Methods*. Thousand Oaks, CA: Sage Publications.

Yip, G.S. & McKern, B. (2016). *China's Next Strategic Advantage: From Imitation to Innovation*. Cambridge, MA: The MIT Press.

Zeithammer, R. & Kellogg, R.P. (2013). The hesitant hai gui: Return-migration preferences of US-educated Chinese scientists and engineers. *Journal of Marketing Research*, 50(5), 644–663.

Zhang, F., Cooke, P. & Wu, F. (2011). State-sponsored research and development: A case study of China's biotechnology. *Regional Studies*, 45(5), 575–595.

Zhang, C., Zeng, D.Z., Mako, W.P. & Seward, J. (2009). *Promoting Enterprise-Led Innovation in China*. Washington, DC: World Bank.

Zhang, X., & Whitley, R. (2013). Changing macro-structural varieties of East Asian capitalism. *Socio-Economic Review*, 11(2), 301–336.

Zhao, L. (2005). Memorabilia of Yun-10 research and development (in Chinese). *Aviation Archives*, 6, 52–53.

Zheng, H., De Jong, M. & Koppenjan, J. (2010). Applying policy network theory to policy-making in China: The case of unban health insurance reform. *Public Administration*, 88(2), 398–417.

Zheng, Y. & Huang, Y. (2018). *Market in State: The Political Economy of Domination in China*. Cambridge: Cambridge University Press.

Zhong, X. & Yang, X. (2007). Science and technology policy reform and its impact on China's national innovation system. *Technology in Society*, 29(3), 317–325.

Zhou, S. (2008). China is expected to invest 690 billion RMB in nine major civilian MEPs by 2020 (in Chinese). Available at http://news.sciencenet.cn/htmlnews/2008/11/213754.html (accessed on November 12, 2012).

Zhou, L. & Shen, Z. (2011). Progress in high-speed train technology around the world. *Journal of Modern Transportation*, 19(1), 1–6.

Zhou, Y., Lazonick, W. & Sun, Y., eds. (2016). *China as an Innovation Nation*. Oxford: Oxford University Press.

Zhu, Z. & Gong, X. (2008). Basic research: Its impact on China's future. *Technology in Society*, 30(3–4), 293–298.

Zweig, D. (2006). Competing for talent: China's strategies to reverse the brain drain. *International Labour Review*, 145 (1–2), 65–90.

Zweig, D., Kang, S. & Wang, H. (2020). "The best are yet to come": State programs, domestic resistance and reverse migration of high-level talent to China. *Journal of Contemporary China*, 29(125), 776–791.

Zweig, D. & Wang, H. (2013). Can China bring back the best? The Communist Party organizes China's search for talent. *The China Quarterly*, 215, 590–615.

Index

Printed in the USA
CPSIA information can be obtained
at www.ICGtesting.com
LVHW061506060823
754430LV00006B/100